Somanatha

The Many Voices of a History

ROMILA THAPAR

VERSO
London • New York

This edition first published by Verso 2005
© Romila Thapar 2005
First published in India by Penguin Books India 2004
© Romila Thapar 2004

1 3 5 7 9 10 8 6 4 2

Verso
UK: 6 Meard Street, London W1F 0EG
USA: 180 Varick Street, New York, NY 10014-4606
www.versobooks.com

Verso is the imprint of New Left Books

ISBN 1-84467-020-1

British Library Cataloguing in Publication Data
Thapar, Romila
   Somanatha: the many voices of a history
   1. Somanatha Temple (Somnath, India) – History
   2. Pillage – India – Somnath – History – To 1500
   3. Pillage – India – History – To 1500 – Sources
   4. India – History – 1000–1526   5. India – History –
   1000–1526 – Sources   6. India – History – To 1500 –
   Historiography   7. India – Antiquities   I. Title
   954.7'5'022'072

ISBN 1-84467-020-1

Library of Congress Cataloging-in-Publication Data
Thapar, Romila.
   Somanatha: the many voices of a history / Romila Thapar.
   p. cm.
   Originally published: New Delhi: Penguin Books India, 2004.
   Includes bibliographical references and index.
   ISBN 1-84467-020-1 (hardcover: alk. paper)
   1. India – History – 1000–1526 – Sources. 2. Somanatha
   Temple (Somnath, India) – History – Sources.
   3. India – History – 1000–1526 – Historiography.
   4. Mahmud, Sultan of Ghazni, 971–1030. I. Title.

DS458.3.T47 2005
954.02'23–dc22

2004020254

Typeset in Garamond
Printed in the UK by The Bath Press

'… On each occasion one should honour the sect of the other, for by doing so one increases the influence of one's own sect and benefits that of the other; while by doing otherwise one diminishes the influence of one's own sect and harms the other. Again whosoever honours his own sect or disparages that of another, wholly out of devotion to his own, with a view to showing it in a favourable light, harms his own sect even more seriously. Therefore, concord is to be commended, so that men may hear one another's principles and obey them …'

—*From the Twelfth Major Rock Edict of the Mauryan emperor, Ashoka, inscribed in the third century BC*

Contents

Preliminaries

This book is an attempt to explore the interpretation of one event that has been projected in the last two centuries as central to the relations between two communities in South Asia, the Hindu and the Muslim. Sultan Mahmud, ruling from Ghazni in Afghanistan, controlled a substantial territory that has come to be called the area of eastern Islam. At the beginning of the eleventh century he raided prosperous temple towns in the northern and western parts of the South Asian subcontinent. He could thus claim the virtue of being an iconoclast in the eyes of some in the Islamic world and at the same time could use the looted wealth to finance his political ambitions in central Asia. Among these raids was the one that has now become famous as the raid on the temple at Somanatha in Gujarat in 1026.

The reading of his motives and of subsequent events, involving him or the Somanatha temple, have been based almost exclusively on statements from Turko–Persian eulogistic poems and court chronicles from Ghazni and later from the Sultanate courts of India. Different readings from other sources on the history of Somanatha after the raid were not incorporated and generally not even consulted. Given the peculiarity of the periodisation of Indian history by James Mill in the early nineteenth century, who divided it into Hindu civilization, Muslim civilization

and the British period, a disjuncture was projected between the
Hindu and the Muslim period in around AD 1200. There has
been a continuous and unquestioning acceptance of this scheme
until recent times when it was sought to be replaced, but
currently there is an attempt to reintroduce it under different
labels. Whereas the history of the earlier period was constructed
through sources in Sanskrit and Sanskrit-based languages, for the
period after AD 1200 there was a switch to Turkish, Arabic and
Persian, which were the languages introduced by the new traders
and conquerors. This was irrespective of there being a continuity
of texts written in the earlier languages and an even larger body
of literature being written in the regional languages. An attempt is
made in this book to introduce data from non-Persian sources
and these contradict some of the statements in the Persian
sources. That the non-Persian sources do not refer to the raid,
nor provide evidence of a trauma among the Hindus which was
said to have resulted from the raid, remains enigmatic.

The book is primarily a historiographical study, attempting to
explain how the interpretation of an event can change when a
wider range of sources is introduced. Inevitably therefore, it also
becomes an attempt to question the received version of the
event: a version that has remained unquestioned for almost a
century and a half since it was first constructed. This approach
has grown out of the historical explorations that have emerged in
the writing of Indian history over the last fifty years. These have
incorporated analyses generating new causal connections and
historical generalizations, beyond the limited concerns of political
history that had dominated earlier historical writing. But
questioning the received version also has a bearing on the politics
of Hindu–Muslim relations in contemporary times, particularly as
the raid of Mahmud on Somanatha has become, in a current
political ideology, an icon of the projected antagonism.

My endeavour is to place the event, its players and its
location in a historical context, and observe how it was
represented over many centuries. This history becomes something

of a commentary, direct or indirect, on all these aspects. It takes on a quality similar to a multi-faceted cutting of a stone. The non-Persian sources are very varied, consisting of inscriptions, chronicles of local courts, epic poems and popular legends. They have to be viewed not only in terms of their own genres but also for possible interconnections. This helps to explain the many dimensions of the event. In the period between the event and the present, the event was encrusted with other happenings or other readings of these activities. These have then to be included in the reconstruction of the history since they have a bearing on how the event and its context were perceived at various periods. When social memory is introduced the point at which a particular reading of the event is used to construct such a memory becomes significant. The history therefore, is also a history of the perceptions of the event.

This requires probing into the many layers that surface in the writing of this history, where the unravelling of one led to yet another and in some instances came as a surprise to me since some of these contradicted the received version and each other. The many voices are sometimes radically different and this raises the question of why only one version was adhered to. I would argue that it was not the contents of this version that defined its accuracy and importance, but rather colonial policy to begin with and, subsequently, the communal politics of a later time, both of which used this version to support their respective ideologies. Yet the many voices are essential to seeing the larger setting of the history of Somanatha and all that is associated with it. The other sources provide evidence of the existence of multiple communities and glimpses of their relationships with each other. These tended to erode the notion of two dominant communities identified by religion.

Despite these many versions being familiar to various groups of people, the received version remains current. The question then is when and why did this version become the sole explanation for what is in fact a complex history? It seems to have grown from colonial historians accepting the Turko–Persian accounts as authentic narratives of the event, irrespective of the evident contradictions even within this single body of writing, and ignoring the references to Somanatha in other texts. The colonial reading projected the event as germinal to an innate hostility between Hindus and Muslims and this in turn underlined the politics of religious communities. This was further imprinted by the theory that the raid had created a trauma in the Hindu mind and that this trauma was the cause of modern Hindu and Muslim communal hatred.

The colonial reading came to be fixed during a debate in the House of Commons in 1843 after the attempt by Lord Ellenborough to forcibly bring back the so-called gates of the Somanatha temple from Ghazni, said to have been looted by Mahmud, as a trophy of the ill-fated Anglo–Afghan wars. The gates were neither of Indian workmanship nor from Somanatha. But the rhetoric of the debate in the House of Commons set the pattern for the reading of the event.

This reading, accepted as authentic history, fed into the creation of a supposed historical memory that was also said to have fuelled the trauma. There was therefore a political use of the event as part of colonial policy. This spread gradually when it also came to influence a segment of the nationalist imagination, with a section among the nationalists accepting the theory. There was in this acceptance an overlap between anti-colonial nationalism and religious nationalism. And in this process the other voices that happened not to support the received version were silenced. Consequently, when India attained independence, the same section of nationalist opinion supported the demand that the temple be rebuilt at Somanatha. There were however other nationalists who were skeptical about the theory and also felt that as a secular state the government should not associate itself with the rebuilding of the temple.

The temple at Somanatha became an icon of Hindu nationalist resurgence. When Hindu religious nationalism organized a mass movement to lay claim to the possession of the supposed birthplace of the deity-king Rama, at Ayodhya, the procession mobilized for this purpose started its journey from Somanatha and traversed a major part of northern India to arrive at Ayodhya. It was claimed that a temple dedicated to Rama marked his birthplace. This was said to have been destroyed in the sixteenth century by the first Mughal king, Babar, in order to construct a mosque at the site. When the mosque was attacked and destroyed in 1992 at the instigation of Hindu religious nationalism, some argued that this was an act avenging the raid of Mahmud on Somanatha. The colonial reading has therefore now been picked up by a dominant political ideology current in India.

The introduction of many voices can point to contested versions of a history, but it is also necessary to comprehend the multiple cultural articulations that went into the making of Indian society. Such a comprehension has become imperative in the India of today where efforts are being made to silence these voices, efforts that have political support in India and from some groups of Hindus settled as migrants in the Developing World, both claiming to speak for all Hindus.

The history that has been reconstructed by religious nationalisms of various kinds in south Asia validates a narrative that gives precedence to the dominant religious community. It does this in part by determining what it regards as its prior and superior origins and identities. In India, two themes in particular are being redefined in an attempt to give a single identity to the main religious community and declare others as aliens. Indian civilization is said to have had an exclusive foundation, the 'Aryan', and even the cities of the Indus civilization of the third millennium BC are claimed as having been authored by 'the Aryans'. This is an effort to define Indian as Hindu and to evoke the myth of racial superiority and linguistic distinctiveness. The creation of Aryanism was an obsession in European thought in the later half of the nineteenth century, as among some

Orientalists and in the German Romantic movement. These ideas were however not limited to the colonial discourse on India for they also influenced some significant nineteenth-century Indian thinkers. It is often forgotten that the intellectual context of the latter was as much the debate with European ideas on Hindu religion and culture as the attempt to revive earlier debates. Their construction of Hindu civilization, therefore, was not a return to a pristine original, but included a reaction against, or an incorporation of, Orientalist views. Aryanism played a part in this. It influenced the reading of Indian texts, especially the Vedic corpus, and some of it is reflected in the notions of current Hindu religious nationalism.

Hindus, it is said, can trace their descent lineally from 'the Aryans' of five thousand years ago, whereas the Muslims and the Christians are of foreign origin. It makes no difference that their ancestry is actually Indian. Their foreignness lies in their religion having been founded in an area outside the boundaries of British India, according to the dictum of one of the founders of the political ideology of religious nationalism referred to as Hindutva.

This provides a prelude to the other major thesis that Muslim rule in India—that is, the rule of Arabs, Turks, Afghans and Moghuls—was foreign rule, despite their having settled in India. Further, as was stated in colonial interpretations of Indian history, such rule was by its very nature oppressive and tyrannical and detrimental to Hindus and Hinduism.

These historical interpretations have fuelled religious nationalisms. The mirror image, virtually, of Hindu nationalism, lies in Muslim religious nationalism that had its own political agenda, one strand of which was to justify the notion of Pakistan. This latter reading of history argues that true civilization was brought to India with the coming of Islam. This requires the eulogizing of Mahmud and the exaggeration of the exploits of Muslim conquerors. Muslim rule is not depicted as oppressive but a distinction has to be made between believers and infidels. Since non-Muslim subjects were infidels, they could be depicted as inferior.

Colonial discourse of the nineteenth century that was seminal to these religious nationalisms began to involve intellectuals of both Hindu and Muslim persuasion in the latter part of the century. These were intellectuals seeking to recreate what they regarded as their respective traditions and although contesting some aspects of the colonial interpretation of Indian culture they were also imbibing some of the premises of the colonial discourse.

The tradition of liberal, independent historical writing on India—that has contributed widely to what is now recognized as an intellectual exploration of the Indian past—is currently under attack by supporters of Hindutva or Hindu religious nationalism. The debate on history, therefore, is less one between historians and more between historians and those who subscribe to the ideology of religious nationalism. Historians have been troubled both by what went into the rewriting of history but even more by the attempts to impose this history in the syllabus of schools and universities.

A Hindutva version of Indian history was propagated through history textbooks used in schools and through government controlled research institutions during the years when the Bharatiya Janata Party and its allies were in power, terminating in 2004.

It is claimed that this new history has been constructed from an entirely indigenous, Indian point of view. It is therefore hailed as a departure from the earlier writing of Indian history which is described as anti-national, Eurocentric and, inevitably, Marxist. But actually this 'new' history merely repeats the theories of nineteenth-century colonial history, particularly in its insistence on the Aryan foundations of Indian civilization and Hindu–Muslim antagonism.

In the last half century, debates over historical interpretations have moved into more creative areas of historical investigation.

The issues that were important to colonial and nationalist theories are either much less important or else the contemporary analyses are changing the earlier interpretations. There is a keener focus now on more precise methods of enquiry and a more critical use of sources, a focus not unfamiliar to historians in other parts of the world.

There is a greater awareness of other perspectives—such as that of the author of the text, as well as of the purpose and audience of the text—and the historian does not stop at only a familiarity with the contents of a text. The scope of history has widened enormously to include the study of changing forms of caste, gender studies, diverse economies of various periods, the role of technologies, processes of state-formation, the social context of religious sects, the history of ideas, the impact of environment and ecology on human activity and vice versa—in fact the normal components of what today is regarded as appropriate to historical investigation. The much wider range of causal analyses resulting from the broadening of the scope of history requires considerable discussion of priorities in causality. Over and above this, the historical context of ideas and historiography has become a prerequisite for historical research.

The studies of the last fifty years have made visible the multiple cultures that are essential to understanding the Indian past and present. A view of history from the perspective, for example, of underprivileged groups is now beginning to be explored and this also punctures the picture of a seemingly endless ancient golden age, as it does invariably in any civilization.

In writing the history of Somanatha, my aim has been to introduce some methods of historical analysis that might be insightful, and more particularly to reflect on the historiographical question of why there has always been such a simple reading of an obviously complex history. As for the argument that the raid of Mahmud was germinal to an unabated hostility between the Hindus and the Muslims in India, it did seem to me that such an antagonism, irrespective of its historical accuracy, would have emerged from complicated relationships and not merely from a one-time raid. I was interested in examining these relationships by using a variety of sources. And if there were multiple relationships involved it was unlikely that the suggested causation would hold.

I was puzzled by the fact that generally only one source— the Turko–Persian texts—was consulted in the reconstruction of the history of Somanatha, and all the more so when I found ample references in other sources of the time to the temple at Somanatha, but interestingly not to the raid of Mahmud. This latter fact has been commented upon by earlier historians but not taken up for enquiry. Each of the sources have their own perspective and internal contradictions, and are actually less concerned with the raid than with justifying their own ideologies in their representations of events and personalities around Somanatha. The differences in these representations emanating from different social groups provide historical insights into society and politics.

These perspectives also suggest the ways in which narratives about the past can be used towards contemporary political ends. The association of the raid with Hindu–Muslim antagonism was rooted in the nineteenth-century readings of this history and was to become useful to the political mobilization of religious nationalism in the twentieth century. The history of Somanatha therefore, has an additional contemporary relevance as well.

Preface

This study of the aftermath of the raid of Mahmud of Ghazni on the Somanatha temple initially grew out of my interest in historiography and began as a paper given at a seminar some nine years ago. On this occasion I had stopped at the fifteenth century, juxtaposing Persian and Jaina sources with Sanskrit inscriptions. Reactions to this presentation underlined the relevance of continuing the narrative up to the present. This then took the form of a lecture and was published in *Narratives and the Making of History*. This was further expanded and was initially intended to be published in the 'Tracts for the Times' series, but, like Alice, it grew and grew, in the process changing its form from a tract into a monograph. Given the nature of the subject, it also required detailed referencing.

My interest in the subject began with trying to understand why there were contradictions in the Turko–Persian chronicles and then, further, why these narratives focused on concerns that were virtually absent in the Sanskrit inscriptions and the Jaina texts although the latter in part focused on Somanatha. The narratives were significantly diverse and conformed to a differentiated historiography. Following up on how the raid or the subsequent events were represented in a variety of sources, I was both puzzled and fascinated by the fact that each revealed a different story from the other, and from that with which we have all been familiar as the received version of what happened. As an exercise in historiography, this has dimensions that need to be explored further. An initial presentation of the paper led to the comment by a colleague that it was a kind of Rashomon syndrome!

I decided, therefore, to write it at some length and present it with whatever conclusions I could reach, but also include in the presentation the questions that remain unanswered. In pointing to the many voices of a history, it is not my intention to suggest that they all have equal authority, or that they can be heard in such different ways as to make a history impossible. It is rather an attempt to hear these voices so that an understanding of this history can be made more insightful.

I would particularly like to thank Neeladri Bhattacharya not only for his detailed comments on the chapters, but also for his helpful discussion about them. Conversations with the late Sarvepalli Gopal guided me through the sources pertaining to colonial and nationalist concerns. K.N. Panikkar read the text and his comments helped me clarify my arguments in the later chapters. Muzaffar Alam's explanations of questions relating to the Persian sources were very useful, particularly as I was reading translations of the originals. In transliterating Persian and Arabic words, I have tried to adopt the conventional usage. I have not used diacritical marks in transliterating terms from non-English languages, as each language uses a different system and this would be unnecessarily confusing to a reader unfamiliar with these systems. Meenakshi Khanna and Agnihota have helped me with locating publications and rechecking a few references. Munish Joshi's interest in the oral tradition opened up another perspective. Robert Skelton, Sushil Srivastava and Ajay Dandekar obtained copies of publications otherwise difficult to get. Idrak Bhatti read and discussed with me a short exposition in Urdu. Malcolm Yapp kindly sent me a bibliography on the question of the gates of the Somanatha temple at Ghazni. I would also like to thank David Nelson and his staff, who look after the South Asia section of the Van Pelt Library at the University of Pennsylvania, for all their help. As always, it was a pleasure working with Uma Bhattacharya on the maps.

The first draft of this book was completed at the Villa Serbelloni at Bellagio, an idyllic place for thinking and writing.

Romila Thapar
New Delhi, 2003

1

The Context

In 1026, Mahmud of Ghazni raided the temple of Somanatha, plundered its wealth and broke the idol. The received opinion is that this event marked a crystallizing of attitudes, both of the plundered and the plunderers, and these remained antagonistic to each other from that moment on. I decided to explore the aftermath of this event to track what crystallized if it did, how the event was recorded, and whether the perception of the event changed. Of interest to me also was the historiography of these narratives through the representation of this and other events, as well as the later construction of what were thought to be the memories of the event.

The intention of this study is to explore the inter-relationship between an event and the historiography that grows around it by placing the narratives in a historical context. An event occurs, and it slowly becomes encrusted with narratives about what happened. Sometimes the claim is made that such narratives have been constructed on the basis of initial memories, or that they encapsulate what once was a memory, or that the historiography reflects what are believed to be facets of memory. The historian cannot restrict the historical analyses only to the event and the way in which it is being viewed in the present. The intervening stages of the creation of narratives around the event or an aftermath that ignores the event, have also to be investigated. The study becomes one of observing the processes by which the intervening stages are established and how these influence the eventual perception of the event.

There are many concerns that weave their way through this analysis of an event: the subsequent history, the historiography and the reconstructed memory. The three are interconnected and the interconnection may illumine our understanding of the event. The first two aspects focus on what happened and how it has been interpreted, and the third concentrates on the point in time and space when memory is introduced into the interpretation. Each narrative is connected to the history of the place, but each narrative is also connected to what it perceives as the politics of power. The narratives, therefore, are at times ambiguous and more frequently conflicting. This also requires some explanation.

In trying to examine these questions, I shall also attempt to explore, even to a limited extent, the historical context of the sources. These have not generally been juxtaposed. The juxtaposition assists in observing the variant perspectives on the event, or else, why the event was ignored in the kinds of texts where one would expect to find some reference to it. Each of these sources had a particular take on their association with Somanatha. Their reliability has to be assessed, especially where there are contradictions; and their historical context and purpose require explanation. The juxtaposition of the sources demonstrates that none can be taken literally. The event is encoded either in a narrative or a historical explanation, and at some point it is seen as important and is enveloped by a constructed memory. Inevitably, therefore, the link between history and what is treated as memory becomes a subject of study. Equally important is the question of who is remembering or recording what, and why; and the differences in what is being recorded. Why this happens needs to be explained. But so also there is the need to understand why the event is embedded, at a particular historical moment, in what is believed to be memory. This involves looking not just at the event but also at the layers of perception and meaning given to its history.

My interest in the subject has been to examine the historiography implicit in the various categories of sources and observe how narratives have evolved in each. In instances where a reference to the event might have been expected but there is an absence of such a reference, an explanation is needed. Perhaps, it involves an exploration of what in our time is referred to as 'the politics of a text', a phrase which I would like to take fairly literally. Since there are many texts that have a bearing on the subject and they come from varying traditions, the politics of these texts are historically revealing.

My intention in this study is not an attempt at a detailed reconstruction of what happened, but rather to see the sources as presenting various perspectives, either directly or by implication, and to search for clues as to how the event was perceived. Such an assessment results in a different reading of the event from that which has been current so far. It emphasizes a number of significant questions: who were the groups actually involved and affected, if the temple did in fact continuously alternate between rebuilding and destruction? What were the relations between these groups and did these change after each such activity? Was it a matter of Muslims desecrating Hindu temples, or were there other motives? Were such acts in some cases deliberately exaggerated for purposes other than receiving religious acclaim? Did they not involve a variety of changing relationships between the two and among the two or more than the two? Other underlying tensions between groups should not be ignored. Such a method of examining these questions can be applied to parallel situations, sometimes involving temples, at other times relating to inter-religious activities of a popular nature.

In analysing the various perspectives on Somanatha after the raid of Mahmud, I would like to explore the idea that the historiography and the narratives that grow out of an event are significant to an understanding of the historical complexity of how the event and the space where it occurs is remembered or forgotten by a range of people. The desecration of a temple in this case, and attitudes towards the memories of such an event, actual or deliberately constructed, need to be examined. The event itself is not being questioned here, but its occurrence does raise further questions. Among the more pertinent are how a historian assesses its impact and how the event is represented in various sources, contemporary and later. The later sources may extend to a millennium after the event. These, in turn, raise still further questions regarding the manner in which interpretations change. The validity of using this event as germinal to antagonism between the Hindu and Muslim communities as projected in modern times, and as a conventional explanation, also requires discussion.

Such questions involve examining more than one set of sources. Some carry detailed information, others make passing or oblique references while others refer to parallel or associated events but omit the one being investigated. Sources that are textual vary in language, style, authorship and purpose and these perspectives have to be co-related. Many of these sources have not been critically re-examined in recent times, now that the interpretation of this period has undergone substantial change from what it was a century ago. Such critical re-examinations are a necessary adjunct to historiography. Where some sources take the form of material remains—archaeological data and art historical artifacts—they require a different treatment, although here too reassessments are often called for. In this work, the sources range across a large number of categories. Even where more than one source is referred to, there has been a tendency in the past to maintain them in distinct compartments and keep the data segregated, whereas co-relating the data suggests new readings of the event.

I shall discuss six broad categories of sources: the largest in number and the one that has been dominant up to now are the narratives and chronicles in Persian and a few in Arabic, written largely in the context of the Turko–Persian politics and culture prevalent in the Ghaznavid domain and later in northern India; the inscriptions from Somanatha and its vicinity written mainly in Sanskrit; Jaina biographies and chronicles, and epics from Rajput courts; the perception of Mahmud at the popular level in a largely oral tradition; the British intervention via a debate in the House of Commons in the nineteenth century; and the Indian nationalist reconstruction of the event. My intention is not to include all possible sources, but to indicate the variety that needs to be consulted in the kind of assessment that I am making.

Of these, the Turko–Persian chronicles have been hegemonic. They have been privileged as factual without adequate discussion of their historiographical intentions and without an attempt to juxtapose these with other sources. The reading therefore has been restricted to the interpretation provided by these chronicles. But even this reading has been literal and limited, and the contradictions within this category have received little attention. Court chronicles as a genre have a clear agenda, possibly even more evident than the agenda of other textual sources, and this needs to be recognized as the cultural context for the statements that they make. The complexities of using this category have often been ignored in favour of a literal, simplistic reading.

Some Turko–Persian narratives were contemporary with the event or nearly so while most were written during the subsequent centuries. Those that were contemporary tend to be fanciful in that they were uncertain about the identity of the image that was broken and introduce stories about it possibly having been a pre-Islamic goddess from Arabia, and indulge in exaggerated descriptions of the wealth of the temple. The later chronicles were more concerned with establishing Mahmud as the founder of Islamic rule in India. If these narratives are viewed in the context of the history of Islam at this time, they have even greater historiographical relevance than being merely representations of early Islamic intrusions into India. This was a period of some unrest in Arabia and Persia, with attempts to challenge the

Caliphate at Baghdad as well as Islamic orthodoxy. Eastern Islam had its own ambitions and Mahmud was an important player in these. The wider geographical dimension points to Turkish ambition—virtually imperial—with which were involved the politics of western and central Asia.

A relatively untapped category—except for obtaining data on the Chaulukyas—but in some ways the most important in terms of the local history of Somanatha after the event, or its perception, are the inscriptions in Sanskrit dating to about four centuries subsequent to the raid. They present a picture of a rich and powerful temple, active in the politics of the area. In one we are told that the town council, in which the priests of the temple were prominent, gave permission to a Persian trader to build a mosque in the vicinity of the temple. The relationship was one of close cooperation. This major inscription, that is essentially a legal document, gives a glimpse of the politics linking trade and temple and provides a different picture from that of the first category of sources.

A less quoted but significant source is the report on the excavation of the temple site, carried out in 1951. This clarifies the rebuilding of the temple, reducing it to three phases, provides comparative evidence different from some narratives, and indicates the actual dimensions of the temple that were not as vast as a few accounts make out.

The Jaina texts deal largely with the establishing of various Jaina sects and shrines in western India and include biographies of rulers who were claimed as patrons of Jainism. Some of these are said to have made grants to the Somanatha temple, but this contradicts the version in the first set of sources where it is sometimes said that the temple on being sacked was converted into a mosque. There is also a difference in the perception of Jaina court writers and Jaina merchants. The latter were anxious for reconciliation through which there would be a return to normality and which would permit commercial transactions. Epics of this period describe relations among rulers in Rajasthan and

Gujarat and the Delhi Sultans, including a later raid on Somanatha.

A repertoire of stories about Mahmud in the oral tradition, collected and recorded in the early nineteenth century, provide other facets on how he and a supposed nephew of his were viewed. These narratives carry a distinctly different perspective and one that seems to have been current among large numbers of people. At the popular level, there are also stories focusing on *pirs*, *faqirs*, *gurus* and other kinds of 'holy men' who are venerated by followers of various religions, and who sometimes invoke Mahmud. These are narratives that have been set aside by historians as fantasies. Such narratives do not have to be treated as historically accurate but they form a separate genre. Like many other similar genres of the oral tradition, the social assumptions that they encapsulate and the versions of events that they present, illumine the historian's understanding of how the event is perceived at levels other than the formal and textual. The incorporation of such popular versions, given that they come with the caveats that accompany the use of oral sources by historians, have emerged from the interstices of the new methods with which some history is being written.

My purpose is less to analyse this range of sources in detail, and more to set out the span and comment on the variations. It is in some ways an exercise in seeing how a historical relationship can be pursued among such sources and the extent to which the versions are apposite to the creation of what are believed to be memories. There is no uncertainty about the event having happened. The ambiguity lies in the evidence and the degree to which it can be seen as the politics of representation, both of earlier times and of the present. The demythologizing of the aftermath of the event can be one consequence of juxtaposing the sources and treating the information they provide in a comparative manner.

These different sources, barring the excavation, have been known since the nineteenth century but have not been juxtaposed and seen as a commentary on the aftermath of the event. This is in part due to the dominance of the narrative from the Persian sources and partly due to the erroneous periodization of Indian history into Hindu, Muslim and British in which the Hindu period was studied only on the basis of Sanskrit texts, the Muslim period on the basis of Persian texts, and the British by using English language sources. It was believed that the use of Sanskrit texts did not proceed much beyond AD 1200 when the Hindu period was supposed to end, leaving the period from AD 1200, which was said to inaugurate Muslim rule, to those reading Persian sources. This illogicality in the understanding of Indian history ensured a piecemeal history in which links and connections could not be made. Nor did it encourage juxtaposing various kinds of sources and assessing their interconnections and information. Periodization tends to freeze the understanding of a time-bound history into a set of attitudes. Fortunately for the reconstruction of Indian history, this approach is now changing. The emphases on multiple sources and their juxtaposition, oral traditions, methods of analyses highlighting cultural and economic history and the social role of religion, are encouraging historians to move away from simplistic monocausal explanations to exploring the complexities of a range of causes in a changing context. This provides better insights into the past.

The debate in the British House of Commons in the nineteenth century arose incidentally when the Governor-General of India was thought to have lent support to a pagan religion. This lengthy discussion was the first occasion when it was forcefully argued that the Hindus had suffered a trauma through the raid of Mahmud on Somanatha, and that the earlier subservience of India to Afghanistan and to Muslim rule had to be avenged. This debate raised the issue of antagonistic religious communities and the supposed memory of a humiliation.

The conversion of the event into a symbol in the politics of nationalism in India in the twentieth century began in western India. Somanatha was said to be symbolic of Hindu subjugation and the ensuing trauma over Muslim rule. The reconstruction of the temple at Somanatha was demanded. This became a contentious issue between what are now described as secular nationalists and those with an agenda that perceived politics in terms of religious identities. This tension was brought to a head by the rebuilding of the temple at Somanatha in 1951.

Recent analyses of these sources point towards a reading of the event and its aftermath different from that which has been current so far. It raises many new questions: did varying groups in Indian society react in varying ways to the event; was the destruction of temples just a matter of religious hostility? Were accounts of such destruction exaggerated for political reasons or were they accurate? Were there in fact monolithic communities labelled Hindu and Muslim or were there variant and changing relationships among a multiplicity of communities which did not see themselves as part of a monolith? Seeking answers to such questions does not simplify the process of analysing historical events. But even the asking of such questions is essential in order to move away from generalizations based on mono-causal explanations that tell us virtually nothing about the past. They merely allow us to impose on the past our requirements of the present and thus obfuscate the reading of the past.

Over the last hundred years, there have been studies that focus on Mahmud or on Somanatha or the history of Gujarat. Some among these have been influential in the reconstruction of this history. The monograph of Mohammad Habib, *Sultan Mahmud of Ghaznin, A Study* (1927), places Mahmud in the wider historical context of central and western Asia and not just of north-western India, thus providing a better perspective of his activities. It argues for looking at motivations other than only the religious in the raids of Mahmud and suggests that commerce motivated some of the activities. But this idea was not explored in later studies focusing on Mahmud. N. Nazim's study, *The Life and Times of Sultan Mahmud of Ghazna* (1931), combs through the Turko–Persian sources, dismisses other sources, and maintains the centrality of religious concerns. The book was soon mined by later writers on the subject and was treated as a useful summary of the Turko–Persian sources.

K.M. Munshi's *Somanatha, The Shrine Eternal* (1951) states his reconstruction of the history of the Somanatha temple and why it was necessary to rebuild it. The more useful part of the book is B.K. Thapar's report on his excavation of the site. These views have been discussed in M.A. Dhaky and H.P. Shastri's book, *The Riddle of the Temple of Somanatha* (1974). A.K. Majumdar's *Chaulukyas of Gujarat* (1956) includes the period of Mahmud's raid, although this is marginal to his main interest, which is the subsequent period with evidence largely from sources in Sanskrit and Prakrit, particularly those linked to the Chaulukyas. A valuable work that is often overlooked in discussions of Mahmud is C.E. Bosworth's *The Ghaznavids: their Empire in Afghanistan and Eastern Iran 994–1040* (1963). This places the activities of Mahmud more precisely and in a larger historical context, both in terms of the territory that he controlled and the interaction of events in western and central Asia associated with the Ghaznavids. A. Wink's *Al-Hind* (1991, 1997) provides a useful general background to the Indo–Islamic world of the time. Trade and commercial interests are discussed in V.K. Jain's *Trade and Traders in Western India* (1990). M.A. Dhaky and H.P. Shastri examined the history of the temple from the archaeological and art-historical perspective in their fine study, *The Riddle of the Temple of Somanatha*. A more recent history of the icon by R. Davis, *Lives of Indian Images* (1997), has a wide coverage of sources which extends the narrative beyond political events, and this is a useful departure from other studies. The focus is on the history of the temple and the icon, as one among others that the book discusses, and consequently surveys the history of events associated with the temple. The induction of a larger range of sources releases the narrative from being a monopoly of the Turko–Persian. The revived interest in the temple during the last two centuries links the story to recent times. Other scholars, such as S. Amin and M.C. Joshi, have discussed popular perceptions and associations with these events, as, for example, those of Ghazi Miyan and references to *Tantras*.

The generally scant attention given in these studies to the Sanskrit inscriptions pertaining specifically to Somanatha is rather surprising for, in many ways, they provide the most pertinent local data. My interest is less concerned with the historicity of the accounts of the site and the history of the icon and more with the nature of the sources and their historiography. These suggest variant ways of looking at historical problems, and the current implications of how such sources are used.

Historical interpretations went back to the first conceptualizing of Indian history as a modern discipline, which unfortunately was moulded by colonial concepts of the Indian past. These were encapsulated, for instance, in Mill's periodization of Indian history into Hindu and Muslim civilizations and, finally, the British presence, superior to both. This underlined the theory of a permanent confrontation between Hindu and Muslim, which became the perspective through which events such as the raid on Somanatha were viewed. One could well ask if this is a historically valid way of interpreting what happened.

The creation of two nation states in the Indian subcontinent in 1947—India and Pakistan—was justified by arguing that there have always been two nations existing in the subcontinent since the arrival of Islam, the Hindu and the Muslim. The eighteenth-century sense in which the term 'nation' was used, essentially meaning peoples, was overlaid with the concept of the nation-state. This assumption sought the sanction of history. A frequently repeated statement, stemming from the colonial historiography of South Asia, is that after the arrival of the Muslims in India from the eleventh century onwards, two communities emerged, the Hindu and the Muslim, who were generally antagonistic to each other. So it was in the fitness of things that their separate identities as potential nation-states be recognized in the twentieth century and two such states be established. This two-nation theory was endorsed by both Muslim and Hindu religious nationalisms, although it was opposed by the broad-based anti-colonial nationalism.

Historical roots and justification were sought for this antagonism and among these was the raid on Somanatha. Mahmud of Ghazni, who had raided other temple towns before this, came as usual from Afghanistan in 1026 and desecrated the temple at Somanatha and looted it of its wealth. It was argued that this became a foundational event that created hostility between Hindus and Muslims since the raid could neither be forgiven nor forgotten. In this conventional view of the history of medieval India, it was argued that the coming of Islam created a Hindu–Muslim confrontation at all levels. This was expressed in the literature through Persian 'epics of conquest' and Hindi 'epics of resistance', the first intended for a Muslim audience and the second for a Hindu audience.[1] Such descriptions obscure and deny the nuances in each category of texts, which might make us hesitate to label them simply as epics of conquest and epics of resistance. Nor does such a view concede that there were epics of conquest and resistance in India prior to the coming of Islam. These were established genres, and in Gujarat, for instance, the *rasos* were long, narrative poems, narrating campaigns between various rulers and the activities of the royal courts.[2] Nor indeed is there a justification for privileging the literature of the court, singling it out for attention and ignoring other forms of articulation. There has been a tendency, therefore, in the conventional interpretation of medieval Indian history, barring a few studies, to

---

[1] Aziz Ahmed, 'Epic and Counter-Epic in Medieval India', *Journal of the American Oriental Society*, 1963, 83, pp. 470–76.

[2] S. Yashaschandra, 'Gujarati Literary Culture', in S. Pollock (ed.), *Literary Cultures in History*, pp. 574 ff.

see it largely in terms of relationships between courts and the antagonism between Hindus and Muslims.

The political act in 1990 of starting the *rath yatra* from Somanatha and travelling to Ayodhya, as what became a preliminary to the destruction of the Babri Masjid at Ayodhya in 1992, was projected as the obvious and visual symbol of this antagonism. The destruction of the mosque was justified by some groups as the Hindu reply to Mahmud's iconoclasm. Such a view is historically untenable, because apart from other factors it nullifies the events that took place in and around Somanatha during the intervening thousand years.

In recent times, the generally accepted view has been summed up in two statements which are often quoted. V.N. Moore in the Preface to his book on Somanatha, published in 1948, states:

> One of the most popular incidents of Indian history is provided by Mahmud of Ghazni, the great iconoclast who led the most famous of his twelve expeditions against India to humble the might of the great Somanatha. Following him successive Muslim invaders tried to raze the temple to dust. Crisis upon crisis marked the chequered history of Somanatha. But each time the devout Hindu rebuilt the monument as soon as the invader had turned his back after indulging in his favourite game of desecration and plunder. For nearly four hundred years this amazing drama of unending struggle between Muslim bigotry and Hindu zeal went on. Till at last in the fifteenth century the Hindus abandoned the shrine in sheer despair, to build a new temple near by.[3]

---

[3] V.N. Moore, *Somanatha*, Calcutta, 1948.

He adds: 'It is the sacred duty of new and renascent India to reconsecrate Somanatha and try to restore its former glory and splendour.' A plan of a proposed reconstruction is appended to Moore's book.

This was in essence the colonial view on the eve of independence. The colonial interpretation of Indian history and society maintained that the inherent hostility between the two monolithic communities had laid the foundation for supporting such a 'sacred duty'. Nuances and differences within such communities, suggesting a multiplicity and plurality of cultures, were completely ignored. Since the time of William Jones in the eighteenth century and Max Müller in the nineteenth century, Indian civilization had been constructed solely on the basis of the Hindu religion and the Sanskrit language. The contributions of Buddhism and Jainism were subordinated and Islam was regarded as alien. That societies and cultures frequently mould the religions that they choose to follow and therefore every religion has a historical root in the society where it has a following, and that its evolution draws upon multiple religions and societies, was a perspective unfamiliar to historians until recent times.

The concept of a single civilization in a vast geographical area and stretching over many centuries is incapable of accommodating the notion of multiple cultures, even if the latter are the real historical features of civilizations. Added to this was the heritage of the Crusades in Europe that encouraged notions of Muslim barbarism and tyranny. Incidents of an unsavoury kind that are common to moments in most histories were treated as characteristic of Islamic history. These were regarded as general explanations of 'oriental' behaviour with little attempt to ascertain the legitimacy of doing so. Yet in a curiously contradictory manner, the Turko–Persian narratives were accepted as historically valid and even their internal contradictions were not given much attention, largely because they approximated more closely to the current European sense of history than did the other sources. Since the event itself was barely referred to in other sources, a comparative study of the sources was thought to be unnecessary.

Indian anti-colonial nationalism was a movement that claimed openness in its cultural policy and included all those who subscribed to questioning colonial rule. This was not the case in the emergence of Hindu and Muslim religious nationalisms of the early twentieth century. Their emphasis was less on questioning the presence of colonial power and more on forging the Hindu and Muslim identities in India, ultimately aimed at the creation of nation-states with dominant religious majorities. The two types of religious nationalisms, propagating segregation in practice, had much in common in their theory of historical explanation.

There were some among the Indian nationalists who endorsed the colonial readings of Indian civilization and culture and their application to historical events. They claimed to be anti-colonial yet many aspects of their interpretations of the past were founded on the theories of colonial historians. Their dilemma has an explanation. They were hesitant in questioning what they perceived as the positive assessments of some aspects of early Indian history that had been made by colonial historians. At the same time, they were also reluctant to apply the methods of critical enquiry to what they regarded as their own religious and cultural identities. However, those historians for whom the historical method hinged on rational enquiry had also to contend with the subtext of aspects of anti-colonial nationalism that were partial to religious nationalism.

Among the nationalists there were some who were active in demanding what finally came to be the reconstructed temple at Somanatha. They saw this as their 'sacred duty' as argued by Moore. Thus, in 1951, K.M. Munshi writes:

> ... for a thousand years Mahmud's destruction of the shrine has been burnt into the collective sub-conscious of the [Hindu] race, as an unforgettable national disaster ...[4]

[4] K.M. Munshi, *Somanatha—The Shrine Eternal*, p. 58.

Statements such as these have tried to establish that there was a consistent 'Muslim' view of the event over many centuries, motivated solely by an anti-Hindu iconoclastic sentiment, and that the Hindus as a collective suffered a trauma because of this event which coloured their view of the Muslims for all time. But were such events so clearly dichotomized in the past? Could there not have been other interests which provide other facets to this event or its aftermath or which seem to have bypassed the event altogether? What is remembered is that which survives even though it has been chiselled anew in each retelling. Perhaps some events are forgotten but recorded, and the record becomes another memory.

The period of Chaulukya rule in Gujarat covered these events. The historian of the Chaulukya period, A.K. Majumdar, pinpoints the initial problem when he states:

> But, as is well known, Hindu sources do not give any information regarding the raids of Sultan Mahmud, so that what follows is based solely on the testimony of Muslim authors.[5]

It was at Munshi's initiative that the temple was rebuilt soon after Indian independence and for some this became a symbol of what was projected as liberation from the past. But the past is an immutable inheritance and we can neither liberate ourselves from it nor change it. What is feasible is the constant re-examination and reassessment of how we interpret the past, provided that the new interpretations suggested have historical legitimacy.

---

[5] A.K. Majumdar, *Chaulukyas of Gujarat*, p. 43.

2

The Setting

Some familiarity with the historical background leading up to the period under discussion may be useful as a preliminary. Since Gujarat was the hinterland to ports and trading centres from the time of the Indus civilization, its history is inevitably chequered. It has hosted diverse peoples and cultures apart from those already settled there and woven them into a society specific to the region.

The location of Somanatha was earlier referred to as Prabhasa Pattana, a well-known *tirtha* or place of pilgrimage in Saurashtra. It was associated with the nearby confluence of three rivers and it adjoined the port of Veraval. Excavations in the area indicate that settlements of small farming communities go back to the third millennium BC.[1] Some continuity into later times is suggested by the characteristic Gujarat pottery—the Lustrous Red Ware. Iron artifacts point to a more advanced phase similar to other sites in the region. The presence of Northern Black Polished Ware, originating in the Ganga valley in the mid-first

---

[1] M.K. Dhavlikar and G. Possehl, 'The Pre-Harappan Period at Prabhas Pattan', *Man and Environment*, 1992, 17, 1, pp. 71–78. J. Nanavati, R.N. Mehta, and S.N. Chowdhury, *Somanatha*, 1956, MS University Monograph 1.

millennium BC and distributed throughout the subcontinent, and
of amphorae sherds which doubtless came from trade with the
Hellenistic world, underline a growing network of exchange.[2]

The *triveni* in the vicinity is the confluence of three rivers—
one inevitably called the Sarasvati and so-named probably after
the myth of the confluence at Prayaga. This confluence lent
additional credence to the site becoming a place of pilgrimage,
such places being frequently located at the source or the confluence or estuaries of rivers. A myth linking the deity of
Somanatha with the *tirtha* of Prabhasa was required and this is
narrated in the *Mahabharata* and the *Puranas*.[3]

The story goes that Daksha had twenty-seven daughters who
were married to Soma, the deity associated primarily with the
moon and with plants. Among his wives, Soma was devoted to
Rohini and neglected the others. On their complaining to their
father, Daksha cursed Soma who became consumptive and
therefore could not perform sacrificial rituals and this, in turn,
prevented the growth of plants. The gods tried to persuade
Daksha to withdraw the curse. But he was only willing to modify
it on condition that Soma promised to be a husband to all his
wives. According to some versions of the story, the modification
resulted in the fortnightly waxing and waning of the moon. Soma
bathed in the Sarasvati at Prabhasa and regained his brilliance—
prabhasa. The myth is tied to the *nakshatras*, or lunar mansions
through which the moon passes, the waxing and waning of the
moon, eclipses, the notion of rejuvenation through bathing in the
water at Prabhasa and to a fertility cult. This latter aspect is
retained in later mythologies that explain the icon as being a Shiva

---

[2] Supriya Varma, 'Settlement Patterns in Kathiawar from the Chalcolithic
to the Early Historical Period', Ph.D. Thesis, JNU, New Delhi, 1997; *Indian
Archaeology—a Review*, 1955–56, 1956–57, 1971–72, 1979–80, 1980–81.

[3] *Mahabharata,* Shalyaparvan, 34.35 ff.; *Vamana Purana*, 41.4; 57.51–53;
Kurma Purana, 2.34.16, 20; *Varaha Purana*, Thirthakanda, 19; *Agni Purana*,
109.10–11; 116.22–24.

lingam and the site as being one of the twelve important locations where the *jyotir lingam* fell. There is no mention of a temple at Somanatha in the *Mahabharata*, but the *tirtha* of Prabhasa is said to be famous.[4] As a place of pilgrimage, it would be a meeting point for many groups of people from various regions, who would relate to each other as equals irrespective of their sectarian or caste identities in a spirit of what has been called *communitas*.[5] Participating in a pilgrimage not only dulls the edge of social differentiations and sectarian demarcations but also creates a temporary identity of community. Such a centre attracted a number of religious sects over the centuries.

In the *Mahabharata*, Prabhasa is also associated with Krishna and the Pandavas. It was the place where Krishna is said to have met Arjuna, where he assembled the Yadavas, and where it is believed that he died.[6] To this extent, it could be regarded as an early Vaishnava centre although it eventually flourished as a Shaiva centre. The association with the Vrishnis in the *Mahabharata* would support its being the location of a *gana sangha* or an oligarchic system. The need to disable the *gana sanghas* is made evident in the *Arthashastra*.[7]

That the region had an economic potential is apparent from the investments of the Mauryan and later kings in its agricultural and commercial development.[8] Candragupta Maurya's governor had a dam built, presumably to provide irrigation for agriculture, and this was one of the few examples of state initiative in irrigation in early Indian history. The governor associated with the western region had an Iranian name, Tushaspa, which would suggest continuing close links with Iran. Girnar, in the vicinity,

---

[4] *Vanaparvan*, 86.18; 119.

[5] V. Turner, *Dramas, Fields and Metaphors*, pp. 57 ff.

[6] *Adiparvan*, 210.1 ff; *Vanaparvan*, 118.15 ff; cf. *Bhagavata Purana*, 11.30.4 ff.

[7] *Arthashastra*, Book XI.

[8] Romila Thapar, *Ashoka and the Decline of the Mauryas*, pp. 118, 231, 317.

was one of the sites for the major rock edicts of the emperor Ashoka. The larger area was controlled by the western Kshatrapas—Rudradaman placed an important inscription in this region. Other inscriptional evidence suggests activities in the post-Mauryan period around Prabhasa. Ushavadata, the son-in-law of a Kshatrapa raja, records the gifting of eight wives to brahmans at the sacred place of Prabhasa.[9]

By the early centuries AD, as was common to many parts of the subcontinent, a large Buddhist centre arose in this neighbourhood, perhaps also attracted by its prosperity through trade. The caves in the nearby hills at Junagadh and Girnar were rock-cut monastic complexes. A clay sealing found near Girnar suggests that the patron of one of the monasteries may have been Rudrasena I.[10] A major Buddhist settlement of the fourth century AD was excavated at Devanimori near Shamlaji which had *stupas* in its vicinity containing inscribed relic caskets, and the site had links with the Buddhist settlements at Junagadh.[11] Buddhist monasteries would have required a reasonably established agrarian or commercial economy to support them apart from catering to those who came as pilgrims. The dam on the Sudarshan lake, first built by the Mauryas, is mentioned as being kept in good repair, at least up to the Gupta period. This would have facilitated a prosperous agrarian base.

But after the mid-first millennium AD, Buddhism had begun to be replaced by the now more thriving Vaishnava, Jaina, Shaiva and Shakta sects. Chakrapalita, the governor of the Guptas, is associated with the setting up of a small temple to Vishnu at Girnar which would date to about the fifth century AD.[12] The

---

[9] *Epigraphia Indica*, VII, 57, No. 13; op.cit., VIII, 78, No. 10.

[10] Ibid., XXVIII, p. 174.

[11] R.N. Mehta and S.N. Chowdhury, *Excavations at Devanimori*.

[12] Junagadha Rock Inscription of Skandagupta, *Corpus Inscriptionum Indicarum*, Vol. III, pp. 56 ff.

Maitrakas, who succeeded the Guptas, gave grants to various religious sects and took titles such as *parama maheshvara* and *paramopasaka*, which could suggest either conversion from one to the other or else the taking of a title in accordance with the religious context of the occasion.[13] They included worshippers of Surya, and sun-worshippers were frequent among the lesser rajas. Hsüan Tsang, visiting Kathiawar in the seventh century, records a decline in the number of Buddhist monasteries as against what were for him the flourishing centres of the 'heretics'—the Shaiva and Vaishnava sects. He refers to the monastery at the top of Mount Ujjanta but makes no mention of any structure at Prabhasa.[14] He does mention that the local people are much given to trade and barter since they live by the sea and there is a thriving maritime commerce.

A visitor in the early nineteenth century, surveying the historical sites in the area, observed that there was a striking Buddhist presence even after the decline of Buddhism. He suggested that the Somanatha temple may possibly have been in origin a Buddhist structure later taken over by the Shaivas, particularly as it lies so close to what was a Buddhist centre at Praci.[15] This is an observation that has not seen many supporters but which might be worth investigating. The Buddhist caves were later occupied by other religious sects and it is not quite clear whether the taking over by other sects was a process of incorporation or the result of a confrontation.

In the eighth century, the Arabs raided Valabhi in Saurashtra. Further incursions into western India were held back by the rulers of the area. Jaina sources of a later period mention removing the

---

[13] G. Buhler, 'Grants from Valabhi', *Indian Antiquary*, 1876, V, p. 206.

[14] T. Watters (ed. and trans.), *On Yuan Chwang's Travels in India*, II, p. 249.

[15] W. Postan, 'Notes of a Journey to Girnar', *Journal of the Asiatic Society of Bengal*, 1838, 7, 2, pp. 865–87.

images of their deities to safe places. Among these was the image of Chandraprabha which flew through the air to Shivapattana, that is Devapattana/Prabhasa, referred to as being a safe area for images.[16] An inscription of the Chaulukya king Bhima II from Veraval, dated to the late twelfth century AD, refers to an image of Chandraprabha and the restoration of the shrine, but there is no reference to the image having been elsewhere originally. This image is associated with the curing of leprosy.[17]

Subsequent to the attack on Valabhi and the campaign in Sind, the Arabs gradually settled down to trade rather than conquest. Further south, the Rashtrakutas made grants to a Buddhist *vihara* and to the Jainas, as well as patronizing what were seen as newcomers from the west, such as the Arabs.[18] The descendants of those Arab traders who had settled on the western coast, coming probably from southern Arabia, were seen as the *biyasara*, many of whom married locally and observed various local customs.[19] They had links with trading centres in west Asia such as Siraf, Oman, Basra and Baghdad and increasingly from Yemen. Inscriptions in Sanskrit, such as those from Rashtrakuta territory, speak of the Arabs as Tajiks, and mention their functioning as administrative officers and even governors appointed by the Rashtrakuta court. In one case, we are told that a Rashtrakuta king appointed a Tajik governor in present-day Sanjan (north of Mumbai) and this governor granted a village to finance the building of a temple.[20]

---

[16] Merutunga, *Prabandha-cintamani*, 5.11.239; trans. C.H. Tawney, pp. 174–75.

[17] *Epigraphia Indica*, XXX, pp. 117 ff.

[18] Ibid. VI, pp. 285 ff.; XXII, pp. 64 ff.; XXI, pp. 133 ff.; XXXII, pp. 45 ff.

[19] V.K. Jain, *Trade and Traders in Western India*, p. 72. n. 6; A. Wink, *Al-Hind*, I, pp. 68 ff.

[20] Chinchani grants, *Epigraphia Indica*, XXXII, pp. 45 ff.; pp. 55 ff.; pp. 61 ff.; pp. 68 ff.

The western seaboard was a bustling, thriving area, with intense trading activities, and therefore became the habitat of settlements of a large range of people. The four core areas were the Indus delta, Saurashtra and the coast of Gujarat, Konkan and Malabar. The first of these declined largely owing to the frequent silting of the branches of the Indus river in the delta, making ports dysfunctional and requiring them to shift their location. The other three areas not only had long distance maritime trade but also traded among themselves and had extensive hinterlands.

Saurashtra had a scatter of chieftains and minor rulers who were heads of clans and governed small principalities. A ninth-century Saindhava chieftain records a grant that he gave to a brahman who was a resident of Someshvara.[21] A reference is made to the Pratihara king Nagabhatta II, ruling in the ninth century, having visited the *tirthas* in Saurashtra, including Someshvara.[22] These references do not imply the existence of a temple but that Prabhasa could have been a pilgrimage centre focusing on the *triveni*. Hemachandra, in a much later account, says that the raja of Junagadh, Ra Graharipu, obstructed pilgrims from going to Prabhasa—perhaps because it was in the hands of a rival chieftain—and is also said to have killed brahmans, attacked sacred places and eaten beef.[23] This was almost a formulaic description of an enemy.

Tradition has it that the god, Soma, appeared to the Chaulukya king, Mularaja, and ordered him to defeat Graharipu and free Prabhasa, which Mularaja did, and then came to Prabhasa to worship Someshavara before returning to Anahilavada.[24] The

---

[21] Ibid., XXVI, p. 185.

[22] Prabhachandracharya, *Prabhavaka-charitra*, quoted in M.A. Dhaky and H.P. Shastri, *The Riddle of the Temple at Somanatha*, p. 32 fn. 27.

[23] Hemachandra, *Dvyashraya-mahakavya*, 20.91–94, quoted in Dhaky and Shastri, ibid., p. 16 n. 58 and 59.

[24] A.K. Forbes, *The Ras Mala*, pp. 39 ff.

Chaulukyas were anxious to control the chiefs and lesser rulers scattered all over Saurashtra. It is likely that many continued as governors and administrators under the Chaulukyas.

The major royal patrons in Gujarat, from the tenth to the thirteenth century, were the Chaulukyas, also known as the Solankis, who ruled from their base at Anahilavada. Some have argued that it was Mularaja who first built a temple at Somanatha, which would date it to the tenth century as Mularaja died in 997. However, he is not conclusively associated with the temple and there is a suggestion that he may have renovated a small earlier one.[25] If Mularaja did build a temple at Prabhasa to Soma, it was likely to have been a small temple as were the others of the time such as the Lakulisha at Ekalingaji, Ambikamata at Jagat, Vishnu at Kiradu, Sasbahu at Nagda and those at Roda: not to mention the still smaller and earlier temples such as the one at Gop. Mularaja's royal patronage would, among other things, have been an attempt to appropriate the cult and its territory by a newly rising dynasty— a process that was repeated in many parts of the subcontinent where new states were being established. Prabhasa was an important pilgrim centre and its initial geographical reach was wide, given that pilgrims also came from the western seaboard.

The existence of a temple in the tenth century would be supported by the inscriptions mentioning royal pilgrims visiting the temple in the late tenth or early eleventh century, and by Al-Biruni's date for the temple, as well as by what is suggested from the excavation of the site.[26] The temple to Shiva/Somanatha at Prabhasa, linked to the Pashupata Shaiva sect, is not mentioned earlier than about the tenth century AD. A Chedi inscription of

---

[25] Dhaky and Shastri, op.cit., p. 16.

[26] *Epigraphia Indica*, I, p. 251, vs. 61–62; Sachau, *Alberuni's India*, II, p. 105; B.K. Thapar, 'The Temple of Somanatha: History by Excavations', in K.M. Munshi, *Somanatha—The Shrine Eternal*, pp. 71; K.T. Telang, 'A New Silahara Copper-Plate', *Indian Antiquary*, 1880, IX, pp. 34 ff.

the late tenth or early eleventh century refers to a Chedi ruler obtaining an effigy of Kaliya, made of gold and gems from the Odras, and consecrating it to Shiva at the temple of Someshvara, after having bathed in the sea.[27] Anantadeva, a Shilahara king, is said to have made a pilgrimage in the tenth century.[28]

Lesser patrons in the form of local princelings, governors and feudatories, of whom some claimed to being Rajput and others who were content to be just clan chiefs, played a contradictory role, some exploiting the temple and the pilgrims and some protecting them. Among the earlier ones were the Vaghelas, Abhiras, Chudasamas and Chavdas, and later times saw the rise of the Jethvas, Jhalas, Gohels, Jadejas, and still later the Mers and Bhils. The local rulers of Kathiawar were often hostile to the Chaulukyas and some of the hostility is captured in the story of how Ranakadevi became a sati at Vadhavan.[29] She had been promised to the Chaulukya king, Jayasimha Siddharaja, but had instead been married to a lesser ruler, Ra Navaghana II. Jayasimha went into battle against Navaghana and captured Ranakadevi. On the way to Anahilapattana/Anahilavada, she stopped at Vadhavan where she became a *sati* and where there is now a temple to commemorate this act. The lesser rulers were bent upon deriving an income from the major pilgrimage centres. The looting of pilgrims going to Somanatha was one source of income for many of these.[30] The Abhira king is called a *mlechchha* because he consumes beef and plunders the pilgrims visiting Somanatha.[31]

---

[27] Bilhari Stone Inscription, *Epigraphia Indica*, I, pp. 251 ff. vs. 59–63. It is thought that these verses were probably added later.

[28] S.N. Pandey, *Saivite Temples and Sculptures at Somanatha*.

[29] *Gujarat State Gazetteer*, Junagadh District, Ahmedabad 1975, pp. 127 ff.; H. Wilberforce-Bell, *The History of Kathiawar*, p. 69; A.K. Forbes, *The Ras Mala*, pp. 122–31.

[30] H. Cousens, *Somanatha and Other Medieval Temples in Kathiawar*, p. 3.

[31] H.C. Ray, *Dynastic History of Northern India*, p. 941.

At the more popular level, the goddess Khodiyar was widely worshipped as special to Saurashtra.[32] Given the large number of small states in Saurashtra, the cult of the goddess became central, especially in domestic ritual when the process of Rajputization began in this area and a *kuladevi* was required by each clan.[33]

The period from AD 1000 to 1300 saw an upward swing of the economy in Gujarat, partly due to the trade with west Asia but perhaps more because of the interest that the Chaulukyas took in encouraging this development.[34] The capital, Anahilavada, was a political centre with extensive commercial links. This is the period of the immediate aftermath of Mahmud's raid on Somanatha and clearly, despite what Al-Biruni says about the raids of Mahmud devastating the local economy, this did not happen in Saurashtra and Gujarat where there were continuing and spectacular profits from trade. Perhaps the devastation was immediately after the raid and for a brief period. Al-Biruni having left India soon after, the recovery may have been effective subsequent to his departure. Agriculture was improved through systems of irrigation as the hinterland of Saurashtra was prone to drought. In Gujarat, generally, even merchants took a considerable interest in the construction of step-wells, reservoirs and tanks. The minister, Vastupala, who belonged to a merchant family, is associated with a large number of *vavs*/step-wells. Merchants would sometimes underwrite the finances for the construction of wells in return for a part of the crop for a stipulated number of years. If there was a drought and it persisted, this could result in the merchant virtually acquiring the land.

Road links between rural areas and markets were established which also helped in better administration. The transportation of

---

[32] H. Tambs-Lyche, *Power, Profit and Poetry*, pp. 22 ff.

[33] Ibid.

[34] V.K. Jain, *Trade and Traders in Western India*, pp. 250–53.

agricultural produce was made much easier. Cotton and indigo were taken to centres for the production of textiles, a substantial item of export. Travellers were provided with amenities that remained a concern of the local administration even as late as the fifteenth century as is evident from bilingual Arabic and Sanskrit inscriptions instructing the local officers in this matter and threatening those officials who did not carry out these instructions.[35] Caravans banded together and protected their cargo by employing private armies. The *banjaras*, pastoral cattle-keepers, often became the carriers of trade and to some extent traders themselves. The more professional traders handling caravans were the *sarthavahas*. Traders of various kinds were included in the terms *vanik* and *vyavaharika*.

Financiers and the more wealthy merchants were the *shreshthis* and they were sometimes large-scale landowners. These may have been the kinds of merchants who might buy the cargo of an entire ship in a single deal.[36] Merchant castes sometimes claimed to be Rajputs in origin. The transformation of the *thakkura* into a *vanik* was not unknown. Organizations of artisans and merchants, such as the *shreni, nigama, puga*, more often translated as 'guilds', were important organizationally both for the production of goods and for their distribution and sale. These covered the entire range of production and sale, from potters and betel-sellers to horse dealers and shipowners. Officers attached to temples and to civic bodies seem to have been financially well-off. They collected a range of dues for the administration of the temple, some portion of which may well have been retained by them.[37]

---

[35] S.H. Desai, *Arabic and Persian Inscriptions of Saurashtra*, Mota Darwaza Inscription of 1455, No. 34, pp. 121–24.

[36] V.K. Jain, op.cit., p. 219 ff.

[37] E. Hultzsch, 'A Chaulukya Grant', *Indian Antiquary*, 1882, XI, pp. 337 ff.; *Epigraphia Indica*, XIV, No. 21, p. 302, vs. 68–82.

Brigandage and piracy, virtually normal to the area, was gradually controlled.[38] Attacks by local chiefs such as the Abhiras on rich commercial towns such as Somanatha Pattana were frequent and the Chaulukyas were constantly running into problems with these rajas on this count.[39] Pilgrims to Somanatha had to pay a tax, and this together with other valuables carried by them for making donations was looted by local rajas. Customs duties could be exorbitant and should have sufficed as a tax income from commerce. But presumably the rajas were used to obtaining coerced presentations as gifts. Sea piracy was common and Al-Biruni refers to the pirates as the *bawarij*. Piracy remained a lucrative source of income even into British times and sea piracy is an indicator of successful maritime trade.

The success of maritime trade is also marked by the presence of extraordinarily wealthy shipowning merchants, the *nakhudas* as they are known to Arab sources, and the *nauvittakas* as referred to in Sanskrit texts and inscriptions. They were Persian, Arab, Jewish and Indian and were from different places such as Hormuz, Siraf, Aden and Mangalore. They commanded the seas and the coasts and saw the pirates as inveterate enemies.[40]

From all accounts, Somanatha was a significant centre for both inland and maritime trade. Its port, Veraval, adjoined the city and was one of the three major ports of the region, the others being Bhrigukaccha/Bharuch and Khambayat/Khambat/Cambay. The period from the ninth to the fifteenth century was

---

[38] Al Biladuri writing in the ninth century refers to piracy. Elliot and Dowson, *The History of India as Told by its Own Historians*, I, p. 118.

[39] Prachi inscription of Kumarapala, *Poona Orientalist*, 1937, I, No. 4, p. 38; 1938, V, p. 123; V.K. Jain, op.cit., p. 48.

[40] R. Chakravarti, 'Nakhudas and Nauvittakas: Ship-Owning Merchants in Coastal Western India', *Journal of the Economic and Social History of the Orient*, 2000, 43, 1, pp. 34–64; S.D. Goitein, 'Letters and Documents on the India Trade in Medieval Times', *Islamic Culture*, 1963, 37, pp. 188–205.

one in which western India had a conspicuously wealthy trade with ports along the Arabian peninsula and with places such as Hormuz, Qays and Siraf in the Persian Gulf. According to visiting traders, the land of the Gurjaras was rich in resources and its merchants traded widely.[41] The antecedents of this trade go back many centuries and, irrespective of changing political control in this area, the trade in essential commodities was never seriously discontinued. Variations were registered for the trade in luxury goods. Arab concern with extending and safeguarding this trade may well have been a primary reason for the initial attempt to control Sind and the western coast.

So important was the trade that it introduced flexibility in relations between different religious groups. Thus, despite the political confrontation between the local rulers and Muhammad Ghuri in the twelfth century, the latter refrained from confiscating the extensive property of Wasa Abhira, a wealthy Hindu merchant, who had his establishment in Ghazni.[42] The Jaina merchant, Jagadu, had a mosque constructed for his trading partners from Hormuz in the fourteenth century.[43] These actions do not seem to have been exceptional. Even if one argues that the motivation was to enhance commercial profit, nevertheless the spirit of accommodating the religious institutions of others was impressive. An interesting contravention of the norms of caste functions was that brahmans were active in this commerce in northern India and particularly in the trade in horses with its substantial profits.[44] Al-Biruni, writing in the eleventh century,

[41] V.A. Janaki, *Gujarat as the Arabs Knew it*; Suleiman, Elliot and Dowson, I, p. 5; Abdullah Wassaf, Elliot and Dowson, III, pp. 31–32.

[42] Muhammad Ufi, Jami-ul-Hikayat, in Elliot and Dowson, II, 201; V.K. Jain, op.cit., pp. 72 ff., p. 107.

[43] Sarvananda, *Jagaducharita*, quoted in M. Shokoohy, *Bhadreshvar*, p. 9.

[44] Pehoa Inscription, *Epigraphia Indica*, I, pp. 184 ff.; Bayana Inscription, ibid., XXII, pp. 120 ff.; Bali Inscription, ibid., XI, pp. 32 ff.

states that Somanatha-Veraval was the port for people going to Zanj in east Africa and to China.[45] Marco Polo comments in the thirteenth century that the people of Somanatha live by trade. He also mentions the trade in horses from Hormuz as being very valuable.[46]

In the thirteenth and fourteenth century, during the Il Khan period in central Asia, trade between west Asia and China increased and there were some tangential advantages for India in the overland trade.

The counterparts to the Arab traders were Indian merchants at commercial centres in Gujarat such as Bharuch, Cambay and Veraval, as also those settled in Hormuz, or for that matter, even in Ghazni after the eleventh century, who are invariably described as being extremely prosperous. Wealthy merchants such as Jagadu, or Wasa Abhira from Anahilapattana, had their agents, often Indian, in Hormuz and Ghazni, respectively, through whom they conducted trade. The trade focused on imports from west Asia that included horses, wine and metals and with exports from India consisting especially of a range of textiles, spices, semi-precious stones, timber and swords.[47]

Metalsmiths and goldsmiths had a high status because of the demand for their products. Undoubtedly, the most lucrative trade was in horses; each horse being purchased by Indian traders for 220 *dinars* of red gold.[48] According to the same source, as many as 10,000 horses were sent annually from ports and trading centres on and around the Gulf to Cambay and other ports in the vicinity,

---

[45] Sachau, op.cit., II, p. 104.

[46] Ibid.; W. Marsden, *The Travels of Marco Polo*, revised by M. Komroff, sections 19, 21, 29.

[47] V.K. Jain, op.cit., p. 90 ff.; S. Digby, 'The Maritime Trade of India', in T. Raichaudhuri and I. Habib, (eds), *The Cambridge Economic History of India*, I, pp. 125–59.

[48] Abdullah Wassaf, in Elliot and Dowson, III, p. 33.

as well as further south along the west coast to Malabar in order
to reach trading centres in the peninsula. Horses were in demand
for maintaining the army's cavalry wing and for ceremonial
occasions. There was a protocol as to who could ride a horse in a
royal procession and this privilege was generally confined to those
of high status. Horses of quality were not bred in India and were
imported either from central Asia via the north-western passes or
by sea from the Persian Gulf.[49] The latter could have been Arab
horses or horses from Khorasan brought to southern Persia and
shipped from there to India. Horses from beyond the north-west
of India had been famous since early times. Bhoja, writing in the
eleventh century, mentions both Tajik and Khorasani horses and
Abu'l Fazl is full of praise for the Arab horse.[50] Although there
was much interest in the maintenance of horses, nevertheless
superior horse livestock in India was short-lived. The constant
demand for horses kept the trade active.

---

[49] An interesting confirmation of the areas especially linked to the horse
trade comes from a very different source. Dr V.M. Meher-Homji drew my
attention to the fact that the only two areas in India where the Acacia-
planifrons is found are Veraval in Saurashtra and the Ramnathpuram-
Tirunelveli districts in Tamil Nadu. Morphologically, this species is closely
allied to Acacia spirocarpa (A.tortilis), the habitat of which is north-eastern
Africa and the Aden peninsula and Arabia. He suggests that this was an
accidental introduction of the plant which was brought as fodder for horses
and therefore took root in the two areas closely related to the trade in
horses. V.M. Meher-Homji, 'Notes on Some Peculiar Cases of Phytogeographic Distributions', *Journal of the Bombay Natural History Society*,
1970, 67 (I), pp. 81–86.

Climate and pastures in India were not suitable for the breeding of high-
quality horses. One strain of good horse livestock in Kaccha is said to be
derived from the accidental arrival of Arab horses and has remained
confined to a particular area. The small Kathi horses of Saurashtra are not
suitable for cavalry purposes. Therefore, horses had to be imported to
maintain the stock.

[50] P.K. Gode, 'Some References to Persian Horses in Indian Literature from
AD 500 to AD 1800', in *The Poona Orientalist*, 1946, XI, 1 and 2, pp. 1–13.

In addition to patronage and revenue from endowments, the income of the more substantial temples included duties on items of trade, a percentage of which was donated to the temples. A twelfth-century inscription of the *nayaka* of Saurashtra, during the reign of Kumarapala, lists the customs dues collected on agricultural produce from the customs house. From these, one silver piece per day was given as donation for the temple. It is said that Shiva is the donee, man is the donor, and the gift brings religious merit.[51] An additional income came from the pilgrim tax imposed by the local administration at Prabhasa, provided the sum had not already been looted by the local rajas and the sea brigands off the coast of Saurashtra.[52] Policing by the Chaulukya administration was motivated by the need to maintain law and order as well as to try to protect the tax money.

Endowments to temples could consist of regular dues in kind, and where these came from a large range of artisanal production, the temple would have had to have commercial outlets. This would have tied the temple closer to trade.[53] The administrative committees of temples would, therefore, have been anxious to encourage trade. Some temples, it is said, participated directly in the trade, and funds from temples formed a sizeable investment.[54] The commercial centres of Gujarat had access to the hinterland of northern India as well. Commercial wealth steadily increased from the tenth century and the noticeable prosperity of Gujarat was due both to inland trade as well as trade with the Arabs and the Persians, particularly at centres in Saurashtra and Cambay. These were points of exchange in the far larger trade across the Indian Ocean, which together with the

---

[51] *Bhavnagar, Prakrit and Sanskrit Inscriptions*, Mangrol Inscription, pp. 158–60.

[52] E. Sachau, op.cit., I, p. 208.

[53] Siyadoni Stone Inscription, *Epigraphia Indica*, I, pp. 162 ff.

[54] Abdullah Wassaf, Elliot and Dowson, III, p. 33.

overland trade through central Asia, was creating an economy that may be called virtually global.[55]

Gujarat in the period from AD 1000 to 1400 witnessed what might be called a 'renaissance' culture of the Jaina mercantile community. Rich merchant families were in political office, controlled state finances, were patrons of culture, scholars, liberal donors to the Jaina Sangha and builders of Jaina temples. Amazingly, these activities were maintained throughout a period which, as assessed in Turko–Persian sources, was one of considerable disturbance—if these sources are to be taken literally—and the disturbance originated with the raids of Mahmud.

After the fifteenth century, there are indicators of change. The concentration of trade seems to shift away from Somanatha. This may have been partly because of the participation of a larger number of Arab traders, and also because Arab traders now had direct access to south-east Asia and could tap the profitable spice trade without the intervention of Indian middlemen. The import of horses into north India was probably facilitated by an improved access to the north-western passes, and dealers in horses doubtless found conditions less disturbed than they had been in the previous period. Temples that had drawn their wealth from trade went into a decline where trade had also dwindled, hastened further by a fall in patronage, both from royalty and from merchants. However, the ostensible reason given in modern times is that their decline was due solely to continual attacks by the armies of the Delhi and Gujarat Sultans. The wealthier temples were attacked, although more sporadically than is popularly thought, but this was not the only reason for the decline. This explanation is, for instance, only partially correct for the temple at Somanatha, given the evidence of archaeology as

[55] J. Abu-Lughod, *Before European Hegemony. The World System AD 1250–1350.*

well as the references to the temple continually being under
worship despite the Persian chronicles claiming repeated conversions of the temple into a mosque during this period. Where the
prosperity of a religious centre is tied to trade, the decline in
trade is bound to affect its affluence.

Apart from the stability of the Jaina merchants, the commercial wealth of Gujarat was tied to traders who had connections
with the seaports and commerce to the west. They were not all
visitors since there were small communities of Arab traders
settled in Gujarat.[56] Many of these were Isma'ili Muslims and had
their own mosques, distinct from those of Sunni Muslims, but in
many other ways they conformed to local usage. The Isma'ilis
resisted the Sunni Turks and, to that extent, seem not to have
been seen as a threat by local rulers. The two communities that
gradually became dominant were the Khojas and the Bohras, both
claiming roots in west Asia. There was some borrowing of non-
Sunni ideas, and some from the religions of Gujarat. The Khojas
were close to the beliefs and practices of the Isma'ilis and Shi'as
while the Bohras had Vaishnava elements in their beliefs,
supporting the theory of incarnations and observing Hindu
inheritance laws.[57] There seems to have been a gradual rise in the
number of Arab traders settled in Gujarat, judging by their
graves found in the vicinity of Veraval-Somanatha and Cambay,
particularly from the thirteenth century.

The intermixing of ideologies and social practices is evident.
Both the Khojas and the Bohras were regarded as heretics by
the Sunni Muslims who later dominated Sultanate politics.
Acceptance of some local beliefs and practices makes it easier for
traders to be accommodated in the local trading diaspora. Some

---

[56] S.C. Misra, *The Muslim Communities in Gujarat*; M. Shokoohy, op.cit.,
p. 10.

[57] S.C. Misra, op.cit.; M.N. Pearson, *Merchants and Rulers in Gujarat*,
pp. 27 ff.

of the Bohra traditions insist that the Chaulukya king, Jayasimha Siddharaja, and his minister, Hemachandra, were secretly converted, but there is no historical evidence for this and it was doubtless intended to give status to the community.[58] The institution of caste was adapted and those that converted as a *jati*/caste would, as was usual, continue to practise some of their distinctive social customs and religious observances. The sense of community was kept intact by the *jama't* which, among other things, ensured the continuation of marriage rules, inheritance laws, and custom.

These societies of Arab traders and the Khoja and Bohra sects that evolved at the time were different from those influenced by the Turks, with their emphasis on conquest and dominance. The Arab interest shifted from dominance through conquest in the initial phase to participation in the local economy in the later phase. For the Turks at this time, dominance was through conquest and through governance. The rising prosperity of Jaina merchants was dependent on the trade with the hinterland and with the Gulf. This meant that Indian merchants had bases in the entrepots of the Gulf and merchants from there visited India. The Indians visiting the Gulf have left us no accounts or narratives of what they saw and did. Fortunately, the Arab visitors and traders did write about the Indian scene.

---

[58] S.T. Lokhandawalla, 'Islam, Law and Isma'ili Commentaries', *Indian Economic and Social History Review*, 1967, 4, 2, pp. 154–76.

3

The Turko–Persian Narratives

Mahmud of Ghazni plundered the Somanatha temple and there are multiple versions of the event in Turko–Persian sources. Some were contemporary or near contemporary accounts while others were written at later times. The most sober version is that of Al-Biruni.[1] He writes that the temple was built of stone and constructed about a hundred years prior to Mahmud's attack (which would date it to the tenth century); that it was set in a fortress surrounded by the sea on three sides—presumably, its wealth had to be guarded—and that the tides surging up to the temple were described as the sea worshipping the icon; that the idol was a *lingam* especially venerated by sailors and traders.

Al-Biruni states that the upper part of the icon was broken at the orders of Mahmud and parts of it were taken back as loot to Ghazni and placed so that people would walk on it. There were many *lingam* temples in Sind and Kaccha, but this was among the more important ones. He relates the myth of Somanatha to explain why it was regarded as a sacred site. It was also a sacred place for the local pirates, active on the coasts of Saurashtra and Kaccha. These were the *bawarij*, and they

---

[1] E. Sachau (ed. and trans.), *Alberuni's India*, I, p. 208; II, pp. 102 ff, 105, 109.

constantly interfered with and threatened commercial shipping.

Al-Biruni was no sycophant of Mahmud and writes that his raids caused economic devastation and the Turks were hated among the people who suffered because of these raids. Yet, what is striking is the resilience with which these areas, such as Somanatha, bounced back to a vibrant economy in a short while. Also, despite hostile sentiments, there were Indians of standing from these areas who were willing to support the ventures of Mahmud and to fight in Mahmud's army not merely as mercenary soldiers but also as commanders.[2] Evidently, these relationships were far more complex than we have assumed and range beyond the concerns of religions and conversions.

To place the raid in a historical context would require considering the wider canvas of Mahmud's ambitions and the part played in these by his raids on India. Mahmud's activities in the Indian subcontinent on the one hand, and in Afghanistan and central Asia on the other, were seemingly dichotomous, but were to a large extent interconnected. To understand why he was conducting raids into India needs at least a minimal familiarity with what was happening on the other side of the border. The purpose of the raids was multiple, of which iconoclasm was undoubtedly a motivation. But other intentions were equally important and for reasons other than religious.

The Turks were in origin pastoralists and raiding was an accepted way of obtaining wealth.[3] This does not exonerate them but does suggest a variant way of using raiding as a means of augmenting wealth. Earlier raids had focused on the capture of animal herds, but now they were concerned with looting urban treasuries and capturing prisoners of war to be sold as slaves or recruited into the army. Predatory raids were necessary

---

[2] Ibid., II, p. 13.

[3] A.K.S. Lambton, *Continuity and Change in Medieval Persia, Aspects of Administrative, Economic and Social History, 11th to 14th Century.*

to maintain the numbers required in Mahmud's army and supply lines. Technological improvements in saddles and harnesses, allowing of greater manoeuvrability on horseback, and the use of firearms, converted the Turks into a disciplined body of fast-moving, horse-riding warriors, well suited to raids. In India too at this time, the adventurer with his mounted band of followers, trying to create a small principality for himself, was a familiar figure. In this process, raiding was a common phenomenon. The myths about the origin of dynasties frequently refer to the founder being such an adventurer who then negotiated a political or military agreement.[4] Raiding and looting may not have been all that alien to these times. But there is a quantitative difference between the raids of local adventurers and those of Mahmud.

The Indo–Iranian borderlands and north-western India had witnessed the continuous movement of peoples going back and forth since early times. Texts and inscriptions refer to regular incursions led by the Achaemenids, Seleucids, Indo–Greeks, Shakas, Parthians, Kushanas and Hunas, prior to the Turks. Some annexed the areas of the north-west while others used these areas as the core of their more extended kingdoms. The conquest of the *tukharas* and the *turushkas*/Turks by Lalitaditya of Kashmir in the eighth century AD is mentioned.[5] Turkish mercenaries were employed by later kings of Kashmir and doubtless the attraction lay in acquiring cavalrymen with horses.[6] Kashmir had close links with Gandhara and to some extent with Tokharistan. This area became a pool for the recruitment of mercenaries for any army that required soldiers with little concern for their religious affiliations.

---

[4] Romila Thapar, 'The Mouse in the Ancestry', in *Cultural Pasts*, pp. 797–806.

[5] Kalhana, *Rajatarangini*, 4.v.166; 4.v.179.

[6] Ibid., 7.v.1149.

The group that did give religion primacy, at least in theory, was that of the *ghazis* for whom the campaigns were justified as a form of martyrdom if death occurred on the battlefield, but as freelance soldiers they were undoubtedly after the loot. The *ghazis* eagerly joined Mahmud because the Indian campaigns yielded riches and the exaggeration of this wealth made recruitment easier. Some mercenaries may have maintained their own horses since this was a horse-breeding area. The trade in horses between northern India and the borderlands is referred to in inscriptions from central India in the tenth century. Ghazni would have been heavily involved in this trade, quite apart from other kinds of exchange.

Mahmud obviously came from a different socio-economic background to that of the temple towns that he raided. His authority in the state that he created incorporating Afghanistan, northern Persia and Khurasan in central Asia, rested on an assertion over two symbiotic but variant societies. One was that of the pastoralists of the steppe lands and, to an equal degree, the other was that of intensive commercial exchange in the oasis towns of central Asia and the trading centres of Persia and Afghanistan. The integration of these two societies would have been problematic, as was Mahmud's attempt to Persianise the culture of his kingdom. Furthermore, the routes across the steppes and the oasis towns within his state had to be kept under control. The major military and administrative backbone was provided by 'slaves', a status thrust on those defeated in battle. Some were accomplished persons in their own right and often rose to high office. Since slavery resulted from military defeat, ethnic or social reasons for slavery were not at the forefront. One wonders whether some of the contempt for the Turk in certain Sanskrit sources arose over equating the social status of the Turkish *ghulam*/slave, with that of the Indian *dasa*, without enquiring into the origins of the former.

Temple towns were unfamiliar to the Turks and where these were not part of the Ghaznavid kingdom, they were seen largely as

targets for plunder. The temples that Mahmud would have first
come across were those of the Salt Range and although they were
wealthy, religious institutions, they were not so on a scale as
substantial as that of Thanesar, Multan and Somanatha. The
plundered wealth was used to finance armies to maintain the
Ghaznavid state. This involved paying mercenaries, the employing
of whom also meant that the army was always on the ready for
action. Of the mercenaries, a not insubstantial number were
Indians and, presumably, Hindus. Indian soldiers under their
commander, referred to as Suvendhray, remained loyal to Mahmud.
They had their own commander, the *sipahsalar-i-Hinduwan*, lived in
their own quarter in Ghazni and continued with their own religion.
When the Turkish commander of the troops rebelled, the
command was given to a Hindu, Tilak,[7] and he is commended for
his loyalty.[8] Complaints are made about the severity with which
Muslims and Christians were killed by Indian troops fighting for
Mahmud in Seistan. Presumably, these were Shi'a Muslims.

Ghaznavid control largely continued in the existing administrative system. Thus, Ghaznavid coins issued in north-western
India have bilingual legends written in Arabic and Sharda scripts.
Some carry Islamic titles together with the portrayal of the Shaiva
bull, Nandi, and the legend *shri samanta deva*. The reference in
the latter remains ambiguous. A *dirham* struck at Lahore carries a
legend in the Sharda script and a rendering in colloquial Sanskrit
of the Islamic *kalima* and reads: *avyaktam ekam muhammada
avatara nripati mahamuda*, 'the unmanifest is one, Muhammad is
his incarnation and Mahmud is the king.'[9] This was a considerable

---

[7] Bosworth, *The Ghaznavids*, p. 101; p. 110 ff.; M. Nazim, *The Life and
Times of Sultan Mahmud of Ghazna*, p. 163

[8] Abu'l Fazl Al-Bayhaqi, *Tarikh al-Sabuktagin*, Elliot and Dowson, II,
pp. 125 ff.

[9] P.L. Gupta, *Coins*, pp. 83–84; A.K. Bhattacharya, 'Bilingual Coins of
Mahmud of Ghazni', *Journal of the Numismatic Society of India*, 1964,
XXVI, pp. 53–56.

compromise since orthodox Sunni Islam, for whom Muhammad was a *paighambar*/messenger of God, would not have conceded that he was an incarnation of God. Doubtless, the reason for bicultural coins was the practical need for new money to carry some familiar features from the old in order to make it more easily acceptable as legal tender in the market.

The loot also financed a different activity, namely, extending patronage to a reasonably sophisticated courtly culture with characteristics different from the court of the Caliphs of Baghdad. This was Mahmud's attempt to make Ghazni into a cultural capital, and he assumed that bringing scholars and littera-teurs to his court—sometimes forcibly—would be the way to do it. Persian libraries were looted, books regarded as heretical were burnt, and others brought back to Ghazni and Samarqand. Together with the books, literary men were brought to the court. Al-Biruni was among these and, after an altercation with Mahmud, was virtually banished to India. This was fortuitous since he has left for us some of the most insightful observations on Indian society in his famous work, the *Kitab al-Hind*. The epic poet of Persia, Firdausi, the author of the *Shahnama*, presented his work to Mahmud, doubtless envisaging him as a generous patron. In this he was disappointed and, on leaving Ghazni, wrote satires accusing Mahmud of being parsimonious. The *Shahnama* narrates the history of pre-Islamic rulers of Iran—the ancient heroes such as Rustam and Jamshed and kings such as Alexander and Ardeshir the Sassanian. Was the poem also meant to provide a series of Iranian role models, essentially from the pre-Islamic past, to direct Mahmud's ambition—in the effectiveness of which Firdausi would also have been disappointed? Ghaznavid patronage encouraged Persian as a literary language and, in a sense, the Turks, who were Turkish speaking, were being Persianised. Eastern Islam, as the Islam of this area has come to be called by historians, developed its own cultural idiom as a result of this mixing of Turkish and Persian cultures.

Plundered wealth was used to settle artisans and craftsmen in Ghazni so that the city and the homes of the elite could be beautified and palaces and gardens built for the ruling family. Irrigation systems were improved and communication made easier. Where the plunder included the capturing of prisoners of war, these were sold as slaves. Mahmud is said to have captured 53,000 prisoners after the campaign in Kannauj and brought them to Ghazni where they were sold, fetching a price of 2 to 10 *dirhams* per slave.[10] By way of comparison, a horse imported into western India sold for many times more. The figure for the prisoners is likely to have been exaggerated as the herding and transporting of that many people from Kannauj to Ghazni would have been immensely difficult in those times.

The potential for monetization through the availability of temple wealth, especially gold and silver, has also been suggested as a mechanism for converting loot to a commercial purpose and the looting has been described as a 'goldrush'.[11] Given the propensity to exaggerate in many of these accounts, the figures for the amount of wealth looted is likely to be excessive. The loot from Somanatha is said to have amounted to 20 million *dinars*, and that from the raid on the Shi'a centre at Rayy in Persia in 1029 was only a little less. The figures mentioned for Rayy are 500,000 *dinars* worth of jewels, 30,000 *dinars* worth of gold and silver vessels and 260,000 *dinars* worth of coined money.[12] Mahmud, therefore, raided both Hindu and Muslim centres—the latter if they were not Sunni Muslim—and if the figures for the wealth obtained are even halfway correct, they are enormous. Possibly, the figures have been exaggerated to glorify Mahmud

---

[10] C.E. Bosworth, 'Mahmud of Ghazna in Contemporary Eyes and in Later Persian Literature', *Iran*, 1966, 4, pp. 85–92.

[11] A. Wink, *Al-Hind*, Vol. I, p. 23.

[12] C.E. Bosworth, *The Ghaznavids: Their Empire in Afghanistan and Eastern Iran 994–1040*, Edinburgh 1973 (2nd ed.), p. 78.

since it is debatable whether these towns could have generated so much wealth and, even after its loss, continued to flourish. But if even a fraction of this wealth were obtained, it would be impressive. The rise of Ghazni was in some ways phenomenal since in the tenth century it was merely an entrepot in the transit trade between Khurasan and Trans-oxiana with India.[13]

The raid on Somanatha by Mahmud is a fact but what is of greater interest is the question of what is made of this event. Why is it continually mentioned and how is it represented and described? The event is enveloped in a variety of tellings, linked to the histories of communities and their identities. It lends itself to descriptive narratives from the eleventh century onwards. Some of these are sober descriptions while others indulge in myth making. One expects some consistency in the various accounts of what happened so that fantasy can be sifted from fact, but the variations are quite striking. The descriptions of the event are diverse and ambiguous and clearly quite often imagination is superimposed on fact. Diverse interpretations and representations are not a refusal to accept the event but reflect different strategies of representation and the various ways in which the narrative is politicized to give shape to identities. Yet what adds to the complexity is that there is also an underlying attempt to try to project a single, authoritative version of the event. In reading these narratives their politics and the role of these politics in legitimizing power and sectarian authority have to be understood. The narratives are not literal descriptions of what actually happened although some claim to be so.

Al-Utbi's account of Mahmud's activities in the *Tarikh-i-Yamini*, written in 1031, makes no reference to the raid on Somanatha, possibly because his account terminated in 1020. His praise of Mahmud helped strengthen the ties to the Caliph at

---

[13] Ibid., p. 36.

Baghdad. The political machinations enmeshing the Caliphate seeped into a wide range of politics elsewhere in the states of eastern Islam. Another near contemporary, Al-Bayhaqi, makes a rather distant reference to it in his *Tarikh-i-Bayhaqi*, although he writes eloquently on Mahmud's family. In contrast, fanciful versions come from two contemporaries, Farrukhi Sistani and Gardizi. Farrukhi's poems in praise of Mahmud are contemporary and mention the event, whereas the account of Gardizi in the *Zain al-Akhbar* was written some twenty-three years after the event. Farrukhi says that Mahmud destroyed the temple by setting it on fire, whereas others who report on this say that he destroyed only the idol although he may have desecrated the temple.

Farrukhi Sistani was a major poet of the eastern Islamic world and attached to the court at Ghazni, which was fast becoming the focus of an extensive kingdom. He excelled in the literary form known as the *qasida*: lyrical eulogies, and even if given to exaggeration, regarded as among the finest poetry in Persian at that time. Eulogies written on kings ensured them a degree of immortality since the *qasida* would be appreciated and would be known to a wide audience as a literary genre. Many of his *qasidas* are on his patron, Mahmud. Farrukhi claims that he accompanied Mahmud on his campaign to Somanatha and provides an itinerary but there is no blow-by-blow eyewitness account as might be expected. Of Mahmud, he writes: 'You have emptied the lands of India of fighting men and horrendous elephants.'[14] The equation of the two is interesting! The flattery of the poet helped in building an image of Mahmud as a person of considerable accomplishment.

Gardizi's writing is more prosaic but he does collate some information on Indian society and caste which suggests that there

---

[14] J. Scot-Meisami, 'Ghaznavid Panegyrics: Some Political Implications', *Iran*, 1990, 28, pp. 31–44.

was a fair degree of interest in the people who lived in northern India.[15] Gardizi was drawing on earlier writers, some of whom had visited India in search of information on medicinal plants and on various religious beliefs and practices. Indian scholars resident at the court of Harun al-Rashid in Baghdad in earlier times had discussed Indian mathematics, astronomy and medicine with their Arab counterparts and doubtless the curiosity on both sides still continued. Gardizi mentions the seven divisions of Indian society, almost echoing Megasthenes who had visited India in the fourth century BC in the Mauryan period. Unlike Megasthenes, this account refers to two divisions at the lowest social level, that of the Chandala and the Domb. And, echoing the description of Fa Hsien who came to India in Gupta times, he states that the Chandala have to announce their presence by striking wooden clappers, so that the 'pure' castes could keep at a distance from them. In the description of religion, apart from the names of various deities, there is some attempt to describe *avataras*, the doctrine of *karma*, and the nature of the divine.

But linked as they were to Mahmud, both he and Gardizi provide a curious explanation for why Mahmud attacked Somanatha, which involves iconoclasm but not initially of a Hindu image, although iconoclasm in relation to Hindu images came to be included. According to Farrukhi, the name Somanatha or Somnat (as it was often rendered in Persian) was a garbled version of *su-manat*—referring to the goddess Manat.[16] She was an ancient goddess of the Semitic pantheon, originally worshipped as Ishtar. Later, she was worshipped in Arabia in the form of an icon and as one of an important trio of goddesses—

---

[15] V. Minorsky, 'Gardizi on India', *Bulletin of the School of Oriental and African Studies*, 1948, 12, pp. 625–40; H.C. Ray, *Dynastic History of Northern India*, II, p. 953.

[16] M. Nazim, *The Life and Times of Sultan Mahmud of Ghazna*, p. 210; Ibn al-Kalbi, *The Book of Idols/Kitab al-Asnam*, pp. 12–23.

Lat, Uzza, Manat—mentioned in a famous verse of the *Qur'an*.[17] These were the goddesses of three shrines close to Mecca and were the daughters of the great God. The shrine of Manat, the goddess of destiny, was by the sea at Qudayd in the same region as Mecca and Medina. In pre-Islamic times, the goddesses were invoked when circumambulating the Ka'ba in Mecca and the pilgrimage was incomplete without a visit to the shrine of Manat. They were regarded as divine beings and, according to some sources, were each represented by a natural stone. The worship of these and other earlier deities was opposed by Muhammad. It is said that he called for the destruction of these idols and the termination of their cults. This was critical for early Islam before it had taken root, since the goddesses were much venerated, and particularly by the Quraysh, the tribe to which Muhammad belonged. According to some traditions, Ali did destroy the shrine of Manat on instructions from Muhammad but, according to others, Manat was saved and hidden.

These were the goddesses involved in what have come to be called the 'Satanic verses' and which became controversial at the time of their composition (as indeed more recently as well). It is said that at one point Muhammad declared, in the form of revealed verses, that the three goddesses could be worshipped as intermediaries of God. This would have made the new teachings of Islam more acceptable to those who still worshipped the old deities. However, through a later revelation, Muhammad declared that these verses had been inspired by Satan so they were expunged from the *Qur'an*, and there was a return to a firm insistence that these goddesses were not to be worshipped. The story may well be apocryphal, as many think it to be. Nevertheless, the attempt to identify the icon at Somanatha with Manat had extensive ramifications for the Islamic world and was

---

[17] *Qur'an*, sura 53.v.19–20; F.V. Winnett, 'The Daughters of Allah', *The Moslem World*, 1940, 30, pp. 113–30.

not just an incidental remark. This becomes evident from the underlying hint of Manat at Somanatha that is present even in the narratives of much later times.

According to Farrukhi and Gardizi, the legend was that the images of the first two were destroyed in Arabia but the one of Manat was secreted away to Kathiawar for safe keeping in a land where idol worship was considered normal.[18] Descriptions of Manat sometimes mention that she was worshipped in the form of an aniconic image of black stone, which could have been confused with the cylindrical form of the *lingam*, the expected icon in a Pashupata Shaiva temple. Others, however, describe her image as sculpted in a female form.[19] Muhammad's objection was not just to the worship of an idol, but to their representing the continuation of the older religion of the tribes of Arabia that he was trying to replace with his own teachings.[20] Separate tribal identities focusing on the worship of such deities were being replaced with Islamic monotheism. Later texts of the seventeenth century maintain that her sanctuary was destroyed together with the other two, but this may have been an afterthought to scotch the legend. Farrukhi adds that the people of Somanatha believed their icon to be so powerful that Mahmud would be unable to destroy it.[21] All these accounts were written with particular perspectives in mind and have to be compared and not necessarily taken literally. Farrukhi also states that the icon at Somanatha had human features as did the image of Manat at the Ka'ba.[22] The former statement would be incorrect if the icon was

---

[18] M. Nazim, op.cit., p. 210.

[19] A.R. al-Ansary, *Qaryat al-Fau*.

[20] W.E.N. Kensdale, *The Religious Beliefs and Practices of Ancient South Arabians*; G. Ryckmans, *Les Religions Arabes Pre-Islamique*, Vol. I, pp. 14, 18–19.

[21] M. Nazim, op.cit., pp. 115–17, 211.

[22] Farrukhi, *Diwan*, quoted in Nazim, op.cit., p. 210.

the *lingam*, unless it was a *mukha-lingam* which has a face emerging from the *lingam*. But there is no mention of such a *lingam* at Somanatha in any source.

The raid was successful, the loot was enormous, and Mahmud set off for home. Despite his claim that as a Muslim he would not redeem the idol for the wealth that the brahmans offered him, he nevertheless looted the temple of its wealth apart from breaking the idol. On his return journey from Somanatha, Mahmud took a route through the difficult environment of Kaccha and Sind, explained by some as due to his fleeing from the Chaulukya king who decided to pursue him, but Mahmud escaped. Mahmud had had a single-minded intention and that was to raid Somanatha. Was this because of his disapproval of Hindu idol-worship, or the supposed worship of Manat, or was it the lure of wealth and booty, or possibly even the wish to intervene in the Arab supply of horses to western India which might have threatened the trade in horses going through Ghazni, or a combination of all these features? That there might have been reasons in addition to iconoclasm that led to these raids is evident from the statement that the campaign against Thanesar was motivated by Mahmud's wish to acquire special elephants for his army.[23] These were priced at 100,000 *dirhams*, far in excess of even the highly priced horse. The Ghaznavids, like the Sassanians and the Seleucids before them, were very taken up by the idea of using elephants in their army against other armies beyond the borders of India.

Returning from the Somanatha campaign via Sind, Mahmud faced an Isma'ili Muslim ruler who had established an Isma'ili centre at Mansura. Attacking him caused much destruction all around.[24] Implicit in the narratives of these attacks on non-Sunni Muslims is a hint of the fear of the heretic. Such a fear was

---

[23] Al-Utbi, quoted in C.E. Bosworth, *The Ghaznavids*, p. 116.

[24] A. Wink, *Al-Hind*, I, pp. 184–89; pp. 217–18.

perhaps based on there having been many movements regarded as heresies against orthodox Islam in the previous two centuries, and some were politically hostile to the Caliph. Among those regarded as heresies were the Shi'a, the Isma'ili, the Qarmatian, the Assassins, the Zanj people and the Druzes.[25] Perhaps under the influence of the pre-Islamic religions of the region such as Zoroastrianism, Manichaeism and Buddhism, some groups supported the concept of an incarnation of deity and the transmigration of the divine spirit and awaited the saviour hero, ideas which were received with some interest by the Isma'ilis and Shi'as.[26] Sufi groups were also known to be distancing themselves from the formalism and legalism of the Islamic jurists.

Given this background, Mahmud's vehement support of Sunni Islam appears to have been partly religious but clearly political as well. The attempt was to shore up the power of the Caliphate at Baghdad and to exploit its patronage to Mahmud, especially in trying to make Ghazni into a major centre of the eastern Islamic world. The rivalry between Baghdad and Cairo over the legitimacy of the Caliphate impinged on the politics of eastern Islam. Mahmud required the support of Baghdad to safeguard his frontiers in west Asia. His support for the Caliphate was engineered to obtain for himself the appropriate titles of the defender of Islam, although at a more down-to-earth level it would also ratify his having usurped his brother's throne.[27] There may have been the echo of what has been postulated as a kind of cyclic movement in the epic of Firdausi, the *Shahnama*, antici-pating the coming of an Iranian and Islamic sovereignty through a king from the east.[28] Possibly, the panegyrics on Mahmud may

---

[25] A. Hottinger, *The Arabs*, pp. 86 ff.

[26] R. Canfield, 'Theological Extremism and Social Movements in Turko–Persia', in R. Canfield (ed.), *Turko–Persia in Historical Perspective*, pp. 132 ff.

[27] M. Nazim, op.cit., pp. 164 ff.

[28] J. Scot-Meisami, *Persian Historiography*, pp. 41 ff.

have led to the thought that he was such a king. This underlined his claims to legitimacy in ruling the empire of eastern Islam, more especially among the Turks who were impressed by the titles. The relatively obscure origins of his family would have made such legitimacy politically useful to his ambitions. His letters to the Caliph suggest a person who combines sycophancy with an aggressive self-righteousness, claiming that he has set forth exactly what God gave him the power to do in bringing victory to the Caliphate. The attempt to consolidate his holdings in north-west India was also conditioned by the threat of the rising Seljuq Turks and of Byzantine power to the west. Later in the eleventh century, there was to be trouble from further west in the assaults associated with the European Crusades.

Earlier, Mahmud had attacked Multan, ruled by an Isma'ili ruler, a sect which was anathema to the Sunni Mahmud. He had then discontinued the use of the Isma'ili mosque but did not destroy it, and the Sunni mosque was put into use. At first, the ruler agreed to become a Sunni, but later retracted. This gave Mahmud the excuse to attack Multan again and put the Isma'ili Muslims to death. Multan was a rich city and the attack resulted in more plunder for Mahmud. The Isma'ilis, whose major concern was trade, were however able to rehabilitate themselves through their trading contacts.[29] The temple at Multan had initially been desecrated in the late tenth century by Isma'ilis and replaced with a mosque. In the next century, they, in turn, were attacked by the Sunni Muslim Mahmud and their mosque fell into ruins.[30] Again, this is said to be a victory for Sunni Islam, but it also brought considerable wealth and would have affected the Arab trade in Sind for a while.

Farrukhi's account would have made of Mahmud a champion iconoclast in support of Sunni Islam. Not only was he attacking

---

[29] A. Wink, *Al-Hind*, I, p. 218.

[30] Ibid., I, pp. 186 ff.

the Hindus, the well-known idol-worshippers, he was also able to carry out the command of the Prophet regarding the destruction of the idol of Manat and, further, was exterminating Muslim heretics. This was not intended to equalize the killing of Hindus and Muslims, but to claim a double championship. Mahmud himself, while communicating his victories to the Caliphate, exaggerated the size, wealth and religious importance of the Somanatha temple and implied that his action had considerable political and religious significance. Not surprisingly, he became the recipient of grandiose titles from the Caliph.[31] This established his legitimacy in the Islamic world and perhaps explains why, although other idols were broken by him and temples plundered, the event at Somanatha carries a special importance and is more frequently quoted. But Mahmud's legitimacy in the eyes of established Islam also derived from the constant reiteration that he was a Sunni who attacked the heretics, the Ismai'ilis and Shi'as in India and Persia. The boast is always that their mosques were closed or destroyed and that invariably 50,000 of them were killed. The figure becomes formulaic, a part of the rhetoric for killing, irrespective of whether they were Hindu *kafirs* or Muslim heretics.

From the twelfth century onwards, there are further embellishments to the story. Wealth taken from the Somanatha temple by Mahmud is quantified in larger and larger figures. The temple was certainly very wealthy, nevertheless, the accounts are highly exaggerated. The temple and the icon are described through a variety of fantasies. That all this information did not tally, and frequently one source contradicted the other, does not seem to have bothered the authors of the narratives.

---

[31] M. Nazim, op.cit., p. 165; C.E. Bosworth, *The Ghaznavids*, p. 53; M. Habib, *Sultan Mahmud of Ghaznin*, p. 2; C.E. Bosworth, 'Mahmud of Ghazna in Contemporary Eyes and in Later Persian Literature', *Iran*, 1966, 4, pp. 85–92.

The description of the form of the idol varies from text to text.[32] Farrukhi states that Manat had human features and so did the Somanatha idol. Ibn Khallikan mentions that it had thirty rings around it, each ring representing a 1,000 years. So the age of the idol was taken back to 30,000 years. Ibn Zafir states that the idol possessed powers of life and death and could even determine one's future birth. Was this a confusion with Manat, the goddess of fate? Those that described it as a *lingam* sometimes said that it was 7 cubits tall, of which 2 were buried in the foundation, and it was 3 cubits in circumference. The entire image was decorated and was surrounded by lesser deities made of gold and silver. A bell hung on a gold chain at the entrance to the sanctum and the chain was 200 *mans* in weight, a *man* being several kilograms. Another description states that the icon was made of iron with a magnet placed above it so that it would be suspended in space—an awesome sight for the viewer.[33] There is clearly a difference of opinion on whether the idol was a *lingam* or was anthropomorphic.

Shaikh Farid al-Din Attar mentions a story where the brahmans plead with Mahmud to preserve the idol, in return for which they would give him immense wealth, but he refused, stating that he is not an idol seller but an idol breaker.[34] A fire is lit around the idol and it bursts, pouring forth 20 *mans* of precious stones. The *lingam* is said to be hollow. This would be unprecedented in the iconography of the *lingam*, or even in an anthropomorphic idol of stone.

---

[32] M. Nazim op.cit., pp. 209–10; Elliot and Dowson, I, p. 97 ff.; ibid., III, pp. 44 ff.; IV, pp. 181 ff. Ferishta in J. Briggs, *History of the Rise of Mohammadan Power in India*, Calcutta, 1966 (reprint), Vol. I, p. 43.

[33] Zakariya al-Qazwini, *Asrar al-Bilad*, Elliot and Dowson, I, pp. 97 ff.; Sadid-al-Din Muhammad Awfi, *Jawami al-Hikayat wa Lawami al Riwayat*, M. Nizam al-Din (ed.), No. 1996.

[34] M. Nazim, op.cit., p. 221.

A later version, which is frequently repeated, refers to the promise made by Mahmud to the brahmans that he would return the idol.[35] When he is reminded of this, he decides to break his promise. So the idol is burnt and reduced to lime which is then put into the betel leaf served to the brahmans. When the latter ask for the idol, Mahmud says it is already inside them. A sequence to this story is that one of the brahmans made an identical idol, buried it outside the temple, and trained a calf to sniff at the site. He then announced that he had had a dream that the idol was hidden in the ground and that the calf would find it. The calf located the spot and the idol was retrieved and duly installed in the temple. Does this story reflect the wish of the priests of the temple to annul the destruction of the idol?

Not all the stories are eulogies to Mahmud. Some have an edge of irony, questioning the values of the world of power and the humanity of Mahmud. These are frequently influenced by Sufi thought as in the case of Farid al-Din Attar. He attempts to project the ideal king as visualized by Sufis. Mahmud being a prominent personality, the values of the Sufis were projected as contrary to his aspirations. Incidentally, Attar refers to the idol in the Somanatha temple as being that of the goddess Lat, and, when destroyed, revealed an immense amount of jewels. Attar's comment is that iconoclasm means that the idol in one's heart should first be destroyed.[36]

The thirteenth-century *Al-Kamil fi al-Tarikh* of Ibn al-Athir mentions that part of Mahmud's purpose in breaking the idol was to demonstrate that the Hindu claim to its being invincible was false. He does mention that the idol is supposed to have healing qualities, but this is not put to the test. According to him, the temple was built on a foundation of stone and was supported by

---

[35] Isami, *Futuh al-Salatin*, pp. 83–90, quoted in Nazim, op.cit., p. 221–22.

[36] Attar, *The Conference of Birds*, pp. 44, 45, 136–37, 160–61, 171–72, 175, 184, 194–96.

fifty-six columns of teak imported from Africa.[37] This was
structurally not likely in such a building.[38] Besides, why would
teak be imported from Africa when it was widely available in the
forests of Gujarat? The temple, he says, houses the greatest of
idols which was a phallic representation of Shiva and was
serviced by 1,000 to 2,000 brahmans and 300 *devadasis* and
musicians, 300 servants and others. It was endowed with 10,000
villages (although another source quotes 2,000) and therefore
had a huge income. This is again an exaggeration since the
monasteries at Nalanda had endowments of only 200 villages at
most, and the Brihadeshvara temple at Tanjavur had an
endowment of 300 villages. The Somanatha temple would thus
have possessed more jewels and gold than many a royal treasury.
Ibn Zafir states that the temple had a pyramidal roof thirteen
storeys high, decorated with fourteen spherical knobs of gold
which glittered in the distance. The floor was made of teak filled
in with lead.[39] It has been argued that these descriptions are
quoted from the letters written by Mahmud to the Caliph at
Baghdad, describing the Somanatha temple.[40] This may account
for the exaggerations in Mahmud's claims to what he had
conquered.

A truly garbled version comes from the Persian poet Sa'di in
his *Bustan*, composed in the thirteenth century.[41] He claims to

---

[37] M. Nazim, op.cit., p. 212; Ibn al-Athir, *Al-Kamil fi al Tarikh*, C.J.
Tornberg (ed.), pp. 86, 241; *Gazetteer of the Bombay Presidency*, I, p. 523.

[38] Dhaky and Shastri, *The Riddle of the Temple of Somanatha*, pp. 10–11.

[39] M. Nazim, op.cit., pp. 211 ff.

[40] M. Nazim, 'Somanath and its Conquest by Sultan Mahmud', *Journal of
the Royal Asiatic Society*, 1928, Part 1, January, pp. 233–38.

[41] *The Bustan of Shaikh Muslih al-Din Sa'di*, pp. 238–44; J. Prinsep, 'Note
on Somnath', *Journal of the Asiatic Society of Bengal*, 1838, 7, pp. 883–87;
A.H. Edwards, *The Bustan of Sadi*, London 1911, p. 109, R.H. Davis, *The
Lives of Indian Images*, New Jersey, 1997, pp. 100 ff.

have visited the Somanatha temple, although there is no record of this. He describes the idol as beautiful and made of ivory and set with jewels in the manner of Manat. The image has a faultless form and therefore many people come to see it. The priests, according to him, are Mogh priests. This might suggest Magha brahmans, but this is unlikely in a Shaiva Pashupata temple since Magha brahmans are associated with the worship of the sun. Possibly, he had heard of the Magha brahmans. He describes the brahmans as fire-worshippers and as expounding the teachings in the Asta and Zend—clearly a confusion with Zoroastrian priests—about whom he might have been better informed in Iran. One of these priests, he says, shows him the image magically moving its hands and he is both impressed and intrigued. Hiding himself in the temple, he makes the dramatic discovery that this was an illusion since the hands were worked with strings, presumably rather like string puppets. Since he was caught hiding and observing the deceit, Sa'di threw the string-puller into a well and escaped. It has been suggested that Sa'di, being a Sufi poet, was susceptible to visions!

A story recorded by Minhaj Siraj, writing in the thirteenth century, narrates that Mahmud's father had a dream in which there was a tall tree growing out of his house whose shadow covered the world. At this point, an idol in an Indian temple on the banks of the Indus, near present-day Peshawar, collapsed.[42] The indicators are only too obvious in this story. It goes on to say that Mahmud converted thousands of temples into mosques and brought back the idol of Manat from Somanatha and broke it into four pieces, two of which were embedded in the palace and the mosque in Ghazni, and one each sent to Mecca and Medina. The latter was doubtless to clinch the matter of the

---

[42] H.G. Raverty (trans.), *Tabaqat-i-Nasiri: A General History of the Muhammadan Dynasties of Asia including Hindustan*, Vol. I, pp. 76, 82–83.

destruction of Manat.[43] Recent excavations at Ghazni have
revealed some Hindu icons but not the kind mentioned in these
accounts.[44] A statue of Brahma in white marble with multiple
heads, standing in a nimbus and surrounded by other figures, can
be partially reconstructed from the finds as well as a few worn-
out statues. It remains unclear as to who brought these and from
where. There would not have been much point in taking back
pieces of the *lingam* to Ghazni, since if it was of the usual form,
there would be little to show that it was an icon.

In a fifteenth-century account, *Habib al-Siyar*, the temple is
described as being of vast dimensions, the idol is said to be that
of Lat, as reported by Attar, and on certain nights more than a
hundred thousand people congregate in the temple. Mahmud's
attack resulted in the death of 50,000 infidels.[45] The excavation of
1951 does not suggest a particularly large temple, and certainly
not large enough to accommodate so many people. Nor is it likely
that people in such great numbers would have assembled there.
But the hyperbole endows these narratives with a sense of the
dramatic.

If the story of Manat was to have any credence, the idol
would have to be either aniconic or a female form. The *lingam*
was generally in the shape of a short column or pillar, or even
smaller. The confusion was doubtless caused by these two
different versions, identifying the deity being represented by the
idol. Gradually, the link with Manat in the Turko–Persian
accounts became more doubtful but, nevertheless, it did not
altogether disappear.

---

[43] Al-Biruni states that the stone idol from the Somanatha temple and the
bronze idol from Thanesar were broken and embedded in the hippodrome
at Ghazni. Sachau, *Alberuni's India*, I, p. 117.

[44] U. Scerrato, 'Summary Report on the Italian Archaeological Mission in
Afghanistan', *East and West*, 1959, 10, 1 and 2, pp. 39–40.

[45] *Habib al-Siyar*, Elliot and Dowson, IV, pp. 180 ff.

The fourteenth century saw a shift in the representation of Mahmud in Turko–Persian narratives. This is not surprising since the historical context had changed. This is in part reflected in the policy of the Sultans towards the destruction of temples. Mahmud came as a plunderer whose purpose, apart from iconoclasm, was to collect wealth to equip his kingdom at Ghazni and beyond. His selection of temples was determined by the quantity of wealth each would provide. The Ghurids and their successors, who created a kingdom in India, were more concerned with establishing their political authority since revenue and taxes would bring in the wealth. The temples that they selected for destruction were the ones that gave legitimacy to local rulers, a legitimacy that the Sultans were attempting to appropriate.[46] The early Turko–Persian accounts are the narratives of the immigrant intended to contain social dissent and encourage acculturation within the immigrant group. With the stabilization of the settlement, the legitimacy of the Sultan to rule takes precedence over the triumphs of the conqueror.

Mahmud being represented as the raider, commanding the passes of the Hindu Kush and carrying out raids to plunder the temple towns of the north Indian plains, was now being superceded by another image, that of the man who laid the foundation of Islamic rule in India. This was of course historically inaccurate. The Arabs were the earliest Islamic rulers, having conquered Sind in the eighth century, and were more effectively settled in western India. Nor was Mahmud able to establish his rule over northern India. But the concern of the new historians of the fourteenth century was with seeking continuity for political power and with Turkish connections. This was also the period when the Sultanates of the subcontinent were becoming politically more stable. However, the lead-up to this period had seen

---

[46] R. Eaton, 'Temple Desecration and Indo–Muslim States', in *Essays on Islam and Indian History*, pp. 94–132.

crises in the Caliphate and a range of dissident groups within Islam. Given that conversion to Islam in India was limited, such crises were possible during the rule of the Sultans in India as well. Mahmud was seen as the starting point of a continuous Islamic rule, and by now the propaganda of his campaigning in the cause of Islam was well established. There was therefore a change of tack and the glorification of plunder, although not discarded, was nevertheless secondary to the glorification of the ideal Islamic ruler. This perspective becomes apparent, for example, in the writings of two among the more influential historians, Barani and Isami.

Both Barani and Isami, important litterateurs, writing at Indian courts, introduce a new perspective, historiographically more significant than the earlier ones. India was no longer merely the backdrop to narratives glorifying Islamic iconoclasm and the forcible acquisition of wealth. India had to be welded into the world of Islam. Both chroniclers were contemporaries, Barani being at the court of the Delhi Sultans, and Isami at the Bahmani court in the Deccan. Both project Mahmud as the ideal Muslim hero, but the perspective is from within India and the context is the Islamic state and society in India and the historical intervention that has made this possible. Barani states that it is the duty of the historian to teach the lessons of history. To this end, there is much less of fantasy and more of polemic.

Barani claims to be writing in order to educate Muslim rulers in their duties towards Islam and the text includes Mahmud giving advice to his sons and to other Muslim kings.[47] For Barani, religion and kingship are twins and the ruler needs to know the religious ideals of kingship if he claims to be ruling on behalf of God. If he is ignorant of these, he cannot claim to be God's deputy. Sultans are required to protect Islam through the *shari'a*

---

[47] Zia al-Din Barani, *Fatawa-i-Jahandari*; P. Hardy, *Historians of Medieval India, Studies in Indo-Muslim Historical Writing*, pp. 25 ff.

and suppress both Muslim heretics and Hindu infidels. But at the
same time, they must be just rulers. Mahmud as the model ruler
is the creation of Barani who was projecting his own ideas of
what a good Muslim ruler should be. Mahmud, interestingly, was
seen as a crusader against the rationalists and the philosophers.[48]
There was little space for the dissidents and the heterodox in this
view of Islam, and intellectuals such as Ibn-i-Sina/Avicenna
would have been silenced.

Isami composes what he regards as an epic poem on the
Muslim rulers of India, starting with Mahmud.[49] In his epic,
Futuh al-Salatin, he emulates Firdausi's *Shahnama*—an epic on the
kings of Persia—doubtless, with the partial intention that the
Bahmani Sultan should be generous towards him in the same way
as Firdausi had hoped for generosity from Mahmud! Isami's epic
is intended to provide the Sultans of India, but particularly the
Bahmani Sultans, with appropriate legitimation. He argues that
kingship descended from Adam to the early pre-Islamic rulers of
Persia—and in this, he includes Alexander of Macedon and the
Sassanids—and continues through Qutb-ud-din Aibak and the
Khaljis to the Tughlaqs. The Sultans of India begin with
Mahmud, who established Muslim rule in India, and continue
with the later dynasties. They are warriors of the faith, pillars of
orthodoxy and militarily triumphant. It is interesting that Persian
antecedents play such an important role in the projection of the
past, despite Alexander and the Sassanids being pre-Islamic.
Invoking Alexander may have been an attempt to underline the
importance of conquest, but the fuller evocation of the Sassanids
sent an altogether different message. Seeking a Sassanid ancestry
was not a claim to conquest but rather a wish to be seen as part

---

[48] This was a comment by Professor Muzaffar Alam. See also his 'Shari'a
and Governance in the Indo–Islamic Context', in D. Gilmartin and B.B.
Lawrence (eds), *Beyond Turk and Hindu*, pp. 216–45.

[49] *Futuh al-Salatin*, discussed in P. Hardy, op.cit., pp. 94 ff.

of the civilized world of Persian culture: a world that was wooed without too much success by Mahmud, but which was now the emergent culture of the lands to the west and was giving a different direction to Indian Islam. From this perspective, the chronicles of the Sultanates were in some ways sequels to the *Shahnama*. The increasing imprint of Persian culture on the Turkish and Afghan aristocracy is noticeable. Whatever the reasons, it is significant that the so-called 'epics of conquest' were changing directions.

Barani refers to Mahmud destroying the idol of Manat (at Somanatha). Isami also mentions Manat but obliquely, in saying that God informed the Prophet that the last remnants of idolatry to be found at Somanatha would be destroyed. This becomes an explanation for Mahmud's raid and Isami adds that Mahmud received divine help when he was lost on his return from Somanatha. Allah and Muhammad both looked upon Mahmud with favour, which is of course the kind of comment that Mahmud would have wished for.

The earlier fantasy of Manat gradually gives way to a more political concern with the legitimacy of Islamic rule in India through the Sultans. But having once raised the ghost of Manat, she cannot be made to disappear and hovers over many of the variations in the narratives. The icon was obviously not of Manat but what is curious is that it was either seen or hinted at as being Manat by a number of people. Her importance lies not in judging the validity of her identity with the Shiva *lingam*, but in the role that the story played in providing an identity to the Turks and linking these central Asian Muslims to significant events in the life of Muhammad in Arabia. By destroying Manat, they may have believed that they were carrying out the wishes of the Prophet to a more efficient degree than the Arabs.

Curiously, the Arabs received little attention. The coming of Islam is not recognized as a political presence until the establishment of Turkish rule. This position is reiterated in Badayuni's sixteenth-century work, *Muntakhab al-Tawarikh*, where kingship descends from Allah to Muhammad to the Caliphs. However, Badayuni does state categorically that he does not begin his history of India with the Arab conquest of Sind in the eighth century AD because this was a transitory event in the history of Islam. It was only when Subuktagin conquered parts of northern India that Islam came to stay. He denies that the idol at Somanatha was Manat and explains that Somanatha was actually 'Shobhanatha', and means the lord of beauty.[50] He adds that part of the broken idol was sent to Ghazni to be placed at the entrance of the Jami Masjid to be trod upon by all those who entered the mosque.

The change in political emphasis on the role of Mahmud is reflected in other stories, as, for example, in the claim that the names of all the kings of India were inscribed on the walls of the temple[51] and therefore its destruction amounted to the defeat of all of them. This was an attempt to portray a single act as symbolic of the conquest of India, a portrayal that is also projected in the claim that Mahmud founded Muslim rule in India. In fact, many of the kings of India would have been unknown to the builders of the temple, and many of the kings of eastern India and the peninsula seem to have been unconcerned with either Mahmud or Somanatha. At approximately the time of the raid, the Chola king, Rajendra I, was marching his armies up the eastern coast, claiming conquests and declaring his triumph by bringing back water from the Ganga. He was apparently unaware of the activities of Mahmud. The obtaining of wealth as the focus of the raid also shifts the political emphasis. In one sixteenth-century account, the raid is explained as due to gold being obtainable near Somanatha and semi-precious stones being available from the trade with Sri Lanka.[52]

---

[50] G.B.A. Ranking (trans.), Badayuni, *Muntakhab al-Tawarikh*, p. 28.

[51] R. Davis, *The Lives of Indian Images*, p. 94.

[52] *Mir'at-i Ahmadi*, quoted in E.C. Bayley, *The Local Muhammadan Dynasties, Gujarat*, pp. 28–29.

With the decline in the power of the Caliphate, states with Muslim rulers had to find their own sources of legitimation. In the Indian case, there was a reiteration of the old narrative of destroying the temple but the action and the purpose were different. These accounts describe various patrons as repeatedly destroying the Somanatha temple and converting it into a mosque. In 1299, Ulugh Khan is said to have attacked the temple, constructed a mosque on the site, and sent the image to Ala al-Din Khalji in Delhi. Ferishta says that in 1395, Muzaffar Khan, the governor of Gujarat, attacked Somanatha and converted the temple into a mosque. Towards the end of the fourteenth century, in one account, we are told that Zafar Khan conducted another campaign against Somanatha, broke the idol, and established Islam.[53] Was this a more recent idol or was it merely the rhetoric of the older event being endlessly repeated? Soon after this, in a later text, it is said that in about 1398, Zafar Khan was informed that the infidels had assembled at Somanatha to re-establish their religion. So he set out with his army, killed most of the infidels, destroyed the idols and the temples and built *masjids* instead, appointed an administration of *qazis* and *muftis* and left a garrison to prevent further action by the infidels.[54] Ferishta says that in 1413, Muzaffar Khan's grandson attacked the temple. Mahmud Begada, the Sultan of Gujarat, claims to have attacked the temple in 1469 and converted it into a mosque.

The narrative of the raid is repeated but with embellished variations through a cloud of hype. Every century or less, some Sultan or general is associated with the breaking of the Somanatha idol and, at various times, the temple already said to have been converted into a mosque gets converted into a mosque once again. According to the Turko–Persian accounts, there seems to have been an obsession with destroying the temple and breaking the

---

[53] *Mir'at-i Sikandari*, quoted in E.C. Bayley, op.cit., pp. 76 ff.

[54] *Tabakat-i Akbari*, quoted in ibid., pp. 79 ff.

idol each time a fresh one is installed. But was there such a pattern of continually breaking the idol and converting the temple into a mosque? There is a basic contradiction in these statements. Had the temple been converted to a mosque subsequent to each attack, then logically (and logic is not at a premium in these accounts), apart from the first attack and conversion of the temple into a mosque by Ulugh Khan, the later attackers were each attacking a mosque. Clearly, various people were muscling in on the narrative of the act to get the benefit of claiming to be the destroyers of the Somanatha temple and responsible for its conversion into a mosque, irrespective of whether the destruction or the conversion was actually carried out. To that extent, it could well have been hyperbole in most cases. These claims are not reflected in Jaina narratives, or the Sanskrit inscriptions, and are contradicted by the excavation of the site as we shall see.

It would seem that after the first raid, the claim ceases to be history and becomes rhetoric. All the more so, since colophons to Sanskrit texts of the late fifteenth century continue to refer to it as a place of pilgrimage and worship. The *Krishna-krida-kavya* of Keshavadasa Hridayarama of Prabhasa refers to the temple of Somanatha in the holy city of Prabhasa in 1473.[55] *The Prabodha-prakasha* of Vishnudasa-Bhima refers to the *nija-avasa* of Somanatha in 1490.[56] They both describe the temple as another Kailasa on earth. If the temple had been converted into a mosque and used as such, it would have had to be repeatedly sanctified and reconverted to a temple, a procedure that finds no mention. The rather squat dome and the unimpressive minarets do not suggest that much effort was made even by Aurangzeb's

---

[55] Dhaky and Shastri, op.cit., pp. 29, 35, fn. 92, 93, *Sorathadesha sohamano pavanapura prabhasa shri someshvara sharada ali antara kailasa* [v.119] in N.I. Desai, *Gujarati*, Dipotsavi Issue, October 1935.

[56] Dhaky and Shastri, op.cit., pp. 29, 35 fn. 92, 94. *Shri someshvara nija-avasa bhumi manhi biju kailasa* [v.174] in K.K. Sastri (ed.), *Prabodha-prakasha*, Gujarat Vernacular Society, Ahmedabad.

officers to convert the temple into a functioning mosque. This appears in striking contrast to other temples converted into mosques, such as the Quwwat-al-Islam in Delhi.

The repeated claim to destroying the temple reads like an exaggerated attempt on the part of the chroniclers to proclaim the greatness of their patrons and to prop up their self-importance. By now, the destruction of the temple had in itself become part of the rhetoric of conquest, and it did not matter too much whether it was actually raided every half-century. Yet, it continued to function as a temple. Popular tradition maintains that the temple was attacked seven times, but this is not borne out by the excavation of the site nor by the non-Persian sources. From the sixteenth century, there may well have been a relative decline in its patronage. Whereas a number of Jaina temples were still financed by merchants, this was not the case with the Somanatha temple. A falling off in the commercial economy of the region would also have limited its patrons. It would seem that there were neither kings nor rajas nor merchants to sustain its status as a second Kailasa on earth, quite apart from whether or not it suffered raids. Nevertheless, it remained a functioning temple with an income, since in the sixteenth century Akbar permitted the worship of the linga in the Somanatha temple and appointed *desais*/officers to administer it. Abu'l Fazl refers to the raids of Mahmud and makes an interesting comment:

> ... fanatical bigots representing India as a country of unbelievers at war with Islam, incited his unsuspecting nature to the wreck of honour and the shedding of blood and the plunder of the virtuous.[57]

This is, at one level, a condoning of the actions of Mahmud but at another, an indictment. Significantly, he does not mention

---

[57] *A'in-i-Akbari*, Vol. III, p. 377.

Mahmud laying the foundations of Muslim rule in India. This legitimation was not required by Mughal rulers who were well integrated into the Indian polity.

In the mid-seventeenth century, Aurangzeb ordered his army to destroy the temple. The order appears not to have been carried out as he issues a further and later order for its destruction and its conversion into a mosque in 1706 just before he died. Some conversion was carried out since the ruins of the temple carry squat domes and stunted minarets. Irrespective of whether it was a temple or mosque, few people by now worshipped there and it was abandoned. Royal patrons were unwilling to restore it, as it was probably too costly to do so, or else the will was lacking. An attempt was made by a merchant, but was discontinued. Ahalyabai Holkar built a small temple in its vicinity in the late eighteenth century, and it was said that the *lingam* had been 'hidden' in an underground chamber. She was probably unable to finance the building of a temple on the scale of the older one. If Maratha resistance to Muslim rule, and a Hindu trauma over Mahmud's attack on Somanatha, were as central as is alleged in recent views, it is surprising that the Maratha rulers did not get together to rebuild the temple as an act of defiance and an expression of sentiment. This would have been easy to do because in any case by now Mughal power had declined.

The account quoted most frequently from the eighteenth century was that of Ferishta who had written it in the previous century. There is again a hint of Manat in his statement that Shiva was worshipped in pre-Islamic Arabia. He collated a number of existing versions indiscriminately and worked out his own, but the contradictions of the earlier versions remain. Ferishta's account is far removed from the event in time.[58]

---

[58] *Gulshan-i-Ibrahimi/Tarikh-i-Ferishta*, trans. J. Briggs, *History of the Rise of Mohammadan Power in India*, Vol. I, p. 43; Vol. II, p. 377; A. Dow, *The History of Hindustan*, Vol. I, pp. 68 ff.

Ferishta describes the size of the idol as being the equivalent of 5 yards in height, 2 yards of which were buried in the ground. Mahmud is said to have struck off the nose from the face, at which point the brahmans tried to negotiate to save the idol but Mahmud would have none of it. He then struck the belly which was hollow and full of gem stones. Yet at the same time, Ferishta describes it as a *lingam* and as such it should not have had a belly. Mahmud sent its pieces to Ghazni, Mecca and Medina. Ferishta repeats an earlier story of Mahmud having appointed a local Indian, Dabiselima/Dabishalim/Dabbisalima, to rule over the Somanatha territory. There were said to be two persons by the same name, a brahman and a prince. The brahman was mistakenly appointed. After many vicissitudes, the prince came to rule. Who this person was or whether such a person existed remains unclear. It has been suggested that this could be a reference to the story of the brothers Vallabhasena and Durlabhasena, and of the latter being appointed by Mahmud to rule the area as his deputy.[59] Ferishta's version became the accepted one in more recent times, having been translated early on into English.

In the Mughal period, the event becomes marginal to the historiographic concerns of Mughal chroniclers who were seeking a wider intellectual horizon and linking Mughal history both to aspects of the earlier Indian past and to the broader Islamic view of history. As a contrast to this, it is sometimes projected as accompanying claims to legitimacy by the lesser rulers and generals.

In the Turko–Persian and similar accounts, there were many inexplicable features. There was a continuing contradiction as to whether the icon is anthropomorphic or aniconic, whether it is male or female, whether it is Shiva or Manat. Iconographically, even if it was a *mukha-lingam* with the depiction of a face, this

---

[59] A.K. Forbes, *The Ras Mala*, p. 61.

might explain the existence of the nose as in some accounts, but the more important part of the icon—the belly from which jewels poured out—would not have been part of the *lingam*. Had it been a *lingam* with a representation of a standing Shiva, there would have been no ambiguity about its being a male figure. A stone icon would not have been hollow. There are many generalized references in Turko–Persian texts to temple destruction and iconoclasm but the Somanatha temple and its idol are always specifically mentioned and described in detail. Interest in the other temples raided by Mahmud is relatively less as compared to the almost obsessive interest in Somanatha. Among Shaiva temples and icons, Somanatha was important, but as one among a dozen others. It was a popular place of pilgrimage and attracted pilgrims from distant places. Was there a lingering wish among these chroniclers that it might be Manat?

The elevation in importance of the Somanatha temple in Turko–Persian accounts subsequent to Mahmud's raid was a way of giving added importance to the raid as well. Was Somanatha being elevated as the Hindu equivalent of Mecca or of Baghdad and Mahmud's raid symbolic of the conquest of India?[60] It is worth keeping in mind that Barani and Isami were writing when Somanatha was still a rich and powerful institution—although not regarded as exceptionally so when compared with royal temples such as those of the Cholas. This adds to the rhetorical flavour of their reference to the raids. We may also ask whether the icon, if identified as Manat, was perhaps of considerable consequence to Muslim sentiment. It would not, therefore, have been merely an account of iconoclasm, since the icon where it is identified as Manat was of importance more to the conquerors than to the conquered. Admittedly, the identification with a Hindu icon was superimposed on that with Manat and was to become the dominant identification.

---

[60] R. Davis, op.cit., p. 94.

In order to repress heresies of all types, some Sunni Muslim rulers believed that they had to demonstrate their willingness and ability to destroy the symbols of heretics and non-believers, and to repeat their accounts, however exaggerated, of destroying these symbols, in order to continually legitimize their rule. The specifics of what was destroyed become unimportant, since the claim is to destruction. Through these narratives, Somanatha comes to be imbued with symbolic significance for Sunni Islam: a significance that is affirmed in an inverse form, as it were, in later times in colonial and communal histories.

The turn in texts such as those of Barani and Isami may also reflect the decreasing power of the Caliphate that led to a greater focus on local Sultans. The reality of politics was being played out in various regions. The centre of gravity was shifting. Serving the cause of Islam required a focus on the deeds of Muslim rulers and these were often exaggerated; the past was to be seen in a religious perspective; and there was a selection of events and arguments to support this change.[61]

Having imbued Somanatha with immense symbolic significance, the authors of the Turko–Persian texts use the event to construct their own fantasies of power. They sometimes convert the idea of attacks on the temple to rhetoric, amplify and exaggerate the loot, fantasize on what happened in order to emphasize the power of those projected as the inheritors of the raid. Descriptions of the destruction of the temple assume immense significance and, in the politics of power, these descriptions uphold legitimation. In another set of texts, as we shall see, the rebuilding of the temple plays a parallel role in legitimizing Chaulukya power.

There was much fantasizing over the wealth of temples, with a vision of opulence that seemed to increase over time. References to the killing of Muslim heretics and infidels are

---

[61] P. Hardy, op.cit., pp. 111–112.

frequent and the figure was often the same—50,000, suggesting that it was notional and formulaic. Mahmud's attack on Hindu temples and on Shi'a and Isma'ili mosques was, at one level, a religious crusade against both the infidel and the heretic. The community of the victors was not a hegemonic, monolithic one but was segmented by the presence of the dissenters. The segment takes precedence over the broader religious identity. But these were also places and people involved in the exchange of goods and wealth in the lucrative and resilient trade with west Asia, an activity that revived after the attack. Traders from Multan were resuscitated by returning to the trade with the Persian Gulf and with west Asia, subsequent to the attack by Mahmud.

Multan, under Isma'ili rule, and Veraval-Somanatha, had an economic viability which was closely tied up with commerce—in the former case, through the Indo–Iranian borderlands as well as through Sind, and in the latter, through maritime trade. This could lead to yet another question. Was Mahmud, in trying to marginalize Somanatha, attempting also to destroy the Arab monopoly over the trade in horses with Gujarat because this was crucial to increasing the trade through Ghazni? Perhaps the Somanatha temple like many others in Gujarat, as mentioned in Arab sources, was also involved in the financing of this trade. Marco Polo, in the thirteenth century, writes of Somanatha attracting trade with merchants from distant places. Hormuz is specifically mentioned, particularly in connection with the trade in horses and is closely tied to the Indian trade. Temple priests involved in these activities are, according to Marco Polo, perfidious.[62]

The narratives from the eleventh to the fourteenth centuries shift in their assessment of Mahmud. From eulogizing iconoclasm as well as the bashing of infidels and heretics and fantasizing

---

[62] W. Marsden, *The Travels of Marco Polo*, revised by M. Komroff, Sections 19, 21, 29.

about the wealth of India, they begin to have a greater concern with projecting the ideal Muslim ruler. This concern became problematic when rulership involved governing a largely non-Islamic society and where even large Muslim communities were not followers of orthodox Islam. Apart from the sizeable communities of Shi'as and Isma'ilis, there were also the Bohras, Khojas, Navayats, Mappilas and many more, whose Islam was neither identical nor orthodox.

The act of conversion not only changes the religion of the person who has been converted but also affects observances and beliefs in the religion to which the person has been converted. This is all the more so when an entire *jati* converts. In such situations identities of status and occupation, customary law, rules of marriage and inheritance, accompany the conversion to a greater or lesser degree. Long established rituals and beliefs are not easily shed and tend to be inducted into the new religion wherever there is scope for flexibility. This is even more frequent when new settlers marry into existing communities as happens, for instance, when traders settle in distant places. New communities are created and new religious sects. Dissent from the orthodoxies of both religions creates heresies that can be either opposed or tolerated, depending on their political and social support or economic potential. The arrival of a new religion is therefore not just a matter of the old confronting the new, but much more a matter of how new relationships are negotiated. This was an active process with the arrival of Islam in India.

The Bohras (known locally as Vahuras) of Gujarat, established as a merchant community, incorporate much of the local tradition in their 'histories'. Thus, even though they were Muslims, their narratives refer to icons that speak of the suspending of a metal image of Ganesha by using magnets. The Bohras suffered as non-Sunnis after the attack of Zafar Khan at the end of the fourteenth century, and possibly because they too incorporated local beliefs and observances into their religious practice and were supporters of the *pir* tradition of popular saints. Subsequently, there were some conversions to Sunni Islam among them.[63] Rules relating both to the believers and the infidels had therefore to be bent or even ignored. Can it be argued that one reason for the shift in the assessment of Mahmud was due to an element of doubt about the accepted role models of Muslim rulers, with the Indian situation throwing up new problems given that the majority of the subjects were non-Muslims? Although the attempt was to depict the coming of Islam as the success of the warrior, the fact that this was so exaggerated would hint at an uncertainty of confidence and the need to negotiate.

The authors of the narratives were poets and court chroniclers. Fantasy would be almost a requirement in the case of the former. The latter would write to please and legitimize the reigning Sultan, often within the context of a distinct perspective. There would have been attempts to revise versions of earlier histories and write narratives reflecting contemporary demands. Even in their courtly segregation from the rest of society, they were aware that the religion of their patron was not necessarily that of the larger population. In the court circles of the Sultans, the identities of Sunnis and Shi'as would have been important. The new religious forms that were evolving in towns and villages, and which under the banner of Bhakti were drawing supporters from various communities identified with Hindu and Islamic sects, had not yet affected the courts. Nor is there much reflection among the elite of the growing centrality of the *guru* and the *pir* and *faqir* with large followings among the populace in general. But the questions that were being asked by the Sufis in their *khanqahs*, not invariably supportive of official Islam, would have had echoes in the courts. The narratives of Mahmud were therefore bound to carry variations, depending

---

[63] S.C. Misra, *The Muslim Communities in Gujarat*, Baroda 1964; J. Blank, *Mullahs on the Mainframe*, Chicago 2001, pp. 36–45.

on how the role of Islam among the elite was being perceived. Variations occurring in narratives claiming to be precise descriptions of an event, would encourage the event and its depiction to become a matter of political rhetoric, even if projected as iconoclasm.

4

Sanskrit Inscriptions from Somanatha and its Vicinity

Another category of major sources of the same period as the Turko–Persian accounts is that of inscriptions in Sanskrit from Somanatha and its vicinity. These reflect the ambience and the activities in and around Somanatha in the period after Mahmud's raid. The perspectives evident from inscriptions are different from other sources, and it is surprising that as texts pertaining to the history of Somanatha, they have generally received little attention.

There are many inscriptions which refer to activities in the area, a few prior to 1026, and more of the period after. Some carry significant evidence of the situation in Somanatha in the later period. They focus on activities related to the Somanatha temple and other temples in the vicinity. They are important as annals of the period since some record the official version of dynastic history and other matters thought to be significant. The intention of these is largely to propagate what might be called an official version of events from the local perspective and this is a contrast to that of the Turko–Persian accounts. The narratives from the two sources sometimes contradict each other. These, in turn, often contradict the narrative from a third major source— the Jaina texts.

One is therefore surprised to read a modern historian writing,

> The inscriptions bearing on the period of Sultan
> Mahmud which have so far been discovered have been
> published in the *Journal of the Asiatic Society of Bengal,*
> the *Epigraphia Indica* and the *Indian Antiquary*, but
> taken together their historical value is almost negligible.[1]

This seems to have been the received opinion until very recently,
hence the scant attention given to inscriptions. The use that is
now being made of inscriptions is an indication of the more
extensive range of sources that characterize contemporary historical research. Collections of inscriptions in Sanskrit and a few in
Arabic from Kathiawar and Gujarat have been published by
various scholars. Some traders from west Asia, when they settled
in the port of Somanatha-Veraval, issued bilingual inscriptions in
Sanskrit and Arabic. Later, when the settlements of Arab traders
grew and administration came under the control of the Sultans,
there were further inscriptions in Arabic, occasionally with a
Sanskrit version. From the fifteenth century, Gujarati came to be
used more widely.

Inscriptions provide a fairly consistent narrative of some
aspects of the history of Gujarat at this time and particularly
during the period from about AD 1000. There are references
initially to various minor rulers, many of whom took the title of
raja but may have been just the chiefs of clans. Others ruled small
principalities. When the Chaulukyas were well established from the
eleventh century, their grants to various grantees—brahmans,
Jainas and others—are recorded.[2] The grants of land made by
Bhimadeva I, especially in Kaccha and soon after Mahmud's raid,

---

[1] Nazim, *The Life and Times of Sultan Mahmud of Ghazna*, p. 17.

[2] H.G. Shastri, *The Inscriptions of Gujarat*; G. Buhler, 'Eleven Land Grants
of the Chaulukyas of Anhilvad', *Indian Antiquary*, 1877, VI, pp. 180–214.

would suggest that Chaulukya authority even in distant places continued relatively undisturbed.[3] The number of grants increases noticeably in the thirteenth century when they are made to temples for their maintenance and expenses and for feeding brahmans. The important inscriptions relating directly to Somanatha begin in the reign of Kumarapala Chaulukya in the twelfth century. Those that have been found at Somanatha-Veraval and the neighbouring areas are under discussion here. There were other temples dedicated to Somanatha, as for instance in Rajasthan, but these have little to do with the temple at Prabhasa-pattana.

But prior to the twelfth century, there are some records that are at least indirectly important to the conditions prevailing in the area. Among these is a grant of land in AD 832 in Junagadh district to a brahman residing at Somanatha.[4] In the reign of Bhimadeva I, who was a contemporary of Mahmud, mention is made of a conflict with the Paramara ruler, the hostilities between the two kingdoms becoming almost a regular refrain.[5] The Kadamba king, ruling in the region of Goa, records his pilgrimage to Somanatha by sea and lists the places he visited.[6] This inscription was issued in 1038 and, presumably, on his return. It could suggest that the temple at Somanatha was not destroyed but desecrated, since it seems to have been repaired fairly quickly and revived as a place of pilgrimage soon after the raid. Had the temple been destroyed, surely some mention of the raid and the destruction would have been made by the royal pilgrim. But there is a puzzling silence on this matter. Neither is the raid mentioned

---

[3] e.g. Copper-Plate Grant of Raja Bhimadeva I of Anahilapura, AD 1029, *Bhavnagar, Prakrit and Sanskrit Inscriptions*, pp. 193 ff. (A collection of inscriptions also referred to as BPSI in some publications.)

[4] A.S. Altekar, 'Six Saindhava Copper-Plate grants from Ghumli', *Epigraphia Indica*, XXVI, pp. 197 ff.

[5] *Pracina Jaina Lekha Sangraha*, II, No. 132, vs. 5–8.

[6] G. Moraes, *The Kadamba Kula*, p. 171.

nor is any credit given to the patron who might have repaired the destroyed temple. The pilgrimage of the Kadamba king is an interesting pointer to the use of the sea route along the western coast and the maritime links among ports. The Chaulukyas were active in building roads in the hinterland of ports to facilitate the movement of goods. As a back-up to this, they tried to suppress the extensive sea piracy around the coast of Saurashtra.

A Goa-to-Somanatha voyage with a halt at Thane (near Mumbai) is recorded a hundred years later in 1125 in connection with a royal pilgrim.[7] In yet another such voyage, the king was shipwrecked but was rescued by an Arab merchant. As a pay-off, the merchant's grandson was appointed to an administrative office and was permitted to build a mosque, the maintenance for which came from the tolls on cargo from Gujarat.[8] The port of Somanatha was well-known and also went by the names of Somanatha-pattana, Someshvara-pattana and Deva-pattana.

Pilgrims going to Somanatha made donations to the temple. But apart from that, they also had to pay taxes and tolls along the way to the local administration and there was little to check the greed of some officers. Where rivers required fording, for instance, tolls were collected for the crossing and excessive charges may have been made. The local administration also collected money as part of the normal taxes from merchants. Visiting merchants were required to pay taxes on the goods they brought, the taxes being assessed on the particular item, the mode of transportation, and the distance from the source. In addition, merchants also paid such taxes on a regular basis to temple authorities.[9] This is corroborated in a twelfth century

---

[7] L. Barnett, 'Inscriptions at Narendra', *Epigraphia Indica*, XIII, pp. 298–316 (p. 309, vs. 7–8).

[8] G. Moraes, op.cit., pp. 171–72, 185.

[9] 'A Stone Inscription of King Allata in the temple of Sarneshvar at Udeypore', *Bhavnagar, Prakrit and Sanskrit Inscriptions*, pp. 67–69.

inscription from Mangrol near Somanatha. The temple was maintained from customs dues calculated on the basis of money offerings to the deity.[10]

In the eleventh century, a queen ordered the remission of taxes paid by pilgrims, but the remission was not effective as taxes continued to be paid until later times.[11] An inscription of 1293 states that if pilgrims to Mount Abu had their belongings stolen, the Thakurs of Abu would have to make up the loss.[12] These taxes could then be used in commercial exchange and a nexus would be created between the temple, the grantor and the mercantile community. Grants made for the initial building of temples, and donations thereafter for their maintenance, accrued merit for the grantor and his ancestors and encouraged the composition of eulogies on the grantor.

Evidence from the inscriptions would point to disturbed conditions existing locally even prior to the raid of Mahmud. However, the Chaulukyas did make an attempt to curb the lesser rajas from plundering the pilgrims, and thereby looting what were intended as offerings for the temple. Kumarapala's governor, Gumadeva, is referred to as the conqueror of the Abhiras who are associated with plundering.[13] The more concentrated animosity of Malwa arose from political competition and the desire to eliminate the economic rivalry of the Chaulukyas and is frequently mentioned in inscriptions.[14]

---

[10] Ibid., 'Stone Inscription of Sodhadi Vao at Mangrol in Saurashtra', pp. 158 ff.

[11] A.K. Forbes, *The Ras Mala*, p. 84.

[12] Vimala-Vasahi Inscription, *Poona Orientalist*, 1938, III, 1, pp. 69 ff.

[13] *Poona Orientalist*, 1940, X, 2 and 3, pp. 123–25.

[14] Amaran Inscription, *Poona Orientalist*, 1938, III, 1, p. 24; Abu Vimala-Vasahi Inscription, ibid., p. 69; G. Buhler, 'Cintra Prashasti of the Reign of Sarangadeva', *Epigraphia Indica*, I, pp. 271 ff., (p. 181, v. 13); G. Buhler and V.G. Ozha, 'Shridhara's Devapattana Prashasti', ibid., II, pp. 437 ff.

Somanatha attracted large numbers of pilgrims and the taxes collected from them made it a lucrative source of wealth for any kingdom. That the Chaulukyas succeeded in controlling the situation to a large extent would seem evident from the increasing commercial prosperity of Saurashtra and Gujarat during their rule. Kumarapala, the Chaulukya king, issued an inscription in the twelfth century, appointing a governor to protect Somanatha, the protection being necessary against the piracy and the looting by the local Abhira rajas.[15] A century later in 1216, the then Chaulukya king was protecting the area from attacks by the Malwa rajas.[16] The regularity of the complaint about local rajas looting pilgrims going to the Somanatha temple becomes something of a litany.

An attempt perhaps to assert control over the Somanatha temple and to thereby stabilize the area against the plunder by local rajas, led Kumarapala to appoint Bhava Brihaspati as the *ganda*/chief priest of the Somanatha temple. A claim to the king appointing him is made by the chief priest. This is recorded in an inscription of c. 1169, originally from the Somanatha temple.[17] The inscription begins in a formulaic style and narrates the birth and career of Bhava Brihaspati. He was the first of a succession of powerful Shaiva priests of the Pashupata sect at the Somanatha temple, who further consolidated their power by marrying within the group and the office became virtually its preserve. It is stated that Bhava Brihaspati came from Varanasi in the Kanyakubja region from a family of Shaiva Pashupata priests. Coming from Kanyakubja is a frequent claim among brahmans in areas distant from the *madhyadesha* or the Ganges heartland. The Girnar brahmans claim the same superiority over others by virtue of being among the *pancha-gauda* brahmans who had an exalted status.

---

[15] Prachi Inscription, *Poona Orientalist*, 1937, 1, 4, pp. 38–40.

[16] Devapattana Prashasti, *Epigraphia Indica*, II, pp. 437 ff.

[17] 'Stone Inscription in the Temple of Bhadrakali at Prabhas Pattana', *Bhavnagar, Prakrit and Sanskrit Inscriptions*, pp. 186–93.

There was considerable geographical mobility among brahmans at the time as is evident from those that travelled from Kashmir and eventually found employment in the courts of the Deccan, such as Bilhana. Bhava Brihaspati, we are told, was widely respected not only in Kanyakubja but also in Malwa and Ujjain.

The inscription states that Shiva sent Bhava Brihaspati to persuade the king Kumarapala to rehabilitate the Somanatha temple which was dilapidated because of its age—*kalajirnam*. That this was not an oblique reference to Mahmud's plunder of the temple is made clear by the next statement. It is said that the temple had deteriorated partly because it was now the period of the Kaliyuga (when temples deteriorate owing to a lack of care), and partly because it was an old structure—*jirna*—and had been neglected and not properly maintained by the officers. The *kusachiva*, the wicked ministers in charge of the administration as well as the local rajas, are said to have almost destroyed the temple through their evil ways and avarice.

A later inscription, referring to Bhava Brihaspati, states that Shiva, observing that *dharma* was disappearing under the rule of bad kings in the Kaliyuga, decided that his abode should be repaired.[18] Shiva reincarnated a part of himself and took birth as Bhava Brihaspati in the family of a Kanyakubja brahman who was a descendent of Shri Vishvanatha. The brahman was opposed to the false doctrines, *pakhanda*, of the time and persuaded King Kumarapala to protect the city and the *matha* of Shiva.[19] The descent of the chief priests is listed. Shaivite divinity

---

[18] 'Stone Inscription at Veraval of Bhimadeva II', ibid., pp. 208–14.

[19] *Pashanda*, sometimes spelt *pakhanda*, initially meant any identifiable group conforming to a set of doctrines and is used in this sense in the edicts of Ashoka. But soon after, from the brahmanical perspective, it came to be used in a derogatory sense, for Buddhists, Jainas and others who were regarded as heretics and followers of false doctrines, and especially for all those opposed to the *Vedas*. Jaina sources, in turn, refer to brahmanical doctrines as *mithya*, incorrect or false, e.g., Merutunga, *Prabandha-cintamani*, 2.7.57.

is also associated with the kings. The inscriptions suggest an active defence of Shaivism against other competing sects. The false doctrine does not appear to be that of the Yavana—the Arab—and his religion, but more likely the traditional reference to the *shramanas* or monk, competing for royal patronage. This is unambiguously stated in Jaina sources. The concern, it would seem, was with retaining patronage in a competitive situation, an understandable concern for those running powerful institutions, whether Shaiva or Jaina. An earlier inscription of 1217 using the symbolism of trees had mentioned that the successor to Kumarapala, Ajayadeva, had rooted out some existing ones and planted in their place the trees of the *Vedas*. Jaina sources maintain that Ajayadeva was a dedicated Shaiva who revoked the patronage of previous Chaulukya rulers to Jaina temples.[20]

Bhava Brihaspati claims that it was he who persuaded Kumarapala to renovate the temple after which it resembled mount Kailasa.[21] The king was reverential towards Bhava Brihaspati in the best brahmanical tradition, showered him with gifts, and bent low before him. Bhava Brihaspati further states that the original temple had been built of gold, had been replaced by one of silver, and finally a stone temple was built. But no date is given for these buildings and the first two, in any case, would be mythical. Nor is it said that the first stone temple was destroyed by Mahmud and another was built to replace it after the raid. Kumarapala's renovations included the addition of fortifications to the north and the south of the temple, enlarging the area of the town, embellishing adjoining temples with golden *kalashas*/finials, and building *baolis*/step-wells. Whether these were actual fortifications may be doubtful since the sea was close enough to spray the temple when the tide came in. Possibly, some form of buttressing was constructed to prevent weathering from

---

[20] Merutunga, *Prabandha-cintamani*, 4.9.175; trans. Tawney, p. 151.

[21] Bhadrakali Inscription, ibid., pp. 186–93.

sea spray. The income of the temple and its chief priest was increased through the grant of the village of Brahmapuri.

The eulogy of Bhava Brihaspati is impressive and his claim to having persuaded Kumarapala to repair the temple was a major achievement—an achievement, however, that runs contrary to the Jaina assertion that Kumarapala's Jaina minister, Hemachandra, was instrumental in the repair of the Somanatha temple. The office of the chief priest of the Somanatha temple remained powerful and much sought after and, where possible, it is referred to in inscriptions. The latter seem to suggest that the succession to this office remained largely in the family. This in itself would make it important for Bhava Brihaspati to claim to have been associated with the renovation and rebuilding of the temple by Kumarapala. There was also the association of the political legitimacy claimed by the Chaulukyas through this act.

A century after the raid of Mahmud, the Somanatha temple was again well-endowed and prosperous and its priests patronized by the Chaulukya kings of Gujarat. The act of renovation and endowment was not restricted to the Somanatha temple but is associated with other temples that had fallen into disrepair. This went on parallel to the accounts of the iconoclastic activities of Turkish generals in Turko–Persian sources. Muslim/Turkish iconoclasm is not given as a reason for repairing such temples, in contrast to some specific cases where such iconoclasm is mentioned. Thus, an inscription of about 1177, perhaps coinciding with Ghurid raids, records that the wife of a king's minister, noticing the breaking of an image of Someshvara by a Turk, had the image replaced and gave a grant for its daily worship.[22] The statement is matter-of-fact with little comment either on the act or on the iconoclasts. An inscription of approximately this period states that Mularaja II defeated the king of Garjanaka,[23] a statement also made in a Jaina chronicle. These are

---

[22] Kiradu Inscription, *Poona Orientalist*, 1936–37, I, 4, pp. 41–44.

[23] G. Buhler, op.cit., *Indian Antiquary*, 1877, VI, pp. 180 ff (p. 186).

thought to be references to the same raids. They are mentioned as merely one among the many campaigns conducted by Mularaja II, the others being against neighbouring kings.

Kumarapala's renovation was an act of veneration for Shiva, but was he also using this symbolically to further his suzerainty over Gujarat? Was this the inversion of Mahmud seeking legitimation through plundering the temple and destroying the icon? Renovation and destruction of the temple seem to have become a kind of counterposed legitimation where renovation is required of the Chaulukyas and destruction is required of the Turks. Are these the counterpoints of legitimation in the politics of the past? The Chaulukyas were not rebuilding the temple as a claim to their autonomy as they were already autonomous.

A number of inscriptions granting land to brahmans and to Jaina temples survive from the twelfth century, suggesting some changes in the economy and polity parallel to those in other parts of northern India. Royal patronage to brahmans was a form of support which had increased in many parts of the subcontinent over the previous few centuries. In 1216, Bhimadeva II erected a *mandapa*/pavilion at Somanatha, sometimes referred to as the *megha-dhvani* or the *meghanada*, the sound of thunder, and he once again protected the site from the attacks of the rulers of Malwa.[24] This may have been a reason for the fortifications built earlier by Kumarapala. In the thirteenth century, the Vaghelas encroached upon Chaulukya power and some claimed kinship with the latter. Arjunadeva, ruling in the new political regime, erected temples, including one at Girnar. Temple building continued apace, supported by each ruler and dynasty, and does not seem to have been affected by the threat of raids on temples. The more impressive structures in Gujarat such as those at Modhera and Mt. Abu are of these times. This is not surprising, given that temples were symbols of much more than religious

---

[24] Devapattana Prashasti, *Epigraphia Indica*, II, p. 437; 'Stone Inscription at the Mota Darvaja', *Bhavnagar, Prakrit and Sanskrit Inscriptions*, pp. 195 ff.

devotion alone and encapsulated a range of other assertions and activities—political, economic and social. The Somanatha temple remained a major centre for Pashupata Shaivism as is clear from inscriptions recording the succession of powerful and wealthy chief priests subsequent to Bhava Brihaspati.

That no mention is made of Mahmud's attack on the Somanatha temple is strange, given the statement that the temple had deteriorated and needed renovation. This is puzzling as there are occasional references to the breaking of temples. An inscription of 1489, linked to the repairing of the Ekalingaji temple near Udaipur, refers to grants of villages being revoked and temples broken (*prasada bhanga*) by the Yavanas. But such references are not so frequent and this questions the rhetoric of temple destruction in the Turko–Persian sources.[25] The explanation for the decline of the Somanatha temple is confined to its age and its mismanagement. Inscriptional sources referring to renovation do not mention the desecration resulting from a raid. Was this due to embarrassment that the icon symbolizing the authority of the ruler and the protection of the deity had been allowed to be broken and removed? The authority of the Chaulukyas at Somanatha in the early eleventh century was not as firm as it was later and the area was being contested by petty rajas. Or was the looting of a temple not such an extraordinary event, given that some Hindu rulers also attacked the temples of those they had conquered, or in order to confiscate the wealth of the temple? Yet the attacks of the Abhiras and Malwa rajas who looted pilgrims are mentioned.

It is possible that the temple constructed by Bhimadeva may have gradually deteriorated through lack of maintenance. There was no major political patron to maintain the temple, until Kumarapala decided to do so. The sculpture recovered from the excavation of the site in 1951 and now housed in the museum

---

[25] Stone Inscription of Ekalingaji', ibid., pp. 117 ff.

near the temple, shows evidence of some pieces having been hacked but, equally, many having weathered badly. The closeness to the sea may well have brought about extensive weathering of the structure and damaged it, quite apart from the contribution, great or small, of Turkish desecration.

Weathering as a result of sea spray is mentioned in Jaina sources while referring to the Somanatha temple. The repairing of a temple does not invariably imply that it had been damaged due to a raid or to Muslim iconoclasm. There is enough evidence of temples having fallen into disrepair and being renovated as an act of merit as, for instance, in the repairs carried out to the temple of Adinatha by the ministers, Vastupala and Tejapala.[26] Jaina merchants were particular about keeping temples in good repair and had the wherewithal to do so.

The lack of mention of Mahmud's raid can also be explained, perhaps in part, by the relationship that emerged between the elite of Somanatha and a trader from Hormuz who acquired land to build a mosque in the vicinity of the Somanatha temple.

This is recorded in a significant and lengthy bilingual Sanskrit–Arabic inscription, dating to 1264, a little over 200 years after the raid of Mahmud.[27] Being in the nature of a legal document concerning property, it was not only drafted in two languages but was dated very precisely in four dating systems— the Hijri, *Samvat*, Simha and Valabhi. The universally used era was the *Samvat* (BC 58–57), the Valabhi being the older local era,

---

[26] 'A Stone Inscription of Adishvara at Shatrunjaya', ibid., pp. 134 ff.; pp. 174–84.

[27] E. Hultzsch, 'A Grant of Arjunadeva of Gujarat', *Indian Antiquary*, 1882, XI, pp. 241 ff.; D.C. Sircar, 'Veraval Inscription of Chaulukya-Vaghela Arjuna', *Epigraphia Indica*, XXXIV, pp. 141 ff.; for the Arabic version see, 'Inscription of 1264 AD from Prabhas Pattan' in Z.A. Desai, *Epigraphia Indica*, Arabic and Persian Supplement, 1961, pp. 10 ff.

and the Simha the more recent local era. The Hijri was used for time reckoning in Islamic documents. The inscription has been edited more than once and has been quoted with reference to maritime commerce.[28] Only very recently has there been an insightful analysis of the inscription as representing an interaction that has social and cultural dimensions.[29] My attempt here is to extend this argument and also see it in the context of the earlier raid of Mahmud. The contents of the inscription provide a perspective on local attitudes in Somanatha to accommodating the requirements of a wealthy merchant, trading from Persia, and in the process much else gets illumined.

The inscription begins with the usual, formulaic opening of a benediction and an invocation of the deity. The benediction, *siddham*, is followed by invoking the deity as Vishvanatha—*om namah shri vishvanathaya*—using the epithets, *shunya-rupa, vishva-rupa*, and *lakshyalakshya*, without form, omnipresent and both visible and invisible. Vishvanatha could well be Shiva, the icon of Somanatha and revered by the Chaulukyas and the Vaghelas. *Vishva-rupa* is sometimes associated with an *avatara* of Vishnu but this link does not seem appropriate in this case.[30] If Vishvanatha was a rendering of Allah in Sanskrit, as has been suggested, then the epithets, which are unusual, would be appropriate. Since the document was inscribed at the initiative of a Persian shipowner, such an invocation would be in order. It has been read as divinity being represented as a locally comprehensible concept.[31] This would involve, as other phrases in the inscription show, an attempt to find the equivalent in the conceptual language of the

---

[28] R. Chakravarti, 'Nakhuda Nuruddin Firuz at Somanatha: AD 1264' in *Trade and Traders in Early Indian Society*, pp. 220–42.

[29] B.D. Chattopadhyaya, *Representing the Other?* pp. 70–78; R. Thapar, *Narratives and the Making of History*, pp. 38–41.

[30] J.N. Banerjea, *Development of Hindu Iconography*, pp. 391, 426, 557.

[31] B.D. Chattopadhyaya, op.cit., p. 76.

community where the mosque was located. The cultural translations evident in this inscription—at the literal level from Arabic to
Sanskrit as also more conceptually—had wider ramifications in
Indian society. They are most evident perhaps in a variety of
religious discourses of a popular kind.

The inscription goes on to say that Noradina Piroja, the
Sanskrit rendering of Nur-ud-din Firuz, of Hurmuja-desha/
Hormuz, a respected shipowner and merchant (or what we today
would probably call a shipping magnate), and *sadr*/head
presumably of his co-professionals, has acquired land in the
vicinity of Somanatha through the help of the local raja, Sri
Chada, the son of Nansimha. Nur-ud-din is the son of a
shipowner, *khwaja* Abu Ibrahim, rendered into Sanskrit as *khoja*
Abubrahim, where *khwaja/khoja* means an honourable or
respected person. Hormuz had become a major trading centre in
the Persian Gulf, written about later by European, Arab and
Chinese visitors, and was particularly reputed for trade in
horses.[32] Hormuz was well connected with Malabar and
Cambay—and this inscription extends the connection to
Somanatha—and was additional to the earlier port at Siraf in
controlling the Gulf trade. The Indian merchant, Jagadu, traded
with merchants at Hormuz and Siraf where he had stationed his
representatives. The implication of these links and the trade that
ensued was that they were part of the larger circuit involving the
Indian Ocean trade.

The transfer of the land mentioned in the inscription takes
place in the reign of the Chaulukya-Vaghela king, Arjunadeva,
and his local governor, the *mahamatya* Maladeva/Mahadeva. They
are referred to in another inscription from Kaccha in 1270.[33]
Given the legal basis on which the land was transferred, it
is thought that it was gifted, but that Nur-ud-din may have

---

[32] P. Morgan, 'New Thoughts on Old Hormuz', *Iran*, 1991, 29, pp. 67–85.

[33] Rav Inscription, *Poona Orientalist*, 1938, III, 1, pp. 20–28.

been required to pay some taxes on it. The land so granted is to be used for the building of a mosque—the word used is *mijigiti*/from *masjid*—which is described as a *dharmasthana*, a sacred place. Chada is also referred to as a *dharma-bandhava* of Firuz. The tone of the inscription suggests a considerable friendliness and closeness between Firuz and the elite of the town, doubtless developed through long and continuous contact. Somanatha was obviously a prosperous trading centre else Nur-ud-din, who is described as a *nauvittaka* (or *nakhuda* in Arabic), would not have found it profitable to construct a mosque at this location. There was evidently much familiarity with the profession of ship-owning merchants and sometimes the abbreviated forms of *nau* and *nakhu* are used in inscriptions.[34] Thirteenth-century inscriptions in Arabic from coastal Gujarat mention merchants and shipowners from west Asia settled in western India. Local shipowners are mentioned in the record of a town council.[35] Nur-ud-din's mosque was not the only one being built in Gujarat under the auspices of the Chaulukyas and their governors. There were mosques at Bhadreshvar, Khambayat/Khambat/Cambay, and other places.

The land acquired for building the mosque was in the area known as the mahajanapali—the quarter of the merchants—and was on the outskirts of the town of Somanatha. But this plot in *mahajanapali* appears to have been part of the estates of the temple of Somanatha. The acquisition of land and its use for building a mosque had the approval of the *pancha-kula* of Somanatha. The pancha-kulas were powerful administrative committees with a controlling membership of a few persons who were recognized as people of authority, consisting of local

---

[34] R. Chakravarti, 'Nakhudas and Nauvittakas: Ship-Owning Merchants in Coastal Western India', *Journal of the Economic and Social History of the Orient*, 2000, XLIII, pp. 30–64.

[35] Ibid.

dignitaries, officials, merchants and important priests.[36] Some *pancha-kulas* came under the jurisdiction of officials, others were appointed by the king, or else approved of by the king, or by the governor, or by members of the local elite which included landed magnates and wealthy merchants.[37] The designation is attested as early as in an eighth-century inscription and *pancha-kulas* continue to be mentioned in later sources.[38] The *pancha-kulas* supervised making grants and imposing and collecting taxes, and were required to negotiate agreements if there was a conflict over land settlements or an argument over payments. They were representative bodies involved with local functioning and administration and were distinct from the official hierarchy, even if occasionally they had government sanction or had officials among their members. In the port of Gogha, in the seventeenth century, the wife of a merchant wishing to build a temple refers it to the *pancha-kula* which includes among its members officers, dignatories, merchants, all of high rank, such as, *vazirs, kazis, thanedaras, desais, thakurs* and *vyavaharas*.

Two members of the *pancha-kula* of Somanatha are specifically mentioned. These were the Shaiva Pashupati priest, the *ganda* Bhava Virabhadra, associated in other inscriptions with the Somanatha temple, and Abhayasimha. Virabhadra appears to have been in line of succession to Bhava Brihaspati and may even have been related to him. He is described grandiloquently as *pashupata-acharya-mahapandita-mahattara-dharmamurti-ganda-shri-para*. (The short form for *purohita* was *para*.) Abhayasimha represented the merchant community that was important enough to have a voice in the *pancha-kula*.

---

[36] Amaran Inscription, *Poona Orientalist*, 1938, III, 1, pp. 20–28; *Epigraphia Indica*, XXII, p. 97; ibid., I, p. 173.

[37] *Poona Orientalist*, 1938, III, 1, pp. 22–28; II, 4, p. 225; B.D. Diskalkar, 'Inscriptions of Kathiawad', *New Indian Antiquary*, April 1939, pp. 693 ff.; A.K. Majumdar, op.cit., pp. 232 ff.; Porbandar Inscription of Visaladeva, *Poona Orientalist*, 1938, II, 4, pp. 225–26.

[38] Ibid.

Witnesses to the agreement were the *brihat purusha*—literally, the local big men—the *thakkuras* and the *ranakas*, and the names mentioned are: Palugideva, Ramadeva, Bhimasena, Someshavaradeva, Chada and the merchant Abhayasimha. In the Arabic version, the names are listed as: Bailakdev, Ramdev, Bhimsinh Thakur, Someshvardev and Jada Rawat, the son of Rawat Nansinh. Some of these were functionaries of the estates of the Somanatha temple as, for example, in the area of *mahajanapali* in which the mosque was to be located. It has been suggested that they might have been lessees of the land. Abhayasimha is thought to have been a valuer of coins and, as such, crucial to the work of the *pancha-kula*. Some members of the *pancha-kula* were important enough to be mentioned by name. The acquisition of land by Nur-ud-din and the building of a mosque in the vicinity of the Somanatha temple and on its estate, seem to have offered no problem, or aroused no resentment against the Muslim shipowner.

The document continues with statements on the provisions made for the maintenance of the mosque and the persons required to supervise this. The latter were members of the *jamatha/jama't*. The endowments were extensive and would have provided generously for the maintenance. This included items for daily worship, the cost of teachers, muezzins and readers of the *Qur'an*, the observance of festivals and repairs to the mosque. These were to come from the purchase of two *palladika* of land—large areas of land—and most likely referring here to temple property. One of these was part of the temple property from the adjoining temple of Vakuleshvaradeva. The other plot of land adjoined a temple, and the house of an artisan located on the land was excluded from the transfer. The measures of land were located in the midst of the town—*somanathadeva-nagara-madhye*—in the vicinity of the Somanatha temple. The first measure of land had been purchased from and through the good offices of two *purohitas* of neighbouring temples, one of which was the *para* Tripurantaka, who was the chief priest of the Navaghaneshvaradeva temple. The boundaries of the land are given, as is normal in documents recording ownership of land.

Other investments for the maintenance of the mosque were an oil-mill and two shops. These were purchased from the following persons: Lunasiha, Dharani and Masuma who were the sons of *thakkura* Sohana, Kilhanadeva son of *thakkura* Sodhala, *rana* Ashadhara, Chhada and Nirmalya. These were lessees or owners of the shops and the mill. Respectable citizens of Somanatha such as these would have, in all likelihood, made a profit on these transactions with a person, who, even if he was a visiting merchant, had close connections with the city's elite. Importantly enough, these transactions took place only two centuries after the raid of Mahmud. It would seem that neither the 'big men' nor the lesser men of Somanatha-pattana were troubled by any associations linked to the raid.

The *jamatha*, as the name suggests, was an association, in this case of persons consisting of those in charge of ships and sailors; the *ghamchikas* or oil-men; religious teachers; the *churnakaras* or whitewashers and masons, necessary for regular repairs; the *Musalamanas*, among whom were included the horse-handlers and drivers of horse-carts. The members of the *jamatha* are likely to have been mainly Muslims. The specific mention of *Musalamana* in association with one category—incidentally, an early and rare use of the word—may suggest that some on this list were Bohras or Shi'as. The occupational groups seem to be caste names as well, possibly those converted to Islam. The *jamatha* was not only a witness to this agreement but was also required to maintain the mosque and ensure the income from endowments. Any surplus income was to be donated to the Makha and Madina *dharmasthanas*, i.e. Mecca and Medina. The Arabic text has a sentence expressing the desirability of Somanatha-pattana becoming a city of Islam with no infidels and no idols, a wish that is tactfully omitted in the Sanskrit version. If Nur-ud-din was an orthodox Muslim, he was perhaps also compromising his orthodoxy in the arrangements he was making and especially if the land was a grant from the estates of a temple. The endowments were additionally to be used for various festivals, including the *vishesha-puja-mahotsava*, the special festivals of Baratisabi—what is now called the *shab-i-barat*—and the Khatamaratri, the overnight reading of the entire *Qur'an*. The mosque of Nur-ud-din is no longer identifiable and it would seem that over the centuries either the income for its maintenance became insufficient, or else it was siphoned off for other purposes by members of the *jamatha*.

The Arabic version of this inscription is not a translation of the Sanskrit. Although it carries the bare bones of the essential information, it is factually less detailed and stylistically has more flourishes of language and formulaic passages of religious sentiment. Beginning with the usual invocation to Allah, it then sets out the precise date. The prayer that 'Somnat' may become a city of Islam carries the sense of the formulaic. Such passages often occur in legal documents intended for Arab legal specialists of that time. The witnesses to the transaction are mentioned. The family of Nur-ud-din is described in exalted terms. He then calls upon Allah to bless the mosque and states that after all the local requirements have been met, the balance from the endowments would be sent to Mecca and Madina.

In building the mosque, Nur-ud-din was establishing his adherence to Islam and the intervention of Islam at Somanatha. But he was doing it differently from Mahmud of Ghazni. As has been pointed out, he was willing to use the idioms and concepts of the local religion to institute his own *dharmasthana* and faith. Furthermore, he was doing so with the cooperation of the local people. He was not adopting the religion of the host culture since the mosque was a symbol of Islam. This is clear from the Arabic version where he wishes that Somanatha may adopt Islam—however formulaic the wish may be. There is no hint of his being objected to because he was a Muslim and therefore linked to the raid of Mahmud. His hosts understood that the space for faith is distinct and assisted him in establishing a space for Islam. Undoubtedly, there must have been conversations and discussions about faith and belief between him and the local 'big men' since some of the latter were priests. Given the long contacts with west Asia, Islam was not new to the elite of Somanatha-pattana and by now it was a religion known to other parts of India as well.

One of the chief priests mentioned in connection with Nur-ud-din's purchase of land was Tripurantaka. An inscription of 1287, twenty-three years after that of Nur-ud-din, and issued during the reign of the Vaghela king, Sarangadeva, refers to the powerful and wealthy Shaiva priest, Tripurantaka. The *prashasti*/eulogy begins with the praise of the Chaulukya kings and the Pashupata priests at Somanatha. Tripurantaka is said to have trained at Karvan in south Gujarat and belonged to a lineage of well-known Shaiva priests. He is said to have visited the major Shaiva centres from Kedaranatha to Rameshavaram. These claims carry an echo of the life of Shankaracharya and are repeated in other biographical references to important Shaiva priests. The inscription states that he also constructed five temples at Somanatha-pattana close to the Somanatha temple and installed many images. The temples were dedicated to his mother, his preceptor, his preceptor's wife, and the remaining two to his wife and himself. Modesty, it seems, did not come to him easily! Only one of the temples can now be identified.

Tripurantaka was appointed to the high office of *mahattara* at Prabhas by the chief priest, Para Brihaspati, of the Somanatha temple.[39] (This Brihaspati was the husband of Uma, the daughter of Para Virabhadra, and should not be confused with the Bhava Brihaspati of the previous century.) Tripurantaka played an important role both in temple administration and in civic

---

[39] D.B. Diskalkar, 'Inscriptions of Kathiawad', *New Indian Antiquary*, April 1939, I, pp. 724 ff.

administration.[40] The inscription describes in some detail his establishing benefactions for the maintenance of the temples. As a *mahattara* he could have had a share in common land and legal rights over temple property. Various professional organizations were required to present items on a daily or monthly basis—such as flowers, rice, butter, oil, betel nuts and leaves, incense and items of daily consumption. The keeper of the temple's storehouse was to be given a stipulated amount every month. Could Tripurantaka be the same priest who was exercising his entrepreneurial talents in helping Nur-ud-din acquire land for the endowment of the mosque? His may not have been the style that would have been appreciated by those who argued in the *Puranas* that because it was the Kaliyuga, the age of decline, Shiva would desert his icons, temples would be destroyed, and all this was part of an inevitable condition.

The inscription informs us that there was a close connection between commerce and the dues demanded by temples. Tripurantaka acquired land for religious purposes which he assigned to a city organization, in return for which the latter issued two grants which are thought to refer to privileges for the temples built by Tripurantaka. These could have been in the form of donations and, apart from money, grain, textiles, oil, sandal-wood and incense were appreciated for their high commercial value. Merchants and customs houses were required to pay a stipulated sum to the temples as a regular tax. One *dramma* per day was to be paid by the *mandapika*/the customs house, and 9 *drammas* per month were paid for the maintenance of a disciple. Tripurantaka purchased three shops (markets?) and converted these into a temple endowment, the temple thereby becoming a commercial property owner. Those who rented the shops had to provide garlands, coconuts and clothes for the procession taken

---

[40] G. Buhler, 'Cintra Prashasti of the Reign of Sarangadeva', *Epigraphia Indica*, I, pp. 271 ff. K. Ray, 'Tripurantaka: A Pasupata *Acarya* at Somanatha, (Thirteen Century AD)', *Proceedings of the Indian History Congress*, 62nd Session, Bhopal 2001, pp. 180–86.

out by the Somanatha temple. He also deposited 15 *drammas* per month—presumably out of the income of his five temples—into the treasury, so that the Pashupata priest had a salary. All the merchants had to donate 1 *dramma* as a contribution to religious festivals.

Apart from holding a high religious office, Tripurantaka seems to have been an impressive dealer in properties and dues, a not unusual combination among those priests, monks and *mahants* who manage the properties of religious institutions. The involvement of temples in commercial enterprises was evidently quite substantial and this, together with endowments and donations, accounted for temple wealth. Apart from matters of faith, the reality on the ground doubtless encouraged the elite of Somanatha to cooperate with Nur-ud-din as it would have enhanced the commercial nexus. This was not an unusual development in the institutions of many religions. The prosperity of Somanatha again made it a target for attack at the end of the century, the repeated excuse being religious iconoclasm.

Temples continued to be built and embellished in Somanatha-pattana in the thirteenth century. Other inscriptions inform us that another active patron of such building activity during the reign of Bhimadeva II was his minister, Shridhara.[41] The king claims to have stabilized the area after the attack from the raja of Malwa and also defended Somanatha-pattana against the heroic Hammira, whose identity is not clear. Mobility among the priests of status, which involved their travelling to and from temple centres of importance, as evident from a number of inscriptions, would presumably have led to much discussion about the new political powers being established in northern India and soon after in the Deccan, as well as the new religious ideas and practices that were being introduced.

---

[41] Devapattan Prashasti, op.cit., II, pp. 437 ff.; 'Stone Inscription of the Mota Darvaja,' *Bhavnagar, Prakrit and Sanskrit Inscriptions*, pp. 195 ff.

Other inscriptions suggest that the office of the chief priest was controlled by the family of Bhava Brihaspati. Vishveshvara, a successor and kinsman, claims to have had the temple renovated by the Chaulukya king who had appointed him the chief priest. He is said to be descended from a family in Kannauj in which Shiva is believed to have taken birth.[42] Association with the deity was intended to underline his status and legitimacy since the family had migrated from a distant place. He repeats the earlier pattern and claims that the pavilion built by the king, as an addition to the temple, was at his persuasion. Virabhadra, who became the chief priest later on, was a son-in-law of the previous chief priest, and his assistant was Abhaysimha, possibly the same as mentioned in the inscription of Nur-ud-din. Virabhadra was the father of Umadevi who was the wife of Para Brihaspati, his successor, and the list of succession includes Tripurantaka.[43] The succession seems to have frequently gone through sons-in-law. There is no reference to cross-cousin marriage which would have furthered the family's control over the temple, its administration and resources.

The inscriptions raise a number of questions. The raid of Mahmud could not have been forgotten 200 years after the event if it had been as traumatic as it is currently said to be. A passing reference has been made by an epigraphist to an inscription of 1263 from Veraval which seems to have said that Mahmud left a governor and a small force at Somanatha-pattana, but apparently neither survived for long.[44] The reference is ambiguous and the

---

[42] 'Veraval Inscription of Bhimadeva II', *Bhavnagar, Prakrit and Sanskrit Inscriptions*, pp. 208–14.

[43] 'Somanatha Pattan Inscriptions', *Annals of the Bhandarkar Oriental Research Institute*, 5, pp. 169 ff.; *Epigraphia Indica*, I, pp. 271 ff.

[44] D.B. Diskalkar, 'Inscriptions of Kathiawad', *New Indian Antiquary*, April 1939, I, p. 584.

text seems unavailable. At most, this can be linked to the story in some Turko–Persian accounts of Mahmud appointing Dabashalim as his governor on leaving Somanatha. If such an inscription existed, the memory of Mahmud had not receded at this time. Curiously, in 1264 another inscription records the building of a wall around the temple of Somanatha by the *mahajanas/* merchants of Devapattana during the reign of Arjunadeva Vaghela.[45] Here again one wonders whether it was a wall or an embankment. Was it a wall built to protect the temple from Turkish attacks or was it an embankment built to protect it from the sea? The decision is likely to have been taken by the same dignitaries who negotiated an agreement with Nur-ud-din Firuz.

Did the transaction recorded in Nur-ud-din's inscription not interfere with the memory of Mahmud's raid on Somanatha, or the threats of the Turkish Sultans if they were as frequent as is claimed in Persian sources, in the minds of the rajas, the priests and the 'big men' who were all party to the decision to permit the building of the mosque on the estates of the temple and in its vicinity? If no mention is made in the inscriptions of Mahmud's devastating destruction of the temple, was it in fact so? Or did Mahmud break the idol, and loot the temple of its wealth, leaving it to the chroniclers to fantasize about this event? Did the local people make a distinction between the Arab traders and the Turks? The Arabs, who were initially invaders, had now come to be accepted as partners in trade and the trade brought large profits. Were the Turks unacceptable because most of them were still coming as invaders? Clearly, they were not all homogenized and identified simply as 'Muslims', as we would do today.

Hormuz was crucial to the trade in horses, therefore Nur-ud-din Firuz, an obviously wealthy and efficient trader, was welcomed. Did the profits of trade overrule other considerations? Were the administrators of the temples and of civic authority also

---

[45] H. Cousens, *Somanatha and Other Medieval Temples in Kathiawar*, pp. 24 ff.

trading and making handsome profits? This was not the sole example of mosques being built by and for Arab and Persian traders in Gujarat, for both Hindu kings and wealthy merchants were known to endow mosques. Among other places, mosques were built at Bhadreshvar and Khambat. The former was an Isma'ili mosque and serviced a settlement of Isma'ilis who continued to live and trade there for centuries.

An inscription of 1218 in Arabic from Khambat relates to the Jami mosque built by Sa'id, son of Abu Sharaf al-Bammi, an Iranian settled in Khambat which was then held by the Chaulukyas. The local people of Khambat—mainly communities of traders—instigated by the Mughs (fire-worshippers?) attacked the mosque and killed eighty Muslims.[46] Most of these communities engaged in commerce, and competition would have been a more likely reason for discord than religious hostility. The mosque symbolized the presence of successful merchants from the Gulf. A complaint was taken to the king, who personally verified the accuracy of the incident. Two persons from each of the communities that had perpetrated the killing were punished and the king financed the rebuilding of the mosque. When the king of Malwa, Subhatavarman, campaigned against the Chaulukyas, he attacked both the mosque and the Jaina temples and looted, as was his wont, the golden cupolas and pitchers of these and other temples. The Jaina temples were restored by the Jaina ministers, Vastupala and Tejapala. This was an attempt by Malwa to destroy the commercial potential of Gujarat. Sa'id, who was by now a wealthy merchant in Khambat, rebuilt the mosque.[47] The construction of a mosque implied that there were a reasonable number of Muslims living in the area, both visitors and a local population. There was familiarity with the incoming religion, and closeness towards it would vary among different social groups.

---

[46] Z.A. Desai, *Epigraphia Indica, Arabic and Persian Supplement*, 1961, pp. 4 ff.

[47] P. Bhatia, *The Paramaras*, pp. 140–43.

Those that attacked the mosque are listed by community and caste and not by a single religious label, as Hindus. Such contestations seem not to have troubled the elite of Somanatha.

The evidence of the inscriptions highlights the fact that in these hostilities, there was no single host and no single enemy. There were many groups at different levels of the social hierarchy who had their own relationships with a large range of others. The alliances and the enmities could change as could the reasons for the relationships. Many groups were competing for power and/or for economic resources. Such competition ranges over a variety of relationships and the values associated with these need not be permanent. Can we then continue to speak of a 'Hindu' reaction to the event created by the 'Muslim', or should we not attempt to sift the actions and the reactions according to social groups and specific situations?

The perceptions and concerns of the authors of the inscriptions are distinctively different from those of the authors of the Turko–Persian texts, even though they are providing evidence for the same area in the same period.

This is also the period when there are quite a few shorter inscriptions recording the building or the removing and renovating of the less important Hindu and Jaina temples said to have fallen into disrepair. The removal of the old temples or their rebuilding was carried out under the direction of local priests and financed by local rajas.[48] According to Cousens, rebuilding became necessary because of the inferior quality of the stone and the technologically weak construction. Poor foundations with limited pillar bases, inferior jointing of stones or methods of keeping them in place, and beams unable to bear the required weight, were all factors that encouraged the collapse of the structures. There was a difference, therefore, between the

---

[48] As, for example, in the Somanatha-pattana Inscription of Bhima II, *Poona Orientalist*, 1937, III, 1, pp. 223–25.

construction of temples financed by royal patronage and affluent merchants and those by local patrons with limited finances.

The evidence from inscriptions indicates that there was no falling off in the number of temples being built. Local deities were sometimes elevated and a temple was constructed for this purpose, or else mainstream deities presided over local worship through existing temples. Grants for the upkeep of temples and images are recorded. It would be worth assessing how many of these went to new installations as against the upkeep of the old. This was also the period when Jaina temples began to be built in larger numbers and were well-endowed and profusely adorned. Mention of 'Muslim' attacks on temples are few in inscriptions, although there are both positive and negative comments on the rule of Sultans in various texts.[49] The context of this writing and the perceptions and intentions of their authors need to be assessed in greater detail. Repairs to a temple were not necessarily required because of iconoclasm, and were in any case dependent on patronage. A wealthy Jaina merchant repaired a Jaina temple at Shatrunjaya in 1531 and the inscription recording the repairs begins with a eulogy of Bahadur Shah of Gujarat.[50]

In the fifteenth century, a number of short inscriptions from Gujarat refer to battles. Most are associated with local confrontations and memorialized in the many *palyas* or hero-stones, memorials to dead heroes, scattered through the countryside. But this was the period of Turkish pressure on Gujarat. An inscription of 1404 from Veraval mentions Brahmadeva, son of Shivanatha, the governor, defending the town against attacks by the Turks and the death of those defending it. One such inscription, dating to 1406, is a small and rather moving one in Sanskrit

---

[49] B.D. Chattopadhyaya, op.cit., pp. 56–60.

[50] 'A Stone Inscription of Adishvara on the Shatrunjaya Hills', *Bhavnagar, Prakrit and Sanskrit Inscriptions*, pp. 134–140.

from Somanatha.[51] It begins with the formulaic benediction used by Muslims—*Bismillahi'r Rahmani'r Rahim*. It gives details of the family of the *vahura/bohra* Farid, the son of the *vahura* Muhammad. We are told that the town of Somanatha was attacked by the Turushkas/Turks. *Vahura* Farid joined in the defence of the town, fighting against the Turks on behalf of the local ruler, Brahmadeva. Farid was killed and the inscription is a memorial to him.

---

[51] D.B. Diskalkar, 'Inscriptions of Kathiawad', *New Indian Antiquary*, April 1939, I, p. 591.

5

Biographies, Chronicles and Epics

A third major category of sources are biographies and chronicles by Jaina scholars that recount events in the history of Gujarat during the period from the eleventh to the fifteenth centuries. Approximately towards the end of this period there are epic poems largely composed by poets at various Rajput courts. The Jaina works are mainly from the Shvetambara tradition and, like the Persian sources, reveal their own politics through the narrative. Not unexpectedly, the authors of these texts have concerns different from those of the Turko–Persian accounts, even though they refer to some events related to Somanatha. The connection is both topographical and geographical. Sites regarded as most sacred by the Jainas were Shatrunjaya and the area around Girnar such as mount Ujjayanta. The pious Jaina was required to contribute towards the maintenance of temples and icons and this included rebuilding or renovating temples where necessary. This provides a link to Somanatha.

Texts written by Jaina authors during this period are of varying kinds. Some are biographies, the *charita* literature, relating mainly to the lives of kings and ministers, and focusing on those who were regarded as exemplars of Jaina ideals such as the Chaulukya king Kumarapala and ministers such as Hemachandra and the brothers Vastupala and Tejapala. The life of a particularly eminent merchant, Jagadu, who was a patron of the Jaina Sangha is part of this literature. There were also chronicles relating the history of various Jaina sects and their succession of Elders. Such chronicles continue into later centuries. The history of the Jaina Sangha and the *acharyas* was viewed from particular Jaina perspectives and in the course of recording the history of a sect other matters of interest came to be recorded. The need to maintain their history was crucial to the legitimizing of these sects. The existence of such histories gave status to a sect and this was generally respected. Despite the legendary material that clung to these chronicles, they can contribute to reconstructing the history of these times.[1]

Although well-known for some decades, these texts have not been used as extensively as they might have been as evidence for the perceptions of the history of this period. This is largely because they are in Sanskrit and Prakrit, and the history of India from c. 1200 is conventionally studied from Persian and Arabic sources. A modern historian writes that these texts have drawn a veil over the activities of Mahmud who, according to this historian, not only subverted some of the powerful dynasties of the region but also mingled their ancient gods with the dust.[2] Quite apart from what these texts may say, this in itself is hardly a tenable historical statement. He adds, that since the Hindus do not possess a sense of history, their so-called histories are nothing more than a collection of legends. Such statements come from an unquestioning acceptance of the views of the

---

[1] A.K. Forbes, in his *The Ras Mala, Hindu Annals of Western India*, attempted to gather together whatever narratives he had access to, in the style of nineteenth-century administrators, and attempted to narrate a connected history of western India during this period from these sources. Many are Jaina texts but he also incorporates the bardic tradition. The result is a nineteenth-century chronicle that draws on earlier traditions, literary and oral.

[2] M. Nazim, *The Life and Times of Sultan Mahmud of Ghazna*, pp. 15–16.

Turko–Persian narratives as history without analysing them and comparing them with other sources of the same period. Epics are not taken as historical accounts, but they do provide information on the assumptions of the author, the audience, and the society to which they relate.

The Jaina texts provide a narrative that differs from the Turko–Persian sources and the inscriptions. Royal patronage to Jaina institutions is applauded and they tend to draw on the munificence, actual or fictive, of the Chaulukyas. But they also refer to the hostility towards the Jainas apparent in the policies of some kings. Thus, the renovations of temples by the Chaulukya king Kumarapala and the minister Vastupala form part of the narrative, but mention is also made of the hostility of Kumarapala's successor, Ajayapala, to Jaina places of worship. The Shrimal Jaina merchants are recognized as another source of patronage. This is indicated, for instance, in the case of repairs and grants to the Bhadreshvar temple in Kaccha by such merchants.[3]

Earlier attacks by the *mlechchhas* on Valabhi are mentioned, and presumably these may have referred to the Arabs for it is said that the Jaina icons were sent to various other centres for safe keeping. The icon of Chandraprabha was sent to Devapattana/ Prabhas.[4] The dispersal of icons became a technique for protecting them since it was believed that they were invested with special powers. Could the story of the Chandraprabha icon and of Manat have somehow got connected to create the narrative which caught the imagination of the early Turko–Persian writers that Manat was sent to Somanatha for safe keeping?

These early narratives revolve around themes related indirectly to trade and the openings for wealth that it provided as well as the legitimizing of kings. Associated with this, inevitably,

---

[3] M. Shokoohy, *Bhadreshvar*, pp. 9 ff.

[4] Merutunga, *Prabandha-cintamani*, 5.11.239; trans. C.H. Tawney, pp. 174–5. R. Davis, op.cit., pp. 194 ff.

was the presence of groups such as the early Chavdas and the Vaghelas who plundered and captured ships off the coast of Saurashtra. The arrival of foreign merchants when the Chavdas were powerful in the ninth century is mentioned.[5]

Hemachandra[6] states that Mularaja established the Chaulukya dynasty. He was said to have gained the favour of Shiva who appeared to him in a dream and ordered him to fight the Abhira raja, Ra Graharipu, ruling at Junagadh/Junagarh, and other *daityas* who were looting and killing pilgrims going to Prabhasa Pattana. The wicked *mlechchha* Abhira king ate beef, was a tyrant, and is described as behaving like Ravana. Graharipu had mobilized not just the Abhiras, but also a motley crowd of other local peoples such as the Medas, Bhils and Kolis. The defeat of these diverse groups would have helped Mularaja to consolidate his power, but this could not be achieved in a hurry and the groups remained irritants to the Chaulukya administration. Mularaja is said to have celebrated his victory over the Abhira by worshipping at Prabhasa.[7] This could be an indication that the temple existed in the tenth century or could confirm the possibility of his having decided to construct a temple.

A short biographical sketch of Bhimadeva I, the Chaulukya contemporary of Mahmud, refers to his campaigns in Sind and to the infighting of local kings or their attempts to mount campaigns against the Chaulukyas.[8] Conditions were disturbed

---

[5] See A.K. Forbes, *Ras Mala*, pp. 36 ff.

[6] Hemachandra, *Dvyashrayamahakavya* 1.12. ff.; 2.1. ff.; 4.59–63, 89; J. Klatt, 'Extracts from the Historical Records of the Jainas', *Indian Antiquary*, 1882, XI, 245–56; 'The Dvaiashraya', *Indian Antiquary*, 1875, IV, pp. 72 ff.; 110 ff.; 232 ff.; 265 ff.

[7] K. Forbes, *The Ras Mala*, p. 45; Hemachandra, op.cit., IV, 59–63, 89: V.49, 102–3; IX, pp. 1 ff.

[8] Merutunga, *Prabandha-cintamani*, 2.7.53; trans. Tawney, pp. 46 ff. Hemachandra, op.cit., IX, 1 ff.

and there was much fighting between local rajas. This is a confirmation of the conditions depicted in the inscriptions. Mahmud
may therefore have been viewed, at least initially, as yet another
contender on the scene, and a temporary one at that. This might
be one explanation why there is no mention of Mahmud's raid in
these texts. From the Jaina perspective, the raid of Mahmud did
not disturb Chaulukya power.

There are, however, two passing references to Mahmud's raid
on Somanatha in other texts. A contemporary of Mahmud,
Dhanapala, the poet at the court of Bhoja Paramara of Malwa,
briefly describes Mahmud's campaign in Gujarat and mentions the
towns looted en route. He makes just a bare reference to
Mahmud breaking the idol at Somanatha.[9] By contrast, he
comments at length on Mahmud's inability to damage the image
of Mahavira in a Jaina temple at Satyapura (in southern
Rajasthan) and in other places. Mahmud, he writes, cannot
destroy the idol of Mahavira for snakes cannot swallow Garuda
nor stars dim the light of the sun. The blows attacking the idol
left marks on it but could not break it for each blow rebounded
on the striker. He maintains that this proves the superiority of the
Jaina icon over other icons, a statement which is not surprising
from a recent convert to Jainism, but which is also frequently
made in such sources. The comparison is made again in passing
by Jinaprabha Suri who states that much as the lord of
Gajjana/Ghazna wished to break the idol of Mahavira, neither
his elephants nor his bullocks could dislodge it.[10]

These are the two limited references, and made in passing,
to the raid on Somanatha (other than in the Turko–Persian

---

[9] *Satyapuriya Mahavira Utsaha*, III, 2; quoted in D. Sharma, 'Some new
light on the route of Mahmud of Ghazni's raid on Somanatha: Multan to
Somanatha and Somanatha to Multan' in B.P. Sinha (ed.), *Dr Satkari
Mookerji Felicitation Volume*, pp. 165–68; *Jaina-sahitya-samshodhaka*, III,
Pt. 2, also quoted in D. Sharma.

[10] D. Sharma, ibid.

chronicles), and they are confined to Jaina texts. Given the number of chronicles and the detailed history of Gujarat that they cover, it is surprising that the mention is so scant. Was it in fact such an important event as is made out by the Turko–Persian sources? Even Bilhana, the poet from Kashmir, travelling to Somanatha barely fifty years after the raid, complains about the lack of learning among the people of Gujarat and the local speech being of poor quality, but makes no mention of the plundering of Somanatha by Mahmud.[11] This is surprising because he stayed for a while in Gujarat at the Chaulukya court where he wrote a play, the *Karnasundari*, in honour of the Chaulukya king. Equally surprising is the absence of reference to the raid in Kalhana's *Rajatarangini*, which otherwise discusses Mahmud's campaigns against the Shahis and in the north-west at some length.[12]

Later sources refer to activities around Somanatha in greater detail and provide a perspective on the period subsequent to the event. Two of the more renowned scholars of the Jaina tradition from Gujarat were Hemachandra and Merutunga, writing in the twelfth and early fourteenth centuries, respectively. Hemachandra's major grammatical work, containing material of interest to Somanatha, is the *Dvyashrayamahakavya*. The first part of this work, drawing on Sanskrit grammar, has a summary of the history of the Chaulukyas; and the second, drawing on Prakrit grammar, focuses on the king, Kumarapala. Hemachandra was the minister to both Jayasimha Siddharaja and his successor, Kumarapala. Merutunga's famous historical compendium, the *Prabandhachintamani*, has narratives advanced as history, some going back to earlier Chaulukya times. The *Sukritasamkirtana* of Arisimha of the thirteenth century, and the later *Vasantavilasa* of

---

[11] Bilhana, *Vikramankadeva-charitam*, 18.97.

[12] VII, 47–69; VIII, 1190.

Balachandra, also have narratives but are less well-known. Some Jainas such as Hemachandra, or the brothers Vastupala and Tejapala, held high political office, and were notable patrons of Jainism. This brought Jaina sects closer to the court and seems to have encouraged attempts at recording the history of the Chaulukyas and, in association with them, the history of the Jaina ministers and various sects in Gujarat as well as mentioning neighbouring kings.

Much of the intention of these works was to edify the congregation and demonstrate the might of the Jaina Sangha.[13] There was nevertheless a demarcation between the Rajput aristocracy and the Jaina elite, although some members of the latter claimed Rajput origin. The demarcation was not merely between a warrior aristocracy and a powerful segment of society espousing a philosophy of non-violence.[14] Cultural differences arose more effectively between an aristocracy of landed magnates connected through a vast network across the region based on lineage links, and an elite drawing status from the acquisition of wealth primarily from commerce and, to a lesser extent, from land. The one was not necessarily a challenge to the other, although it helped when the ruling aristocracy patronized the religion of the traders or appointed scholars of that persuasion to high administrative office.

Hemachandra was not only much appreciated as a minister but was also an impressive presence at the Chaulukya court of Jayasimha Siddharaja and his successor Kumarapala. Jayasimha, ruling in the twelfth century was, we are told, active in punishing those who destroy temples and disturb brahmans and *rishis*. He terms such people as *barbaras*/barbarians, *yatudhanas*/sorcerers, *rakshasas* and *daityas*/demons, and *asuras*.[15] The *rakshasas* are

---

[13] G. Buhler, *The Life of Hemacandra*, p. 3.

[14] L. Babb, et.al., *Multiple Histories*, pp. 15–38.

[15] Hemachandra, *Dvyashraya-mahakavya*, 12.3 ff.

said to have destroyed the temple of Svayambhurudramahakala at Shristhala. Jayasimha captures the culprit whose wife then pleads for his life and, on being released, he becomes a devoted follower of the king. These may have been people outside caste society whose land had been encroached upon and were resisting the encroachment. One expects to find the Turushkas and Yavanas included in the list, but interestingly it mentions only the local rajas. The extortion of taxes from pilgrims going to the Somanatha temple even by an officer of the *pancha-kula* is objected to by a queen. She has the taxes terminated, although this meant that the state lost a huge income of 72 lakh.[16] This would seem to be an exaggerated figure but nevertheless hints at the kind of revenue expected from these taxes. The queen then proceeds to Somanatha and offers her weight in gold and other gifts to the temple. Jayasimha, not having a son, made a pilgrimage to various holy places, including the Somanatha temple.[17]

But whatever his sentiment about the pilgrimage, it did not prevent the king from building a mosque in Khambat, presumably for the use of the Arab traders who visited there and added substantially to the commercial profits of this important port. Incidentally, the mosque was destroyed by the Paramara king, together with some Jaina temples, when he campaigned against the Chaulukya.[18]

The story of how Jayasimha prevented an invasion of the *mlechchhas* (presumably this refers to the Turks) is narrated, and a high degree of mythologizing—not lacking in humour—becomes essential to the narrative. The king arranges that when the ambassadors of the *mlechchha* are received in court, two *rakshasas* would descend from above bearing a message for him,

---

[16] Merutunga, *Prabandha-cintamani*, 3.8.94; trans. Tawney, p. 84.

[17] *Dvyashraya-mahakavya*, 15.40 ff.

[18] P. Bhatia, *The Paramaras*, p. 141.

suggesting that he is an incarnation of Rama and inviting him to Lanka. The ambassadors are overawed by the spectacle and, instead of delivering a message of war, make their submission and flee.[19] The link with the Rama incarnation of Vishnu is yet another example of what might be called a form of parenthesis through mythology and not to be taken literally. In a condition of aggressive competition for power among a range of kingdoms, such mythologizing becomes current.

A significant episode concerning the Somanatha temple is related in more than one Jaina text and focuses on activities connected with the king, Kumarapala Chaulukya, and his minister, Hemachandra.[20] There appears to have been some rivalry between Hemachandra and the Shaiva chief priest at the Somanatha temple, Bhava Brihaspati. There is therefore a discrepancy between the statements of the minister as given in the Jaina texts and those of the chief priest expressed in an inscription. The Shaiva–Jaina rivalry had a visibility and a presence elsewhere too, and sometimes took a violent turn as in Tamil Nadu and Karnataka.

Kumarapala wished to perform an act that would immortalize him and asked Hemachandra what it should be. Hemachandra replied that either he should conquer the world or repair the temple to Somanatha at Prabhasa. Hemachandra persuaded the king that as a good Shaiva, he should attend to the maintenance of the Somanatha temple and should have the existing dilapidated wooden temple replaced by a stone temple. The temple, it is said, had almost collapsed because of weathering by the sea spray that lashed against it. The temple is clearly mentioned as dilapidated and not as destroyed. In connection with the repairing of another temple, the Kedareshvara Mahadeva, collapsing because of its

---

[19] Merutunga, *Prabandha-cintamani*, 3.8.118; trans. Tawney, p. 110.

[20] G. Buhler, *The Life of Hemacandra*; Merutunga, *Prabandha-cintamani*, trans. Tawney, 4.9.140 ff., 142 ff.; pp. 126, 129 ff.

age, it is said that Kumarapala castigated the local raja for plundering pilgrims rather than repairing the temple.[21] So he ordered his own minister to repair the temple as he did in the case of Somanatha. Curiously again, there is no mention of Mahmud in connection with the decline of the Somanatha temple. The *pancha-kula* was sent to the site and an auspicious time calculated for starting on the new temple. Two years later, it was completed and the king was received by Brihaspati, the chief priest of the temple. Both Hemachandra and Kumarapala took part in the rituals of its consecration. If the earlier temple had been built of wood or substantially of wood, the change to stone was more than a renovation. This is a puzzling statement, for although some temples were built of wood, there were others— small but impressive—in stone as well dating to an earlier period.

Hemachandra, being a Jaina, was challenged by the courtiers to worship the icon of Shiva. This he did with the appropriate rituals as prescribed in the *Shiva Purana* to the astonishment of those assembled. After the consecration of the temple, Kumarapala dismissed the courtiers and the chief priest and, together with Hemachandra, entered the sanctum. Here he asked Hemachandra who was the true deity to guide one to *moksha*, a liberation from rebirth. Hemachandra decided to use his spiritual powers to call upon the deity of the temple, Shiva, to manifest himself. With this in mind, he meditated and so powerful was his meditation that he was able to invoke Shiva. When Shiva appeared before the king as a resplendent ascetic in a halo of immense light, and stated that Hemachandra knew the way to *moksha*, Kumarapala was so overwhelmed by this miracle that, instead of its strengthening his faith in Shaivism, he was converted to Jainism.

---

[21] Hemachandra, *Dvayshraya-mahakavya*, XX, 92, 94, 97, 99–101; 'The Dvaiashraya', *Indian Antiquary*, 1875, IV, pp. 269 ff. S.P. Narang, *Hemachandra's Dvayshrayakavya: A Literary and Cultural Study*, p. 112, n. 3.

Thus, in this account, Kumarapala renovated the temple as a Shaiva but was converted to Jainism after its renovation because of the miracle performed by Hemachandra. The focus here is again on the superior power of Jainism. The Shaiva *acharya* would not have been able to perform the miracle and it required the power of the Jaina *acharya* to do so. And so great was the power of the Jaina *acharya* that he could even invoke Shiva. As a good Jaina, Kumarapala is said to have become a vegetarian, declared a ban on killing animals for fourteen years, and built 1,440 temples. He refrained from appropriating the inheritance of widows even though this was a substantial loss of revenue amounting to 72 lakh.[22] This figure again would seem to be formulaic. Kumarapala's rebuilding of at least two important Shaiva temples may well have been, among other things, an attempt to get an endorsement of his right to rule since he was not the son of the previous ruler.

The miracle of Shiva appearing at the request of a Jaina *acharya* becomes the central concern of the Jaina sources relating to Somanatha. This was viewed as about the most significant happening in support of Jainism and therefore an act of much importance in the confrontation between Jainism and Shaivism. The history of other events concerning Somanatha was of far less significance. This might also explain the frequency of biographies of Kumarapala among Jaina texts.[23]

Kumarapala did not forsake Shaivism but followed the policy of many Indian rulers who have frequently been patrons to a range of prominent religious sects. In one inscription, he is described as a *paramarhat*.[24] Shaiva texts insist that Kumarapala converted back to Shaivism. The *Skanda Purana* relates the story of how the brahmans appealed to Hanuman, requesting him to

---

[22] Merutunga, *Prabandha-cintamani*, 4.9.143; trans. Tawney, p. 133.

[23] Jina Vijaya Muni (ed.), *Kumarapalacharitasangraha*.

[24] *Epigraphia Indica*, XI, pp. 54–55.

prevail upon Kumarapala to return to Shaivism. Hanuman gives them a talisman that destroys the capital at Anahilapattana. This results in the reconversion of Kumarapala.[25] A sixteenth-century text narrates that Hemachandra was defeated in a debate and sentenced to death whereupon Kumarapala reconverted to Shaivism.[26] Such stories, perhaps based on wishful thinking, concede that at some point Kumarapala was a Jaina. The hostility seems to have continued. It is strange that the brahmans did not ask Hanuman for a talisman against the Turks. Kumarapala's successor, Ajayapala, is said to have desecrated Jaina temples and looted others and supported the Shaiva religion. His son, also a zealous Shaiva, worshipped at Somanatha.[27] This would date to the latter part of the twelfth century. According to more than one *mahakavya*, a later Chaulukya king, Mularaja II, fought against the Turushkas, but little is said about this, the more important campaigns seem to have been against other, local neighbouring kings and tributary rulers.[28]

In the thirteenth century, the Somanatha temple was visited by a number of literary luminaries that included Vastupala, Harihara, Someshavara and Nanaka.[29] Clearly, the temple was prosperous. The chief priest Virabhadra, pleased by Nanaka's learning and piety, granted him a percentage of the revenue from Mangrol, presumably part of the temple estates.

---

[25] *Skanda Purana* III, Brahmakhanda Book II, Dharmaranyakakhanda Chs. 36 and 37; quoted in A.K. Majumdar, *Chaulukyas of Gujarat*, pp. 329 ff.

[26] Gadadhara, *Sampradaya Pradipa*, quoted in A.K. Majumdar, *Chaulukyas of Gujarat*, pp. 329 ff.

[27] Someshvaradeva, *Kirtikaumudi*, II, 53.

[28] Ibid., II, 56 ff.

[29] B.J. Sandesara, *Literary Circle of Mahamatya Vastupala and its Contribution to Sanskrit Literature*, pp. 55–56, 91–98.

Another set of Jaina sources suggest indirect expressions of an awareness and sensitivity, resulting possibly from Mahmud's action, although the raid on Somanatha is not actually mentioned nor is the Turkish presence in north-western India. These relate to the perceptions of a different group of people not connected with the court, nor with the competition for patronage between the Jainas and the Shaivas. These are merchants, to some degree apolitical, with their major concerns being a return to normality so that commerce could continue as before.

A story is related in a fourteenth-century text of the merchant Javadi, who is upset that the clay image he is worshipping is being washed away by his libations. He is advised to go to Gajjana/Garjana where the original image can be found. He quickly makes a fortune in trade and goes in search of the Jaina icon that takes him to the land of Gajjana.[30] The ruler of Gajjana was a Yavana and is won over by the expensive gifts presented to him by Javadi. The icon is located, permission is given for it to be taken back to where it belongs, and the ruler of Gajjana worships the icon before it is taken away. There is a complication with its installation at Girnar, creating immense problems for Javadi and his wife, before the retrieved icon can be installed.

Gajjana is evidently Ghazna and the story attempts a reconciliation of the Yavana to image worship. The Yavana could have referred back to Mahmud or to the more recent attacks of Ala al-Din Khalji on the Jaina temples at Shatrunjaya. Is there a hint of the return of the broken pieces of the Somanatha icon taken by Mahmud to Ghazna? It is also an attempt to restore the status quo ante with regard to the iconoclasm of Mahmud. There are other similar stories where the ruler of Gajjana or some other Yavana king is persuaded not to attack Gujarat. Such stories often incorporate attempts to show the power of the Jaina *acharya*, and

---

[30] P. Granoff, 'The Householder as Shaman: Jaina Biographies of Temple Builders', *East and West*, 1992, 42, 2–4, 301–17. R. Davis, op.cit., pp. 194. ff.

especially of Hemachandra. They are reconciliation stories, with a certain element of wishful thinking, as in the story of Javadi. The initial removal of the icon is hurtful and creates anguish. Its return should ideally be through reconciling iconoclasts to the worship of icons. The Yavanas, although they do not worship icons, are not described as horrendous.

The pattern of events at Somanatha with the revitalizing of the area economically, despite the raid of Mahmud and the settling of Arab traders and the building of a mosque in the area that suffered a raid, was not unique. Settlements of Arab trading communities extended from Sind all the way south along the west coast. These gave rise to variant forms of Islam, and became part of the landscape from about the twelfth century. Inscriptions from the tombs of those buried in these places or at the mosques, indicate that they came from various parts of southern Iran, the Gulf, and southern Arabia. As such, they would have been culturally distinct from the Turks settling in northern India. The interaction between various ethnic and social groups in Gujarat suggests a far more diverse picture than has been assumed so far. One example of this, for which there is both textual and architectural evidence, focuses on the city of Bhadreshvar in Kaccha.

If Bhadreshvar can be identified with Bhiswara, as some would argue, then it was raided by Mahmud; but after the raid, the local Jaina ruler was re-established. The *Jagaducharita* of Sarvananda is a much quoted biography of a Jaina merchant and shipowner, Jagadu, who belonged to the Shrimal group and was an important person in the trade with the Arabs. He is said to have been fabulously wealthy, trading with Hormuz, and this allowed him to compete with Arab merchants from Khambat, although his base was in Kaccha.[31] He has been identified as the

---

[31] G. Buhler, *The Jagaducarita of Sarvananda, a Historical Romance from Gujarat*, quoted in M. Shokoohy, *Bhadreshvar*.

Jagadeva or Jagdevasha who is said to have governed the city of Bhadreshvar through a royal charter of the Chaulukyas in the twelfth century.[32] Before Jagadu ruled over the city, it was attacked by a certain Pithadeva, a neighbouring ruler, whom some would identify with the Muslim Sumra chief, Dadu Phitu, perhaps from Sind. Jagadu acquired an army from the Chaulukya king and with this reconquered the city and came to rule over it.

The Islamic remains of Bhadreshvar are inscribed and date to the twelfth–thirteenth centuries. They indicate that Islamic communities were settled there for some time and they were largely Isma'ili. It would seem that these communities did not side with the attacker and continued to support Jagadu.[33] He renovated the temple and the votive inscriptions date to between 1166 and 1178. Much of the city had also to be reconstructed. This included Jagadu building a *vav*—an elaborate step-well—and a mosque that was, according to the text, in recognition of the wealth brought in by the *mlechchhas*. An inscription on the mosque would suggest a date of 1160—a century prior to the mosque of Nur-ud-din at Somanatha. Despite his closeness to the Arab traders, Jagadu continued his campaign against the Sumras, as did the Chaulukya army.

The politics of these events are therefore complex. The Chaulukya kings were patrons of Jaina merchants but were at war with the Sumra chiefs. The Jaina merchants wished to retain both control of the city since it was a major trading centre as well as the goodwill of the Arab traders who brought in a substantial income. But, at the same time, they wished to prevent the taking over of the city by the Sumras which would have resulted in a loss of wealth for the Jaina merchants. The Arabs remained at Bhadreshvar but did not interfere in the hostilities between Jagadu and the Sumra chiefs. As Isma'ilis, the Muslims of

---

[32] M. Shokoohy, *Bhadreshvar*, pp. 8 ff.; 38 ff.

[33] Ibid., p. 9.

Bhadreshvar may have differentiated themselves from the Sumras. Alliances and enmities were not based on identities of Muslim and Hindu, but on the identities and requirements of each of the smaller sects and communities. This appears to have been the case in various places in western India that had Muslim mercantile settlements. Another indication of this can be seen in their adoption of local styles of building, dress, food, and custom. The architectural style of the mosques is an example of such adoption. If architectural style can be read as a statement of cultural identity, there is little doubt that the patrons of the mosques in Bhadreshvar were quite willing to adopt the local temple style.[34] The structures borrow heavily from Hindu and Jaina temple architecture. Part of the reason for this is that they used local craftsmen, but all the same, barring a few characteristic features, there was little imposition of an alien style. The elegance and decoration of the pillars, copied from Hindu and Jaina temple architecture, is striking, particularly as these were not Hindu temples refashioned as Muslim mosques but were originally built as mosques. There is some difference between the Indian relationship with the Arabs and with the Turks and this needs to be recognized. The Arabs, after their initial conquests which were only successful in the lower Indus plain, established themselves as traders and negotiated relationships with their local counterparts to the benefit of both. They built mosques as new structures in this area and not from the debris of temples, and often in the local style.

The tradition of composing *prabandhas* and *vamshavalis*, narratives and chronicles, at various courts was continued with the composition of *mahakavyas*, epic poems, at some Rajput courts. These were conscious imitations of epic genres and some forms of earlier Sanskrit court literature. They were composed in

---

[34] Ibid., pp. 38 ff.

the languages current at the courts and often these were early forms of Hindi, Rajasthani, Gujarati. Epic poems on Rajput valour that have received some attention constitute a complementary but alternate source to Jaina texts. Among these are the much quoted *Prithviraja-raso*, the *Prithviraja-vijaya*, the later *Hammira-mahakavya*, and the *Kanhadade Prabandha*. The first two focus on Prithviraja Chauhan's conquests, including the battle with Muhammad Ghuri towards the end of the twelfth century. The third relates to a Chauhan ruler's defence of his kingdom against the Khalji Sultan. The last concerns the attempt of Ala al-Din Khalji to annex Gujarat, and, in this process, his general Ulugh Khan, raided the Somanatha temple. The relations between the Sultan and his general with the ruler of Jalor are the subject of this epic. These epics are different in style, composition, and content from the Jaina texts. The narrative of Hammira was written by a Jaina poet, the other three were by brahman court poets and bards. They have been treated as Hindu 'epics of resistance' to Muslim conquests,[35] but their construction touches on many facets that introduce sentiments other than resistance.

Aziz Ahmed's notion of two opposing literary genres divided by language, religion and readership needs to be examined more analytically. Some of the items included in what he calls the 'epics of conquest' have been discussed in an earlier section of this book. Here the 'epics of resistance' which are quoted will be briefly examined in terms of their content. The physical confrontation is actually not between the generalized categories of Muslim and Hindu, but between Turk and Rajput, and this changes the form and often privileges politics over religion. Even the category of Rajput can be narrowed down further to refer largely to the Chauhans/Chahamanas, and similarly the Turks to the Ghuris and Khaljis. The epics have a geographical location in the areas where there was a Rajput–Turkish competition for

---

[35] Aziz Ahmed, op.cit., R. Davis, op.cit., pp. 89 ff.

power. This makes them less 'Hindu epics' and more 'Rajput epics'. These particular epics were not known in many parts of what would be called Hindu India. The nature of this confrontation encapsulates a large range of relationships of varying kinds, of which religion is one feature among many others.

These epics had their genesis in a bardic tradition that battened on the almost formulaic expressions of enmity and friendship, although the identities of the persons involved in both changed over time and in association with new sets of events. These were, in a sense, professional constructions of epics as a genre, neither reliable history nor entirely poetic fantasy. Among other features they celebrated the hostility of groups in competition. Some anti-Muslim sentiment is evident, since the Turk was the enemy, but this does not annul the contrary sentiment of friendship with the Muslim, or indeed the loyalty of the Muslim to the Rajput where such loyalty is recorded and narrated. The bardic origins were transmuted into courtly literature following the fortunes of the clans that established dynasties. The mutation of epic into court literature was a process that went back much earlier in time. It is not as if the Turkish invasions gave rise to this genre of texts for the first time. Few disputes between the Rajputs and the Turks, as depicted in these texts, focused entirely on the power of the religious icon or its temple, which may partly explain the absence of reference to Mahmud's raid on Somanatha.

Chand Bardai's celebrated *Prithviraja-raso* highlights themes similar to the *Kanhadade Prabandha* and other epics when it maintains that Prithviraja lost to Muhammad Ghuri because the Rajputs were often disloyal to each other, that his father-in-law opposed him, and that his minister crossed over to the enemy. The Rajput hero dies, loses his territory, and women immolate themselves. Prithviraja is taken prisoner and eventually dies but not before he has also killed Muhammad Ghuri—a version that resorts to poetic licence. Prithviraja's campaigns against other rulers, such as the Chaulukyas and the Chandellas, were said to be campaigns against significant enemies, although these dynasties were treated with some disdain by the poet, as for instance, the uncomplimentary references to the neighbouring rulers, such as those directed to the Chandella dynasty. These episodes weaken the reading of the text as essentially an epic of resistance against the Muslim. It is more an explanation of defeat in the guise of a eulogy and often expressed with sensitivity.

Jayanaka's *Prithviraja-vijaya* is a eulogy on Prithviraja's initial victory over Ghuri, but it does not continue the story to the second battle and the defeat of Prithviraja by Ghuri, so the notion of resistance is restricted to politics and military confrontation at the first battle.[36] This was Jayanaka's offering to Prithviraja who had specially invited the author to come from Kashmir and spend time at his court. Ghuri is portrayed as a *mlechchha*, eating beef and therefore evil, which would be expected in a conventional description of an enemy[37] and echoes the description of Graharipu confronting the Chaulukyas in the Jaina texts. But even here there is a distinction between the Turk who is an invader and therefore evil and other Turks, such as the envoy of Ghuri, who is learned, attractive and acceptable. The Chahamana king's defence of the holy site of Pushkar, in the vicinity of the capital at Ajayameru/Ajmer, attacked by the Chaulukya king, is described as an immensely heroic act,[38] and an analogy is made with Rama. Incidentally, Merutunga has a different version of the confrontation between Prithviraja and the *mlechchhas*, the latter presumably being the Turks led by Ghuri. The story goes that Prithviraja was defeated by the *mlechchhas*, nevertheless their king decided to reinstate him in his kingdom. Therefore they all returned to Prithviraja's capital. But on arriving there, they found many paintings depicting pigs

---

[36] Jayanaka *Prithviraja-vijaya-mahakavyam*, I, 49–54; 10, 41 ff.

[37] I, 49; X, 41–42; VI, 1–28.

[38] Ibid., V, 81 ff.; I, 33.

killing the *mlechchhas*. This so infuriated them that they killed Prithviraja.[39]

It is again curious that neither the *Prithviraja-raso* nor the *Prithviraja-vijaya*, for both of whom the Turk was the enemy, refer to Mahmud's raid on Somanatha. Nor do they portray Prithviraja's campaign against Ghuri as avenging the raid of Mahmud.

The *Hammira-mahakavya*, written by the Jaina poet Nayachandra Suri, is again an epic of court intrigue and battles of the late thirteenth century. The hero, with the interesting name of Hammira—a Sanskritisation of the Arab title Amir—is a Chauhan king.[40] Kalhana refers to Mahmud as Hammira.[41] The currency of Hammira as a personal name among Rajputs suggests an admiration for the qualities associated with those referred to as Amirs. Nayachandra Suri and Padmanabha would presumably have been familiar with compositions from the court of Gujarat, such as the works of Hemachandra and Merutunga and the corpus of biographies of Kumarapala. Yet the Rajput epic was different from the Jaina *prabandha* since the ambience of the Rajput courts was also different.

Much space is given in the *Hammira-mahakavya* to Hammira's conquests of neighbouring kingdoms and his plundering of many cities.[42] As in the case of the Turko–Persian chronicles, battle, plunder and loot were the hallmarks of a heroic king in the literature of the courts. In the last third of the epic, his confrontations with Ala al-Din Khalji are narrated. This becomes a litany of the duplicity and disloyalty of fellow Rajputs, including his ministers

[39] *Prabandha-cintamani*, 5.11.216.

[40] As also Suratrana was of Sultan. R. Thapar, 'The Tyranny of Labels', in *Cultural Pasts*, pp. 990–1014.

[41] *Rajatarangini*, VII, 53–64; 47–69 n.

[42] *Hammira-mahakavya*, IX, 1–27, 39–47; X, 8–10; X, 88; XI, 1–2; XIII, 69–166.

and generals, some of whom joined Ala al-Din. A noticeable exception was his adviser, Mahimashahi, who was loyal to him till the last. Mahimashahi is described as a Mudgal/Mughal/Mongol. Apart from Mahimashahi, Hammira had other Mudgal courtiers loyal to him and hostile to the Turks. According to this text, the reason why Ala al-Din sent his army against Hammira was because he was not paying the stipulated tribute to the Delhi Sultan and had given shelter to the Muslim Mudgals.[43]

The entry of Mudgals/Mughals/Mongols adds to the complexities in relationships. Barani refers to them as neo-Muslims who had taken service with the Khaljis and settled in various parts of Delhi and some had also been granted villages. They were central Asians more recently converted to Islam. They were part of the Khalji army that invaded Gujarat. The Khalji general, Ulugh Khan, uprooted the idol of Manat—the deity of the Hindus—that had earlier been broken by Mahmud but reinstalled by the brahmans of Somanatha. Ulugh Khan despatched the idol to Delhi where it was taken round the city to entertain the people. On their way back from Gujarat, the Mongols revolted against the Khalji general, who treated them badly because he suspected that they had not deposited in the royal treasury the required one-fifth share of the loot from the campaign due from them. The Mongols resented the ill-treatment, rebelled, and killed a few of the commanders. Some of the rebels were captured, others fled and took service with Rajput rajas. Evidently, some were serving at the court of Hammira.[44]

The *Kanhadade Prabandha* was composed by Padmanabha, a Nagar brahman, who identifies himself as a *kavi*/poet attached

---

[43] Ibid., IX, 101 ff.

[44] Ziya al-Din Barani, *Tarikh-I Firuz Shahi* (ed.), Saiyid Ahmed Khan, pp. 251–53; P. Jackson, *The Delhi Sultanate: A Political and Military History*, pp. 80–81. I am grateful to Professor Muzaffar Alam for informing me about this passage and translating it.

to the court at Jalor (Marwar) in the mid-fifteenth century. The epic refers back to events of two centuries earlier.[45] The language is Prakrit, overlapping with Old Rajasthani and some Gujarati, that suggests its access to a more popular audience than that of the Jaina texts.[46] The poem is a eulogy to yet another Chauhan ruler, Kanhadade Chahamana, who had ruled in Jalor in southern Rajasthan and was an ancestor to the current ruler.

The trouble that brings about the hostility between Kanhadade and Ala al-Din Khalji begins with Madhava, a brahman who was close to the Jalor court and who claimed that he had been insulted by the king of Gujarat. Madhava seeks to avenge the insult by bringing the Turks into Gujarat as conquerors. He therefore goes to Ala al-Din Khalji and offers to assist the army of the Sultanate in conquering Gujarat.[47] (Merutunga also states in his *Vicharashreni* that Madhava betrayed the Vaghela king of Gujarat and assisted in the Khalji attack.)[48] Ulugh Khan, the general of the Sultan, sets out with his army, accompanied by Madhava. They are not permitted to pass through Jalor by Kanhadade but skirt around it and arrive in Pattana. Since Madhava knows the secret entry into the city, the Khalji army enters and plunders the town. The author compares this not to the earlier sack by Mahmud of Ghazni, as one would expect, but to the sack of Lanka by the armies of Rama.[49] Madhava is seen as the cause of the conflict and is killed by the defenders of Somanatha.

---

[45] K.D. Vyas (ed.), *Kanhadade Prabandha*; trans. V.S. Bhatnagar, *Kanhadade Prabandha*. D. Sharma, *Early Chauhan Dynasties*; See also R. Davis, op.cit., pp. 191–94.

[46] I.M.P. Raeside, 'A Gujarati Bardic Poem: The Kanhadade Prabandha'.

[47] *Kanhadade Prabandha*, Canto I, v, 15 ff.

[48] *History and Culture of the Indian People*, VI, 'The Delhi Sultanate', p. 19.

[49] *Kanhadade Prabandha*, I, 78–86.

Ulugh Khan carries away the *lingam*, intending to take it back to Delhi as a trophy, although it is also said that he wanted to break it and grind it into lime, actions associated in Persian accounts with Mahmud. The capturing of the image is possible because Shiva has deserted his icon and gone to Kailasa and, in any case, it is now the Kaliyuga—'the age of the losing throw' as it has been called—when the images of deities can be wilfully broken. Surprisingly, there is no mention of Mahmud or the earlier raid on Somanatha. The temple clearly has not been converted into a mosque. The theme in this version seems less to be the desecration of the temple, and more the attempted conquest of Gujarat by the Khaljis. It could be argued that perhaps the temple had become a symbol of legitimation of the kings of Gujarat after Kumarapala's renovation, therefore the conquest of Gujarat required the capturing of the icon at Somanatha, but seems not to have required the destruction of the temple. Hence, the focus on the icon. The capturing of the icon amounts to the symbolic capturing of the legitimacy to rule, apart from an Islamic victory over Shaivism.

The story continues with Parvati and Ganga appearing to Kanhadade in a dream, urging him to rescue the *lingam*. The icon seems to remain important even though Shiva had deserted it. Kanhadade retrieves the *lingam*, which is then safeguarded by being converted into five icons. Each is sent to five places for installation.[50] One of these is in Saurashtra and was most likely Somanatha, which would again indicate that it had not been converted into a mosque by Ulugh Khan as Persian sources maintain. Could this also be an attempt to mirror the act of Mahmud who is said to have taken the pieces of the icon back to Ghazni and sent some to Mecca and Medina, although the desecration of the icon in this case was a form of 'inverted' legitimation?

---

[50] Ibid., I, 251 ff.

There is a contradiction between this version and the account as given by Barani. The rescuing of the icon is Kanhadade's claim to legitimizing his authority. This would be important to a member of a lesser Chauhan lineage facing constant and intense competition from other Chauhans as well. He created five icons from the one and distributed them in Marwar by way of marking the kingdom he aspired to or sanctifying the kingdom he was ruling.[51] The narratives can then be read as the claims made by both Turks and Rajputs to the legitimacy of rule by capturing the icon, a legitimacy that in the case of the Rajputs was further empowered by their worshipping it. The proximity of Jalor to Gujarat doubtless heightened the focus on Somanatha, which in the other epics has little significance.

Protracted battles follow between the armies of the Sultanate and the Rajputs. By way of a settlement, Ala al-Din suggests a marriage alliance between his daughter, Piroja, and Kanhadade's son. The Sultan's daughter gives a lengthy explanation of how the two of them have been repeatedly married through a series of previous births, which provides the kind of background to the proposal that would make it more acceptable to the Rajput. Previous incarnations are ways of incorporating the Other. The prince regards the proposal as insulting to a Rajput.

A frequent gesture of conciliation among enemies is the offer of a daughter in marriage and this occurs as a theme in more than one such narrative. This is an intrinsically important matter in caste society and where caste status is inappropriate, the avoidance of such a marriage precludes the lowering of caste status. Marriage alliances among Rajput lineages could be means of acquiring territory and the right to rule over it. The offer of a daughter in marriage was also the acceptance of the superior status of her husband, but this was not the case in this proposal of marriage. The Turks generally did not give their daughters to

---

[51] R. Davis, op.cit., p. 193.

the local rajas in marriage, although the practice was known among the Turks ruling in Malwa at about this time.[52] Predictably, the offer is rejected by Kanhadade's son as being inappropriate for a Rajput.[53] Ala al-Din is interested in his daughter's version of her past lives, and he is even said to have visited Jalor and been much respected because he behaved like a Hindu. One is reminded here of the wishful thinking involved in the story of the Yavana king worshipping the icon retrieved by Javadi, as recounted earlier. But the conflict continues. The prince dies in battle and his head is brought to the Sultan, but when the latter turns towards it, the head turns away. Piroja immolates herself while holding the head, conceding superiority to the son of Kanhadade. Piroja's self-immolation exemplifies a love that goes beyond political and social boundaries. But at another level it is an interesting comment on the political shadow-boxing among competitors.

A relative departure from earlier narratives and linked to the confrontation with the Turks is the immolation of *kshatriya* women in the ritual of *jauhar*. However, even this in some ways was an extension of the much earlier ritual of becoming a *sati*, expected initially of a *kshatriya* woman on the death of her husband on the battlefield. At one level, the *jauhar* becomes the formulaic coda in the narratives, given that the purpose of the story was to applaud the culture of the Rajput male.

The *Kanhadade Prabandha* is another narrative of court intrigue, intention of conquest, courtly romance and, in the context of hostility between Rajput and Turk, a description of failed attempts at negotiating relationships. If it was an epic concerned largely with the carrying away of the Somanatha icon and its retrieval, it is surprising that the same action on the part of Mahmud is not referred to as a forerunner of the theme. Nor did that earlier

---

[52] D.H.A. Kolff, *Naukar, Rajput and Sepoy*, pp. 96 ff.

[53] *Kanhadade Prabandha*, Canto III.

action inspire a parallel epic. Some features do not seem very conducive to resistance. For example, the taking of the name Hammira. It could mean that the Rajput was as good as the Turk, but would the title of the enemy be appropriated and honoured among the elite if the intention was to resist that enemy?

There is an attempt to narrate a heroic confrontation between Turk and Rajput but the attention is more on the activities of the courts and the ambience of Rajput society. In terms of campaigns against neighbouring rulers and looting and plundering cities, other Rajput kingdoms are as much at the receiving end of hostilities as are the Turks. This is not surprising since the history of the pre-Islamic period also has its share of royal plunderers where, in doing so, these kings were behaving in a manner that had come to be accepted as part of their assertion of authority. There is less of a directly religious antagonism towards the Turks except in the *Kanhadade Prabandha*, and there the tangled story of the attempted reconciliation weakens its projection as a narrative of resistance.

Although there are occasional references to the *dharma* of the Rajputs being opposed to the demands of the Khalji, the focus is not centrally on religious differences. The themes that recur are the importance of lineage and familial descent where lineage is underlined to claim political status, legitimacy, and heroic qualities, and where lineage claims are unavailable to the Turks; where the aspirations and antagonisms are over control of territory and overlordship; and where marriage alliances are important for stabilizing power and Ala al-Din is seen as transgressing Rajput patriarchy.[54]

Marriage alliances among *kshatriyas* served many purposes: endorsing caste status, making political connections and settling

---

[54] R. Sreenivasan, 'Alauddin Khalji Remembered: Conquest, Gender and Community in Medieval Rajput Narratives', *Studies in History*, 2002, ns. 18. 2, pp. 275–96.

disputes, establishing loyalty and bonding, and acquiring territory and land. Hierarchy of rank reflected hierarchy of authority and access to resources. The intrusion of the Turks interfered not only with controlling territory but also the demands of loyalty. The refusal of the relationship between the Khalji and the Chauhan, therefore, may have been due not just to a difference in religion but also to the threat of ending a system of interlocking controls. Such relationships were complex and were not always understood by outsiders. They were whittled down in colonial history to merely matters of political ambition and religious differences.

These are epics that encapsulate confrontations of various kinds and have an ancestry in pre-Islamic compositions and inscriptions where confrontation is justified, legitimated and applauded. Hero-lauds are recited and some are represented visually on the many hero-stones—memorials to dead heroes—in various parts of the subcontinent, where the enemy is the local marauder, cattle-lifter, sea pirate or contender for power.

Rajput epics are not just a counterpoint to 'Muslim invasions' for they are also the literature of those that emerged successful from the rivalries within Rajput society. There is another dialogue implicit in these texts and that is connected with the popular ballads and legends that had considerable currency.[55] These were about adventurers who acquired kingdoms through battles, diplomacy, matrimonial alliances and ascribed it all to the blessing of the goddess. This context introduces narratives that relate back to earlier traditions and where 'the Other' from event to event is stereotypical, and not necessarily Muslim. For some the context is an earlier Jaina ethos or mythology, although the action has echoes of contemporary society. These are often local epics

---

[55] For the tradition of the *raso* in Gujarat, see S. Yashaschandra, 'From Hemacandra to Hind Svaraj', in S. Pollock (ed.), *Literary Cultures in History*, pp. 574 ff.

whose geographical range is not too great as indeed the geographical limits of the kingdoms they speak about are also small. It could be argued that the genesis of these epics lies in a particular ethos and the visibility of a warrior aristocracy. The Muslim content of the Turkish invasions in this context would be an additional feature and more marginal than central. Interestingly, the Arabs, although Muslims, play no role in these epics; and the Mongols, also Muslims, but who were opposed to the Turks, are treated as reliable or sometimes not-so-reliable friends. Where the Turk was seen as a contender, he was depicted as the enemy.

Individual acts of heroism are applauded, but the main interests are attempts at diplomacy and the success of courtly politics even if on occasion they involve a degree of deceit. Local rulers contesting power with those seeking to establish larger kingdoms was not a new phenomenon, neither in Gujarat, as we have seen, nor in other parts of the subcontinent, and the process has antecedents. Eulogies to those contesting authority are narrated as part of longer compositions. The prevalence of the *vamshavali*, or the chronicle tradition, and the *charita*, or biographies, as forms of political legitimation had become characteristic of new kingdoms. Epic poems are also forms of legitimizing power and status or attempts at explaining why these were lost, and they differ from chronicles in as much as they often focus on the acts of individuals and not without the exaggeration required of the genre.

Literature of what can be read as sentiments of resistance existed in earlier times.[56] The *Gargi Samhita* section of the *Yuga Purana* has a searing attack on the Yavanas who are accused of various kinds of vile behaviour by brahman authors of the *Purana*, and this was probably aimed primarily at the Indo–Greek

---

[56] R. Thapar, 'Indian Views of Europe: Representations of the Yavanas in Early Indian History', *Cultural Pasts*, pp. 536–55.

and other rulers of the north-west. The behaviour of the enemy was said to be gruesome and the authors would have nothing to do with the Yavanas. This is not surprising since Yavana practices hardly conform to brahmanical norms. Yet, interestingly, these same Yavanas were assimilated into other groups such as the Buddhists and the Bhagavata sects. Votive inscriptions at Buddhist sites attest to Yavana donors. The Buddhist attitude as depicted in the *Milindapanho* is one in which a monk attempts to persuade the king, Menander, to become a Buddhist. As compositions encapsulating resistance, if one chooses to see them as such, texts such as the *Gargi Samhita* are the expression of only one section of society and reveal a sentiment that would not be shared by all. It has been suggested that the negative depiction of Muslims in inscriptions, for instance, is the articulation of upper-caste brahman attitudes since they were the most affected by the Muslim ruling class disrupting their norms.[57] This can also be seen as a continuation of earlier attitudes towards those who came from a society not governed by the rules of *varna* and therefore regarded as outside the social pale.

In juxtaposing sources, it is worth keeping in mind that simultaneous with these epics were the equally popular compositions of what have been called Sufi romances, composed in Hindavi, and in which Sufi and similar themes were illustrated through local folk tales.[58] The fourteenth-century *Chandayan* of Maulana Da'ud was based on an Ahir folk tale and followed a known literary genre. Malik Muhammad Jayasi's *Padmavat* was a rewriting of a well-known story. The *barahmasa* poems on love and separation through the seasons of the year composed by

---

[57] C. Talbot, 'Inscribing the Other: Inscribing the Self; Hindu–Muslim Identities in Pre-Colonial India', *Comparative Studies in Society and History*, 1995, 37, 4, pp. 692–722.

[58] A. Behl, 'The Magic Doe: Desire and Narrative in a Hindavi Sufi Romance circa 1503', in R. Eaton (ed.), *India's Islamic Traditions*, 711–1750.

Hindu and Muslim poets were perhaps even more popular. Qutban composed the *Mrigavati*, a story involving a prince and yogi. Such narratives intermeshed myths, religious notions, social conventions and literary forms derived from Indian traditions with similar sentiments from Islam. By this time, well-known Sanskrit texts had been translated into Persian such as the *Shukasaptati* and works on *Hathayoga*.[59]

The Rajput relationship to the Turks establishing their power in northern India is complex and cannot be reduced to just a relationship between Hindus and Muslims or as one determined solely by religious attitudes. It has been effectively argued that it is debatable whether religion was the predominant factor in the relationship or whether loyalty as a value and in practice was more significant, among other factors.[60] Conquest has multiple dimensions and those under threat face a loss of power, of access to economic resources, of religious icons and a way of life. All these have to be defended. Given the network of Rajput lineages, with each competing for a greater appropriation of power, status and economic resources, the major factors in relationships tend to be questions of loyalty and deceit. This is not to exclude motivations resulting from religious differences, but to locate these differences within the more complex picture involving other concerns as well. A more analytical and comparative study of these epic poems may reveal what they are actually saying. If they are to be read as epics of resistance, there has to be a perceptive analysis of what is being contested, who are the

---

[59] Muzaffar Alam, 'The Culture and Politics of Persian in Pre-Colonial Hindusthan', in S. Pollock (ed.), *Literary Cultures in History*, pp. 131–98; C. Ernst, *Eternal Garden: Mysticism, History and Politics at a South Asian Sufi Centre*, p. 31.

[60] B. Metcalf, 'Too Little and Too Much', *Journal of Asian Studies*, 1995, 54, 4, pp. 951–67. For a later period see, N.P. Ziegler, 'Some Notes on Rajput Loyalties During the Mughal Period', in M. Alam and S. Subrahmanyam (eds), *The Mughal State*, 1526–1750, pp. 168–210.

contestants, and what is the nature of the resistance. To read them as primarily representing Muslim conquest and Hindu resistance is to do them little justice.

In looking at events brought about through Yavana attacks on Gujarat, the Jaina texts are underlining their ideology. Jaina temples survive, whereas Saiva temples are destroyed or marginalized. Unlike Mahavira, Shiva has abandoned his icons. Nevertheless, this appears to be contradicted, in that the Somanatha temple despite its vicissitudes seems to be constantly in worship, is frequently visited by kings, and its renovation is used to legitimize royal power and as an opportunity to demonstrate the power of Jaina spirituality. If the Turko–Persian accounts, the Jaina texts and Sanskrit inscriptions are juxtaposed, it would almost seem that the temple was switching between being a mosque and a temple every century. This has happened with religious structures in other parts of the world when their identity was transmuted, as in the case of the mosque/church at Cordoba, or the St Sophia in Istanbul. Was this the case at Somanatha? Or can it be argued that the insistence on the destruction of temples in the Turko–Persian accounts may be exaggerated? The Somanatha temple does not seem to have been actually used as a mosque until the seventeenth or possibly even early eighteenth century and then too not seriously, despite earlier claims to its having been converted into a mosque time and again.

The Jaina narratives frequently speak of the dilapidated condition of the temple through wear and tear, weathering from sea spray, and bad maintenance. Even they do not refer to wilful destruction. Inscriptions refer to the neglect and greed of those supervising its maintenance. Its condition can be set right with adequate renovation. Given the two references in earlier Jaina writing to Mahmud's raid on Somanatha, surprisingly, these are not mentioned when reference is made to the poor condition of the temple before Kumarapala's renovation, which would have enhanced his prestige had the raid been of major importance. But this is not the intention of the Jaina narratives. This can also be read to suggest that the icons alone were at the receiving end of fanatical fury, rather than the entire temple, which would underline the sectarian difference. Often, the prosperous Jaina merchant is responsible for repairs and restitution, with some exceptions where royal patronage becomes necessary. Such activity is almost assumed to be normal for the wealthy Jaina, the building and repairing of temples and icons being among the more pious deeds required of him.

The Jaina view maintains that attacks are to be expected in the Kaliyuga. This is the last of the four ages in the cycle of time, where the first is the age of perfection and there is then a gradual decline until the fourth age which terminates in a catastrophic happening and, eventually, the first age returns again. Kaliyuga is the age of decline and degeneration.[61] Icons will be broken, but there are wealthy Jaina merchants eager to restore such temples, and icons are miraculously mended where there are sincere devotees to care for them. There is a coming to terms with iconoclasm, both in its destruction and in its being an agency that requires images to be restored, where the restoration is miraculous. Jinaprabha-suri speaks of images being broken by a Muslim army, but being miraculously restored.[62] Other instances suggest a matter-of-fact attitude as in the case of a thirteenth-century inscription recording the replacing by a woman donor of an image broken by Yavanas. Interestingly, there is no comment on the breaking of the image.[63]

The Jaina texts do not demand that violence be met with violence as this would be contrary to the theory of Jaina ethics. Possibly, as a major trading community they were anxious that

---

[61] R. Thapar, *Time as a Metaphor of History*.

[62] *Vividha-tirtha-kalpa*, section 29, discussed in P. Granoff, 'Tales of Broken Limbs and Bleeding Wounds: Responses to Muslim Iconoclasm in Medieval India', *East and West*, 1991, 41, 1–4, pp. 189–203.

[63] Kiradu Inscription, *Epigraphia Indica*, XI, p. 72.

negotiations, rather than warfare with the ruling authority, whoever it may be, should remain continuous so that trade would not be disrupted. Many of the Jaina and Hindu traders had close contacts with their Arab counterparts, close enough for it to be embarrassing if any of the three adopted hostile stances against each other's religion. Attitudes were neither consistent nor unchanging. When the Turks attacked the Jaina temples at Shatrunjaya in 1313, the representative of Alp Khan governing Gujarat had them restored and provided financial assistance. A Jaina comment on the destruction of temples by the Turks was that such things happen in the Kaliyuga.[64] This permits some flexibility in relations with political authority, and these have to be continually adjusted. Jaina relations with Akbar were friendly and, in a text of the period, a Muslim governor of Gujarat is described as a second Rama, protecting people from the evils of the Kali age.[65]

Inevitably, the question was asked as to how images came to be harmed. The answer often revolves around such things happening in an age of evil—such as the present Kaliyuga—the bad faith of kings and deities not always giving enough attention and support to their own images.[66] The power of the image would depend on how well it has been consecrated and on the devotion of the person worshipping it. Images seem to come to life in sectarian disputes and the narratives of their intervention are symbolic of what is being aspired to.

An interesting parallel to the Jaina narratives is the *mahatmya* (a presumed history of the temple) of the Ekalingaji temple near Udaipur in Rajasthan, composed in about the fifteenth century.[67]

---

[64] P. Dundas, *The Jains*, pp. 124 ff.

[65] P. Dundas, 'Jain Perception of Islam in the Early Modern Period', *Indo–Iranian Journal*, 1999, 42, 1, pp. 35–46.

[66] P. Granoff, op.cit., 1991.

[67] *Vayu Purana*, 12.196; 108–16; 26.59, quoted in P. Granoff, op.cit. 1991. R. Davis, op.cit., pp. 194 ff.

In a dialogue between Narada and Vayu, a question is posed that if an image, when consecrated, becomes the habitat of the deity, how can it be destroyed by the Yavanas? Why do the gods not prevent this? The answer covers more than one facet. It is said that there has been and will continue to be a conflict between *devas*/the deities and the virtuous ones, and the *daityas*, *asuras*, and other evil ones. The Yavanas are a part of this conflict, which will continue until the end of this Kaliyuga or time cycle. The current Yavanas are presumably repeating what the earlier ones have done and doubtless the Yavanas still to come will be doing the same. The Yavanas destroy images as do the *asuras*; and the *devas*/the gods do not prevent this, since the conflict is eternal and cannot be stopped. It is now the Kaliyuga (which had its beginning many hundreds of years ago) and iconoclasm is to be expected because the world turns upside down in this age. The Yavanas are already carrying the burden of being cursed. Whenever rulers are lax in their duties or devoid of faith in Shiva, the Yavanas will break images. When an image is broken, then a new one should be made and consecrated in its place. There does not seem to be a miraculous mending of broken images.

If the icon symbolizes the authority of the ruler as well as representing the deity, can the iconoclasm be said to be motivated by religion or also by the reading of the icon as a symbol of those in authority and power? The icon represents the deity's endorsement of the king and should therefore not be broken is the answer from pre-Islamic times.[68] If what is described is expected in the Kaliyuga, and this age has been calculated as beginning 4,000 years before the coming of Islam to India, the Kaliyuga has to be treated as an undated, continuous present. Waiting out the Kaliyuga is an immense length of time for it extends to 432,000 years.

The Kaliyuga is described in the *Puranas* as a dystopia, an age of moral decline and the overthrowing of social norms as set

---

[68] Varahamihira, *Brihat-samhita*, 46.8.

out in the *dharmashastras*—the normative texts encoding the social and sacred obligations of various castes.[69] This was not a description of a particular period of time, although it has been argued that it referred to the turn of the Christian era when the Yavana, Shaka and Kushana rulers patronized non-brahman sects. Kaliyuga comes to be used for any period that registers a decline in the norms of the *dharmashastras*. It is said that kings behave like thieves and therefore the rule of the unrighteous prospers. They fail to protect their subjects as good *kshatriyas* should. *Dharma* declines with the rise of many heresies, taught by those wearing ochre robes, and moving around as skull-bearing mendicants. They spread untruthfulness, lust and the habits of the *mlechchha*—those outside the pale of caste society—and it is an age when women outnumber men. The enemies here seem to be the non-brahmanical sects, the Jainas, the Nathapanthis, the Shakta worshippers, and such like, those opposed to brahmanical norms.

Attention has been drawn to the statement in some *Puranas* that when places of pilgrimage, *tirthas*, replace asceticism as a means of liberating the soul from rebirth, *moksha*, the gods begin to destroy shrines.[70] Yama, the god of Death, complains that the efficacy of certain shrines, especially those dedicated to Skanda, purifies people and this results in overcrowding in heaven. Space is so confined that people have to stand holding their arms up. Even women and *shudras* start arriving in heaven. Shiva's comment is that they are no longer evil. Elsewhere, it is said that Parvati created Ganesha to divert men from worshipping Shiva, for Ganesha can oppose *dharma* and keep people out of heaven. The intervention of Ganesha led to people seeking wealth rather than purification. This is said with reference to the shrine of

---

[69] e.g. *Vishnu Purana*, IV, 24, 70–101.

[70] W. Doniger, *The Origins of Evil in Hindu Mythology*, pp. 253–58. My attention was drawn to this by Kumkum Roy.

Somanatha. The destruction of shrines is thus not always due to the passivity of gods, but can also be due to their connivance. Even if this is read as an explanation for why shrines are destroyed, the absence of resistance is striking.

The Shaiva texts appear to register an acceptance of images being broken and temples desecrated in the Kaliyuga, with little attempt at a spirited defence. Jaina texts make a far more active assertion by admitting to attacks by Turkish iconoclasts but insisting on miraculous restorations. These attacks seem to provide the perfect opportunity for continued proof of the greatness of Jainism.[71] If it is said that the texts imply that the Turks are behaving like *asuras*, the Shaivas and Vaishnavas seem to be more resigned to this behaviour than the Jainas. One may well ask why the saviour figure of Kalkin, the tenth and last Vaishnava *avatara*, is not invoked to counter the Turkish attacks on temples.

References to gods distancing themselves in the Kaliyuga raise other questions. Is the presence of the deity dependent on human worship or is this irrelevant to the god? Does the authority of the deity therefore also derive from the degree of worship that it attracts? Does worship decline because there is a decline of *dharma* in the Kaliyuga or because alternative avenues of authority begin to gain recognition? One among these, for example, has always been the renouncer or the ascetic, who accumulates power through ascetic practice. Can this be seen as competing with divinity?

Interestingly, these attitudes are different from those reflected in the Sanskrit inscriptions. Although the inscriptions do not record a resistance to Islam, rather, some of them point to an accommodation, nevertheless in terms of restoring icons and temples, there is little concession to its being the Kaliyuga. On the contrary, there is an emphasis on the continuity of building

---

[71] P. Granoff, op.cit., 1991.

temples at sites old and new. Bhava Brihaspati and Tripurantaka, as Pashupata Shaiva priests, seem unconcerned by the events around the Somanatha temple, their focus being the continuation of worship and the revenue that could be channelled to the temple from this and other activities. There were always royal patrons and other affluent people ready to build temples and restore worship so as to enhance their authority and status through such patronage. The building of temples and the installation of icons were not merely rejoinders to Turkish threats and attacks. Building new temples and restoring dilapidated ones were frequent activities even in regions as yet untouched by Turkish attacks. They were statements of the political strength, religious articulation and economic prosperity of the region and of its patrons.

The references to idol breakers are more frequently to Yavanas and Turushkas and not so often to Tajiks. There appears to be a difference at this time in the attitude towards the Arabs as compared to the Turks. The Arab invasions in Sind tended to give way to the settlements through trade all along the western coast of India. The Arabs by now were not essentially interested in founding a state but in protecting their trade. Settlement meant abiding by the governance of Indian rulers and eventually founding communities by marrying locally, adopting some local customs, and being assimilated. These communities, such as the Bohras and Khojas in western India, the Navayats in the Konkan, and the Mappilas in Malabar, were not uniform in their belief and culture although they all professed Islam. Their distinguishing feature was the identity of the region expressed through language, customary law, food and dress. There were also a few settlements that were not so deeply influenced by the culture of the region. The Turko–Persian chronicles had a point therefore when, from their perspective, they set aside the Arabs in the establishing of Turkish power in India.

Possibly in contrast, the Turks, who were first recruited as mercenaries into the armies of Kashmir, or who traded with the brahmans of Pehoa, gradually nurtured ambitions of conquest and power that changed the earlier relationship. This was partly influenced by their political ambitions of empire and by their recent approximation to the politics of empire as played by the Caliphs. Coming from central Asia and acting a new role, they first sought to appropriate Persian culture and were then faced with another cultural idiom in northern India.[72] The appropriation of new cultures is a long and slow process.

In the early texts of north India, the identity of the Turks is tied to pre-Islamic identities. Interestingly, the words initially used for Muslims in India did not come from Arab sources even though they were the first Muslims to settle in the country. The words used most commonly were Yavana, Shaka and Turushka, with Arabs being called Tajiks.[73] The first, referring to anyone coming from the west, such as the Greeks to begin with, could have been applied to the Arabs as it occasionally was, but seems to have been used more often for the Turks. Shaka and Turushka were earlier terms for people from central Asia. The term *mlechchha* is, according to context, used more frequently to refer to someone outside the pale of caste society and dates back to much earlier times. Interestingly, these identities do not relate them to religion but to a certain historical continuity not least based on geography. Similarly, the original meaning of Hindu was an inhabitant of al-Hind, the land across the Indus as viewed from the west. The religious connotation came later. The historical continuity of these names, starting before Islamic times, bears reflecting upon in terms of how various groups perceived each other, as also the probability of earlier perceptions giving form to later ones. Representations and perceptions of the Other, as has been frequently demonstrated, are highly complicated.

---

[72] A. Schimmel, 'Turk and Hindu: a poetical image and its application to historical fact', in S. Vryonis (ed.), *Islam and Cultural Change in the Middle Ages*, pp. 107–26.

[73] R. Thapar, 'The Tyranny of Labels', loc.cit.

The Jaina chronicles, the Rajput epics and other texts of the period subsequent to the raid on Somanatha, would have been the likely ones recording a Hindu trauma. However, what remains enigmatic is that there is little reference to nor reflection of a trauma. The Jaina texts confidently insist that Turkish raids on their sacred centres have failed to dishonour their images. Sources from Shaiva authors appear not to record an upheaval resulting from the raid on Somanatha by Mahmud. There is a hint in accounts referring to merchants of reconciliation and negotiation being a way of reacting to Turkish attacks. Of the Rajput epics, the *Prithviraja-vijaya* may qualify as reflecting Rajput resistance to the Turk, the other epics being largely in the earlier genre of court poetry that covered many activities of which relations with the Turks was only one.

The destruction or the decline of sacred spaces has been a regular historical process, as also the reconstruction of such spaces where necessary, as in other parts of the world. Inevitably, as a historical process, it was viewed and experienced differently from the way it is today. Aspects of hostility against the Turks are registered but they are not too different from the hostilities between contending rulers in the history of those times. This is not to suggest that there was no resentment against the new enemy but to keep in mind that competitors are treated with hostility and not all enemies are viewed as equal.

The literature of medieval courts is frequently enveloped in a recognizable idiom, sometimes religious. But the idiom is not necessarily the reality and it may veil the inevitably complex reality. The historian therefore has to sift the literal from the trope. This requires that the historian listen to many voices, where available, before assessing the cause of a historical process. It also requires the evaluation of a range of possibilities in ascertaining causal links. Even more relevant is the need to appreciate that there may be alternative experiences of a particular past and that these should be included when reconstructing that past and appraising the priority of causes.

6

The Perceptions of Yet Others

Parallel to the Turko–Persian versions of Mahmud's raid on Somanatha and the Rajput epic poems, there are some other versions reflecting the more widespread and popular perceptions of Mahmud and those connected with him in an interesting mix of traditions. The mix tells its own story. Those that seem to have been familiar in a general sense with the Turko–Persian tradition refer to Mahmud in the context of the raid, but others, even when they refer to him, ignore the raid. There may well be more such statements that have yet to be garnered and investigated by historians.

The data is valuable as it provides a perspective from sources that have only recently begun to be taken seriously by historians. Their neglect was because they were legends and this denied them a place as possible sources in investigating the past. This is not to argue that legends state what actually took place in the past, in fact often far from it, but to suggest that they can provide another dimension to history in as much as legends can be examined as perceptions of past events. An attempt can be made to understand why such perceptions took shape, how they differed from the perceptions of chroniclers in the past, and what were the politics of these genres. Popular legends provide a perspective dissimilar from that of court chronicles, given that their authors and the audience to which the compositions were addressed were different. The agenda of each therefore varied. Their contribution is not necessarily to reconstruct events as they actually happened but to understand why some people propagated and believed certain versions about these events. Our notions of what constitute historical sources have undergone a change and these narratives and references, although fanciful, do provide some understanding of the perceptions of the groups from which they have originated. They need to be subjected to the kinds of analyses that are becoming common in the recording and use of oral traditions.

I am taking as my examples some stories from the popular tradition in which Mahmud figures, directly or indirectly. One is a story narrated by Watson, which some have identified as the *Kissa Mangroli Shah*. Another has become the focus of a place of pilgrimage connected to the *pir*, Ghazi Miyan. These stories are in some ways stereotypical but the stereotypes used are of interest. Apart from these, there are also the compositions of itinerant singers, preachers and performers of what are perceived as magical formulae and invocations to deities and holy men, some of which, strangely enough, invoke Mahmud.

In the early nineteenth century, James Tod in his *Travels in Western India*, refers to a ballad on the fall of Patan Somanath that he heard in Saurashtra.[1] It was a fragment of a poem in Hindi, a garbled version of what was said to have been originally a poem in Persian. The story concerns a Haji who came from Mecca and saved the life of a widow's son when he had to be sacrificed to the deity at Somanatha, and the Haji invited Mahmud to raid Somanatha. Reference is made to the heroism of the Gohila brothers in this connection, but Tod states that the Gohilas settled in Somanatha long after Mahmud's

---

[1] J. Tod, *Travels in Western India*, pp. 345–51.

raid.[2] Mahmud left a governor after his raid and the local Hindus tried to dislodge him but failed.

About fifty years later, Watson went in search of this ballad and obtained some fragments that he records as an oral tradition about the event. It may not have been the same ballad but had some similarities and doubtless interpolations of the later date. He writes that the story was recited to him by a certain Shaikh Din, who had rendered it into verse. The poem was complete in itself, was written in the late nineteenth century in a mixture of Hindustani and Gujarati, and involved a story of a Haji, the raja of Patan and Mahmud of Ghazni. The mixture of language was paralleled by an assortment in the narrative of folklore, snippets from the Turko–Persian chronicles, and echoes of the Jaina texts all enveloped in Sufi imagery. The ballad therefore reads as an amalgam of varied elements of the story of Mahmud from various sources.

It is said that before the coming of Mahmud there was a time when Muslims were living in Somanatha-pattana, few in number and oppressed by the Hindu raja. This took the form of an order that one Muslim had to be offered as sacrifice each day to the *lingam*. The Prophet appeared to a certain Haji in Mecca and told him to go to Prabhasa Pattana to end this practice. He was also directed to write to Mahmud at Ghazni and ask him to attack Somanatha. The Haji was refused a place on a boat so he used his special powers to stop the boat from moving until the boatmen agreed to take him. This power of the Haji to stop the movement of the boat, of camels, of soldiers, runs like a refrain throughout the story. Once the boat sets off, they arrive miraculously overnight at Mangrol near Somanatha. The boat could not reach the shore, so the Haji floated on a deer skin and came ashore. His pious acts earned him the title of Mangroli Shah.

---

[2] That this story is still being upheld by some people would seem evident from the painting at the entrance to the present temple depicting a Gohila hero defending the temple.

The Haji then sent a message to the raja to convert to Islam, which he refused to do. The raja came with his army when there was a complaint about the Haji having transfixed the camels of some travellers. But the Haji transfixed the soldiers too. The Haji then went to stay with an old woman, the widow of an oil-presser who was a Muslim, since he did not eat food cooked by a Hindu—an interesting reversal of roles! She was distraught as her only son and sole support was due to be sacrificed to the Somanatha idol the next morning. The Haji reassured her and replaced the boy. He saw the idol which was suspended in mid-air. The Haji meditated and, when asked to prove his power, turned to the sculpted image of the bull Nandi, outside the temple, and brought it to life so that it ate the offerings of fruit and flowers placed before it. The bull announced that it was henceforth in the service of the Haji.

At this point, the *lingam* cracked and the spirit of the deity emerged in human form. The Haji gave it a bucket and it drew into the bucket all the water from the tank attached to the temple. These miracles naturally disturbed the raja, so he ordered the people to stone the Haji who remained unhurt. The Haji merely glanced at the idols in the temple and they broke. The Haji then went to reside in the shrine of Masum Shah. The oil-presser's son was finally sacrificed but it was clear that this was a bad omen for the raja.

The Haji then wrote a letter to Mahmud, asking him to attack the raja and save the Muslims. The letter was sent with the oil-presser's widow who, through the power of the Haji, was able to fly. She flew to Ghazni and insisted on seeing Mahmud, who, even though he was suffering from an inflammation of the eyes, did receive her. He placed the Haji's letter on his eyes and was immediately cured. He agreed that he would come with his army and the woman flew back to the Haji.

Mahmud attacked the raja of Somanatha and was victorious in battle. The raja sued for peace but Mahmud insisted on his converting to Islam, which the raja refused to do. A twelve-year siege followed with frequent skirmishes. Meanwhile, the Haji died and was buried at Mangrol. Mahmud and his army were tired of the siege yet there was no way of its letting up. Mahmud was then advised to pray at the Haji's tomb and seek his blessings. This brought him help from the Haji. Mahmud pretended to abandon camp and was thus able to trap the raja's army. He stormed into the fort, breaking down the heavy iron gates. Mahmud was offered wealth in return for not destroying the idol, which money he took, but all the same crushed the idol and fed it to the raja as lime in his *pan*/betel leaf. He then expelled the raja and killed his followers. He left his governor, Mitha Khan, who later raided the temple. Before leaving, Mahmud built a shrine to Mangroli Shah.[3] The story, as retold by Watson, may well have been garnished in the retelling.

There are many nuances to this story that convey sentiments different from the sources considered so far. A Muslim population oppressed by Hindu rule would seem to be a conceptual inversion of the colonial construction of history as also of the Turko–Persian accounts. The story suggests that at a popular level in the late nineteenth century and among some Muslims who were probably vaguely familiar with the contents of the Turko–Persian accounts, although they may not have read them, it was thought necessary to somehow justify Mahmud's attack, even if the story narrating the justification had no historical basis. The piety of the Haji is pitted against the political authority of the raja and of Mahmud. His piety raises him above the average person and motivates him to offer himself as a victim to the deity. That the raja could not kill the Haji and that the latter could transfix the soldiers of the raja with the sanction of spiritual authority—in this case, the Prophet—was the victory of piety

---

[3] J.W. Watson, 'The Fall of Patan Somanatha: Ballad of the Fall of Pattan', *Indian Antiquary*, 1879, VIII, pp. 153–61; quoted in Nazim, op.cit., pp. 222–24.

over power, a theme that is frequently repeated in such compositions. This attempt of the raja depicts his oppressive attitude and
therefore Mahmud had to be called to contain the raja's power
and any claims that the raja may have had to using an alternate
piety emanating from Shiva. Mahmud, representing another focus
of power, had to humble himself before the piety of the Haji
before he could succeed. This is the projection of a very different
Mahmud from that of the Turko–Persian texts. The story of
reducing the icon to lime and putting it in the *pan*/betel leaf fed
to the court, may have been a floating story also told of other
places, and was incorporated into both the oral tradition and
some Turko–Persian sources.

Conquerors are often slotted into existing myths or
presumed histories, the association providing prestige and
attempting to give a hint of historicity to the story. The narrative
of an invitation to a ruler of Ghazni to avenge the wrongs on
local subjects in northern India is repeated in a later story. This
version was recited by what was recorded in colonial ethnography as the Bhangi caste, and echoes in part the story recorded
by Watson. Because of the tyranny of Prithviraja, a father and
his daughter fled to Ghazni. The daughter married into the
ruling family and the father persuaded the ruler of Ghazni to
attack Prithviraja.[4]

Shaikh Din's story has some echoes of one connected with
the existence of a shrine that could have had associations with
the legend or been its source. The grave of a Haji Mangroli Shah
is located at Mangrol near Prabhasa Pattana and dates to about
AD 1300. An inscription in Persian, fixed to the floor of the
dargah/hospice of Mangroli Shah Pir, identifies it as the tomb of
a *pir*. Later inscriptions confirm this. He had an Iraqi name and
his family may have come from there. He is said to have died in

---

[4] W. Crooke, *The Tribes and Castes of the North-West Province and Oudh*, I,
pp. 289 ff.

1299,[5] the date of Ulugh Khan's attack on Gujarat and Somanatha. The ballad dates Mangroli Shah to the early eleventh century whereas the inscription states that he died a martyr's death in AH 699, that is AD 1299. But the context of his becoming a martyr remains unclear. Was he a heretical Isma'ili Muslim and therefore killed by Ulugh Khan? Was he of Arab origin, and like others after him, helped to defend the town against Turkish attacks, and was killed in the process? Possibly the ballad was composed around the grave and grew with each recitation.

These stories have generally been dismissed as not having an authentic historical backing of evidence. Nevertheless, they do tell us much about popular assumptions regarding Mahmud at the time when they were composed. They were current in societies of the locality and circulated when Mughal power had been replaced by British power. They have all the stereotypes of the folk tale in which declining authority (in this case, Mughal rule and that of the Sultans) is propped up with the story of a glorious victory in the past, albeit hard won. The political edge to a late 'Muslim' version becomes clear. Loss of actual power is compensated for by an assertion of the magical power of piety. It is essentially a statement on how political power is subservient to the spiritual power of piety and even Mahmud could not achieve what he wished to without supplicating the *pir*. This is a theme that occurs frequently in many narratives in India, especially those of a popular variety.

The association of the *pir* with powers beyond the normal is generally explained as part of the Sufi tradition, which it was. But such beliefs have a long ancestry that goes back to the earlier pre-Islamic times. There is a continuing tradition of the renouncer acquiring moral authority, sometimes to the extent of threatening

---

[5] S.H. Desai, *Arabic and Persian Inscriptions of Saurashtra*, No. 2, pp. 2, 8; No. 55, 56.

the gods, and thereby becoming the locus of power even greater than political power. This is illustrated, for instance, in the many myths of ascetics whose asceticism imbues them with so much power that the gods (frequently Indra) have to break this power through sending *apsaras*/celestial maidens to seduce them. Stories abound of the superhuman powers of those that renounce the world, and renunciation did not require a removal from society. It is this authority that is also being evoked in yet another story.

This story has recently received attention as a popular version of how aspects of the history of Muslim conquest in India were perceived over the last four centuries.[6] The *Mir'at-i Mas'udi*, written by Abd al-Rahman Chisti in the early seventeenth century, professes to be a biography of Salar Mas'ud. He is said to be the brilliant son of Mahmud's sister, born in 1014 at Ajmer (which links him to the Chisti saint), and who conquered parts of the western Ganges plain in his early teens and was martyred at Bahraich when nineteen.[7] The account claims to be based on various narratives about Mahmud but draws particularly from a supposedly lost text, the *Tawarikh-i-Mahmudi*, by Mulla Muhammad Ghaznavi who, it is said, belonged to the court of Mahmud and wrote on his activities. Mas'ud is described as accompanying Mahmud in his raid on Somanatha and taking the initiative in feeding particles of the idol to unsuspecting brahmans—a story that is by now a stereotype. He acts in the formulaic manner of proposing a choice to the infidels between

---

[6] Shahid Amin, 'On Retelling the Muslim Conquest' in P. Chatterjee (ed.), *History and the Present*, pp. 24–43.; T. Mahmood, 'The Dargah of Sayyid Salar Mas'ud Ghazi in Bahraich: Legend, Tradition and Reality', in C.W. Troll, *Muslim Shrines in India*, pp. 24–43; I.H. Siddiqui, 'A Note on the Dargah of Salar Mas'ud in Bahraich in the Light of the Standard Historical Sources', in ibid., pp. 44–47.

[7] Elliot and Dowson, op.cit., II, pp. 513–49.

conversion and death, but there are no references as to which of
his enemies chose what. Historians researching the history of the
period regard the text and its contents as spurious. Even the
standard collection of sources of this period refers to it not as a
historical source but as a historical romance.[8]

This is also suggested by the confusion in the chronology of
his biography. Some are of the opinion that he had close links
with the followers of Chisti and came to India a couple of
centuries later together with the Sufi, Khwaja Chisti, and not
with Mahmud. This would negate the story of his being
Mahmud's nephew. The descriptions of his capture of various
cities, as for instance Delhi and Satrikh, are not corroborated by
other sources, although the author claims that his history of
Mas'ud was known to Hindu historians as recorded by Acharya
Mali Bahadur, said to be a brahman from the hills. No such
Hindu histories are known. This is the attempt of the author
Abd al-Rahman to claim historicity for what he says. Other
textual sources do not mention such a nephew. One of
Mahmud's twin sons was named Mas'ud, but no such legend is
linked to him and he was not associated with the Ganges plain.
In the struggle between the twins for the throne of Ghazni, this
son was supported by the Indian commanders and troops
serving in the Ghazni army. This may explain the suggested
Indian connection.

Salar Mas'ud is depicted stereotypically as a Ghaznavid hero
in the Turko–Persian chronicle style, with exaggerated descriptions of victories over infidels all over the place. There is little
attempt to assess the validity of the sources quoted, for this was
not required of the tellers of tales in that period.

His early exploits are enveloped in fantasy, a feature that was
associated with narratives in the Sufi tradition, where resort to the

[8] Ibid., p. 514.

spiritual for information was regarded as normal.[9] But the description of these exploits has also to be seen as a counterbalance to the form that Salar Mas'ud took in the popular imagination as the *pir*, Ghazi Miyan. The stories of his exploits as a warrior may well have surfaced at the time when Ghazi Miyan was acquiring popularity as a protector of the lowly. The biography may have been an attempt to give the *pir* appropriate Islamic credentials.

What are of greater interest are the alternate and more widespread and enduring versions of the activities of Salar Mas'ud, who in these versions, comes to be known as Ghazi Miyan. These narratives about him have circulated through itinerant musicians and storytellers, especially the Dafali *faqirs*, and have gained currency and popularity among those who do not read the texts. They are different from the *Mir'at-i Mas'udi* as are their observations on Mas'ud and his activities.[10] In one version, Ghazi Miyan was disillusioned by his uncle Mahmud's plunder of Somanatha and decided to spend his life in the service of humanity. He is described as upright and virtuous but the rajas and courtiers he had to contend with were treacherous. As with many such figures, he is associated with defending the poor and the lowly against the tyranny of the powerful. He is said to be pure in body and mind and observed many of the taboos regarding food normally associated with upper-caste Hindus.

From among the mass of hagiology about him in northern India comes the story of his martyrdom, happening just as he is about to be married. The interrupted wedding, or the killing of the bridegroom at the point of his marriage, is a known theme in folk literature in many parts of the world, and, as it has been said, it gives poignancy to the death of the young martyr. One version

---

[9] Shahid Amin, op.cit; Abd al-Rahman wrote extensively and in some of his other books he used the same strategy to establish the authority, spiritual or moral, of these texts. Personal communication from Muzaffar Alam.

[10] Shahid Amin, op.cit.; T. Mahmood, op.cit., p. 27.

has it that he was killed by the rajas against whom he was fighting, and killed not on the battlefield but in the vicinity of a tank by a temple to Surya, a location to which he had long been attached.

The more popular ballads narrating his martyrdom state that Jashoda, the wife of Nand, the head of the cowherds among the Ahir, arrived at his house just as he was being prepared for his wedding ceremony. (Jashoda and Nand are the names of the foster parents of Krishna among the Ahir as well.) Jashoda asked for help against the wicked raja Sohal Deo/Sahar Dev, who was killing the Ahir cowherds and their cows. Ghazi Miyan rushed to save the cows from being slaughtered and was killed in the conflict. His wish to save the cows is emphasized and this also presents him as a pastoral hero. This is particularly striking since the protection of cows was generally projected as an act of heroism aimed against the beef-eating Muslims. Ghazi Miyan, apart from being a protector of cows, is said to have owned a vast herd of cows and had a large following among the Ahir. It is possible that this story came from Ahir sources when they adopted Ghazi Miyan as a *sant/pir* and it became a way of justifying their veneration for him. Given the expanse of forests in the region at that time, cattle-herders would be found in significant numbers.

Ghazi Miyan's tomb at Bahraich has been a place of pilgrimage for large numbers of Hindus and Muslims since the fourteenth century and it remains the location of the celebration of his anniversary to this day. A Hindu Ahir rebuilt the grave and it began to attract even larger numbers of pilgrims. Various Delhi Sultans, such as the Tughlaqs, are believed to have visited his grave, in one case accompanied by Ibn Batuta who comments on the vast crowds gathered there. Some, such as Sikandar Lodi, objected to the worship of the *pir* as being non-Islamic and tried to ban it,[11] but his objections made little impact. By the sixteenth

---

[11] Briggs, trans. *Tarikh-i-Farishta*, I, p. 587, quoted in Shahid Amin, op.cit.

century, it was immensely popular as a cult. It remains to this day a place of pilgrimage, cutting across the boundaries of formal religions. As in most places of pilgrimage, caste status becomes irrelevant and the presence of Ahirs does not exclude brahman pilgrims, particularly as the shrine is associated with healing properties. The unfinished wedding is remembered and offerings take the form of wedding gifts, amounting therefore to a handsome income for the shrine.

Many strands of thought and action, taken from a variety of beliefs and experiences, have gone into the making of these narratives. It has been suggested that the presence of Shi'as in Avadh may have emphasized the theme of martyrdom, as indeed cattle-herding and raiding were frequent in Vaishnava legends. As has been pointed out, assessing the historicity of the story has one kind of relevance, but more importantly what it indicates is the popular perception of an event and the associations evoked by what was perceived as a central figure. Ghazi Miyan is almost a generic figure found in every part of the subcontinent and is the kind of *pir, faqir, wali, sadhu, guru, siddha* who draws on a liberal Sufi tradition as well as the Puranic and Shakta traditions.[12]

He is included among the *panj pir*, the five original 'saints' of popular Islam. The symbolism of five is archaic in India, going back to the *Mahabharata*. It is also associated with early Islam. The five names of the *panj pir* could vary, but Ghazi Miyan was virtually always present. Evidence collected a century ago points to the worship of Ghazi Miyan as having a spectacular following, drawn largely from lower castes and Dalits but also including those from across the spectrum of the formally recognized religions of India. The range included those claiming to be Muslims but who worshipped Kali; some claiming *kshatriya* status and employing brahman priests; some among those who

---

[12] See, for instance, W. Crooke, *The Popular Religion and Folklore of Northern India*, I, pp. 202 ff.

observed food taboos and would not eat food cooked by Dalits; bards and tellers of tales claiming to be degraded brahmans, worshipping Hindu gods as well as Ghazi Miyan. The musicians most closely associated with the shrine at Bahraich (Dafalis) are both Hindu and Muslim and mix their rituals.[13]

That such narratives were commonplace and mythologies often intersected is suggested by the parallel story in the epic of the hero Pabuji from Rajasthan. Pabuji's wedding ceremony is interrupted by his having to save a herd of cows from a cattle raid carried out by the Khichi connected to the Bhati clan and kinsmen by marriage.[14] The rustling of cattle was a source of wealth. In some versions the interrupted wedding leaves him celibate for he goes to join the gods in a follow-up of this event. Pabuji, on an earlier occasion, was associated with killing Mirza Khan who was disliked because he raided cattle; but apart from this, there were the normal blood feuds, most often over land, cattle or women. Pabuji was a Rajput, but is venerated and treated as a deity by Rebari herdsmen and many other pastoralists. Priests of the scheduled caste also officiate at his rituals. The worship of Pabuji extends beyond Rajasthan to parts of Gujarat and the Indus plain. Apart from the continuing and varied oral versions, an account of the story is given in the *Khyata*, a seventeenth-century chronicle of Nainasi. It has been suggested that a possibly historical date for Pabuji could be the fourteenth century.[15] Coincidentally, the guru, Gorakhanatha, also features in the narrative.

The centrality of protecting cows in narratives emanating from cattle-herding and pastoral societies is natural to such societies. In Rajasthan, the legend of Pabuji focuses on his

[13] W. Crooke, op.cit., pp. II, 35 ff.; 233 ff.; 240 ff.; 383 ff.; III, 106 ff.; 172 ff.; 280 ff.; 345 ff.; IV, 229 ff.; 258 ff.

[14] J.D. Smith, *The Epic of Pabuji*, pp. 4 ff.; pp. 400 ff.

[15] Ibid., pp. 74 ff.

actions as a *bhomiya*, a person who dies protecting the cattle of his village when they are raided and is worshipped after his death. Cattle raids were common in such herding societies as this was a quick means of increasing the herd and thereby acquiring wealth, and raids were carried out by brigands and rajas alike. Therefore, the *bhomiya* was an exalted hero.[16] The shrine to the *bhomiya* was parallel to the *paliya* or hero-stone which sometimes depicts a cattle raid. The cult of each *bhomiya* is maintained by the *bhopa*, who conducts the rituals at the shrine and narrates the legends.

The cattle raid and the protection of cattle become central to the activities of cattle-herders such as the Ahir. Since these oral epics are closely tied to particular societies, they are concerned with invoking these local hero-deities to help in easing the problems of everyday life. Hence the extensive popularity of and respect for such figures that cut across formal religious boundaries. When this happens, the cult is no longer restricted to a particular society but draws in a universalizing worship, as happened with Ghazi Miyan.

Parallel mythologies emerge in different parts of the sub-continent. The interweaving of worship and belief evolves naturally from the religious sentiments of people and is frequently the most viable religious expression of the largest number. The well-defined, formal categories of Hindu and Muslim that derive from textual definitions, experience an erosion of their boundaries and a mingling of their beliefs through faith in such figures. At the level of the majority of people, the interface between Hinduism and Islam often resulted in a distancing from the formal structures of both religions and created new religious articulations. These articulations have yet to be adequately recognized among those who study the history of

---

[16] R. Bharucha, *Rajasthan: An Oral History, Conversations with Komal Kothari*, pp. 94–117.

religion in India.[17] The most impressive aspect of the veneration for Ghazi Miyan is that even for the Hindu pilgrim, the relationship of Ghazi Miyan with Mahmud—irrespective of whether there was one—is irrelevant to their perception of him.

Explorations of grass-roots religious forms have brought to the surface some features that differ strikingly from the received opinion about the impact of Mahmud in India. The evidence becomes visible through a different way of looking at what is regarded as tradition. It does not concern itself with the views of an elite for whom the past and the present have been read as reflecting Hindu and Muslim communal identities. In the popular tradition, 'Hindu' and 'Muslim' are read differently from the reading of sources discussed in earlier chapters. This is evident from preliminary investigations of another group of texts and oral tradition.[18] This exploration points to what has been recognized as the impact of Islam on the Tantra tradition, a

---

[17] That there is an urgency in doing so derives from the fact that these religious articulations, far from being recognized in their own right, are now being forced into either a formal Islam or Hinduism. The story of Ghazi Miyan is being retold solely as the story of Salar Mas'ud with an insistence on the historicity of his being the nephew of Mahmud even though this legend has been dismissed by historians. He is described in this version as responsible for the second attack on the supposed Rama temple at Ayodhya. This, it is maintained, was subsequent to the first attack by the Indo–Greek king, Menander. That temples did not exist at the time when Menander ruled is irrelevant to such 'history'. Nevertheless, this 'history' is being taught in schools run by Hindu communal organizations all over India. See also, B.D. Chattopadhya, 'Cultural Plurality, Contending Memories and Concerns of Comparative History: Historiography and Pedagogy in Contemporary India', in *Studying Early India*, pp. 277–80; Krishna Kumar, 'Hindu Revivalism and Education in North Central India', *Social Scientist*, 1990, 18, No. 10, pp. 4–26.

[18] M.C. Joshi, 'Islam in the Hindu Tantras', *Journal of the Asiatic Society of Bombay*, 1983, pp. 51–56.

tradition that had its origins in pre-Islamic times and was an agency of acculturation in the many differentiated cultures of earlier periods: a process that continued with the coming of Islam. Obviously, it requires a more detailed study, but the leads given even by a partial exploration are potentially valuable.

Among the sects with an extraordinarily large following were the various manifestations of the Natha Panthis and those that followed the teachings of the Shaiva and Shakta religions through various Tantric compositions. These could be oral compositions related to *mantras* or the exegesis on these that often took the form of written discourses. The Natha Panthis claim Adinatha as their first teacher (if not Shiva himself) who had Matsyendranatha among his disciples. They maintain that their *mantras* had been given to disciples in many languages and as far afield as Gauda, Kerala, Karnataka, Andhra and Gujarat. Among the teachings, those attributed to Gorakhanatha—the next in succession, as it were—generally dated to the fourteenth century or earlier according to some, are the better known. But to provide a reliable chronology is difficult and *mantras* were continually reformulated or added to. The Natha Panthi sects were closely associated with Shakta traditions as expressed in the *Tantras*. The disciples came from any religious persuasion—Shaiva, Vaishnava, Buddhist, Islam, or any other—but many tended to be from the lower ranks of society, which partly accounts for their great popularity. However, upper-caste disciples were known as well. Worship focused on the goddess in the Shakta and Tantric tradition and had a long continuity from the early past. But such traditions incorporated the worship of Sufi *pirs* and Vaishnava and Shaiva *sadhus* and *gurus*. These sometimes had dual names, such as Mouneshwar/Moinuddin.[19] If the Sufi saint was said to

---

[19] Y. Sikand, 'The Changing Nature of Shared Hindu and Muslim Shrines in Contemporary Karnataka', *South Asia*, (ns) April 2002, XXV, 1, pp. 49–67.

ride a tiger as some did, it was a parallel image to Devi riding a tiger. Some Natha *siddhas* evoke Rama and Allah together.

Some of the *mantras*/verses and mystic spells, and *yantras*/mystic diagrams, can be traced to the arcane elements in the teachings of the religions that were current at the time, and are familiar to daily life even to the present. They were and are used for a variety of situations: in times of sickness, or in what is believed to be a warding off of evil, for removing obstacles, as love-spells or as magical incantations to defeat enemies, or in the performing of miracles to venerate the holy. These spells, in as much as they can be explained, are understood as an inter-meshing of Shaiva, Vaishnava, Buddhist and Islamic mystic belief and practices. The language is either a rather faulty Sanskrit or often Hindi or other regional language. The *mantras* are sometimes in what is called *sandhyabhasha*, a cryptic, secret language, intelligible only to the initiate. On occasion, the languages are mixed, as for instance, the mixing of Sanskrit and Arabic where Baba Shah Qalandar is asked to take care of the Dattatreya *pitha* or place of worship.[20]

Shakta religious practices found their way into many religions although the belief systems varied. Their openness encouraged interpolations, modulations and adjustments. Because they were the religions earlier thought to be associated with lower castes and non-castes, they were often overlooked by historians, a situation that is now changing. But it is as well to remember that they were the religions of the majority of people and their presence is essential to any attempt at a complete picture of Indian society and its religions. Investigating the identity of the deities and persons commonly invoked, and by which groups of people and for what purposes, would be enlightening.

The Natha Panthis had close relations with some sections of the Shaktas, as for example, those associated with the *Shabara*

---

[20] A. Bharati, *The Tantric Tradition*, pp. 164 ff.

Tantras. These were compositions frequently linked to magic, to evoking *yoginis*, folk deities, *kshetrapalas*, guardians of the fields, and gods such as Kali and Ganesha. It is thought that they also had a connection with the Kapalika sect of the Shaivas.[21] According to some, Shabara is a minor deity of magical potency and the *mantras* are chanted to induce magic. Among *mantras* in the *Shabara Tantra*, one example is that which begins with a primary invocation in the formulaic *Bismillahi'r Rahmani'r Rahim*, followed by invoking a large number of *pirs* such as Baba Adam, Hazrat Ali, Isma'il Jogi and Chisti. This, in turn, is followed by invoking kings among whom Mahmud of Ghazni features, and by listing deities such as Shiva, Narasimha, Brahma and Hanuman.[22] Since such invocations are more frequent in the oral tradition, it is difficult to date them precisely. The introduction of the names are thought to be of about the seventeenth century but the intermixing could well be from an earlier practice. It could have been linked to the settling of Sufis in India from the early second millennium, and this would have created an appropriate context.[23] Sufi and Tantric traditions could run parallel or there could be overlaps. When this happened, there was a mingling of ideas and rituals. The centrality of the *guru* or preceptor was common to both.[24] Thus, Isma'il Jogi and Gorakhanatha often feature together. Some followers of Gorakhanatha were initially Muslims and this sub-sect was associated with Isma'il Jogi. Pilgrimages were made to Hinglaj in Baluchistan from all over north India. This was the location of the shrine of Hinglaj Mata, especially sacred to a section of the

---

[21] T. Goudrian, *Hindu Tantric and Sakta Literature*, pp. 120–21. S.B. Das Gupta, *Obscure Religious Cults*, pp. 106 ff.

[22] Harishankar Sastri, *Brihat Savara Tantra*, pp. 3, 8, 21, 48. Quoted in M.C. Joshi, op.cit.

[23] M.C. Joshi, op.cit.

[24] N.N. Bhattacharya, *History of the Tantric Religion*, pp. 308 ff.

Tantrics. Those Nathas, who had originally been Muslims, worshipped the goddess as Bibi.[25]

Some verses in the *Shabara Tantra* refer specifically to Mahmud of Ghazni. One has been quoted as saying that Mahmud was the son of a Turkish mother, and was a Sultan who protected the fort at Ghazni. He rides a white horse and holds the magic wand. The context of this invocatory verse is to cure an ailing child, and should Mahmud fail to do so, he will be declared ungrateful to the milk of the mother of Hanuman—possibly a parallel with his own mother. To be accused of such ingratitude was equivalent to being abused.

Another example quoted is more specific:

om namo adesha guru ko
turkani ka put mahmanda bir
nari ka put narsingha bir
age chale mahmanda bir
piche chale narsingha bir

Here, Mahmanda—identified as Mahmud—is described as the son of a Turkish woman and is a *bir*. He marches in front and is protected by the *bir* Narasingha. In another example, the feats of the *bir* Mahmanda are referred to, and he is requested to remove obstacles and fulfil the wishes of the person reciting the *mantra*.

The use of the word *bir* has its own significance. It is generally used in Hindi and Punjabi as a local rendering of the Sanskrit *vira*, meaning a hero or a male relative. In the context of Tantra, it can also be used to refer to someone who has attained the second level of the three *sadhanas* or practices of Shakti worship. It requires the practitioner to be fearless, resolute,

---

[25] A. Hiltebeitel, *Draupadi Among Rajputs, Muslims and Dalits*, pp. 332–33.

inspiring and ready for initiation.[26] It is somewhat unclear as to why Mahmud should be treated as a *vira-sadhaka* if that was the intention. At one level, it is ironic that this should have happened to a staunch Sunni Muslim, but at another, it raises the question of how his activities were perceived such that he should have been associated with Tantric *mantras*. Was it because he was remembered as a warrior and warrior ascetics were part of the extended world of those attracted to the Shaktas and Natha Panthis?[27] Some sects of the Natha Jogis were known to take to arms. Warrior ascetics were linked not invariably to high-status aristocratic groups but to groups of lesser status.

One of the mechanisms of incorporating new religious beliefs and practices can be seen in the history of the Natha sect.[28] The itinerant Natha yogis travelled across north India and became influential among large numbers of people, especially through the teachings attributed to Gorakhanatha. They borrowed and amalgamated as they went along. This is indicated in the following verse:

> *kamarudesha kamakhya devi jahan base isma'il jogi.*
> *isma'il jogi ne lagai kyari, phul bine lona-chamari*
> *duhai adi guru ki ...*

Kamarupa (Assam) was where Kamakshi was worshipped. It was one of the four original centres of Shakta worship and therefore particularly sacred. Her temple (together with others such as Somanatha) is also included among the twelve places where the *jyotir linga* fell and these were therefore regarded as special places of pilgrimage for Shaiva and Shakta worshippers. Lona Chamari or Nona Chamarin was sometimes feared as a witch among the

---

[26] N.N. Bhattacharya, op.cit., p. 317.

[27] D. Lorenzen, 'Warrior Ascetics in Indian History', *JESHO*, 98, 1978.

[28] N.N. Bhattacharya, *History of the Sakta Religion*, p. 163.

Chamars of northern India, but in other contexts was venerated. The names of even the lesser figures occur in the popular verses and often in invocations. The reference to Adi Guru has been read as a reference to either Shiva or Adinatha. The incorporation of Isma'il Jogi with the worship of Kamakshi is significant.

Such sects were interwoven into the Shakta and Tantric religions and drew on Hindu deities as well as the veneration for Islamic *pirs* and popular Islam. Their invocations included Allah as well as a large number of known and respected *pirs*, *gurus* and Hindu deities, thus drawing towards themselves a large following that cut across religions. That this articulation seems to begin around the fourteenth century AD needs investigation. Aspects of the Bhakti tradition were also attracting a following. These were the counterpoints to the formulations of the orthodox and the elite, and need to be integrated into the representation of the religious expression of India at this time.

The induction of Mahmud into the oral tradition is a matter of interest. Oral traditions adapt events and the tradition becomes part of the historical process although not necessarily of history. It is often different from the literate tradition since orality gives it a greater flexibility and allows change. It reflects a diversified non-homogenous society. Quite how and why Mahmud of Ghazni became a part of the galaxy of the pious remains mysterious, particularly since the Sanskrit texts of the elite are silent about him. Perhaps this was precisely the point that the popular compositions were making. Interestingly, he is attributed with magical powers, generally benign, and is neither an object of fear nor hate.

These compositions and their popularity question the validity of seeing religions in India as monolithic, uniform and self-sufficient islands of belief and worship. The history of religions in the Indian subcontinent would suggest otherwise. If historical sights are set even a fraction below the orthodox religious texts and the patronage of the royal courts, a different religious cosmos is revealed. The evident demarcation is not between formal religions, but, if at all, between the exclusively elite religions with their patronage and worldview as against the more universal and popular articulation of requirements from religion. Even this demarcation is not absolute, for it often fades from one to the other, contingent upon historical circumstances. It is the articulation of those whose joys and sorrows are the same and are conditioned by who is ordering their world.

The pilgrimage to Bahraich was not confined to popular religion since the Sultans and the elite of Varanasi also visited the shrine. Similarly, elements in the narrative of the *Kissa Mangroli Shah* show evidence of at least a passing familiarity with the Turko–Persian stories of the raid of Mahmud and the Jaina stories associated with the temple. But such a familiarity is limited in its borrowing and refigures what it borrows. It does not accept in entirety the versions emanating from the royal courts. The religions of the elite tend to emphasize their boundaries, whereas religious expression at a wider level synthesizes belief and practice and has no problems in transgressing boundaries. The transgressions were of religious and caste boundaries and were expressed in personal worship as well as participation in public activities such as pilgrimages and festivals.[29] This calls for a reconsideration of the construction of the history of religion in India, where the religious articulation of the majority of the people has yet to be described, understood and analysed.[30]

In references to Mahmud, the event in the first two narratives is visible but is placed in entirely different contexts from those of the other sources. In the Shakta–Tantric versions, the event no

---

[29] Some of these aspects are discussed in S. Visuvalingam, *The Marriage of Lat Bhairava and Ghazi Miyan: Sexuality, Death and Transgression in Hinduism and Islam* (forthcoming).

[30] R. Thapar, 'The Tyranny of Labels', in *Cultural Pasts*, pp. 990–1014; D. Gilmartin and B.B. Lawrence (eds), *Beyond Turk and Hindu: Rethinking Religious Identities in Islamicate South Asia*.

longer has visibility although the person associated with it is present. The evident differences in these and other sources point to diverse projections of those involved in the event and the aftermath. In all these versions, the character and function of Mahmud has changed with his submission to, and incorporation into, an ethos of piety, magic and defence of the poor. The event and the personality become part of a long historical process. The disjuncture in these readings is brought about by an intervention that insists on only a single homogenous reading, arising out of the political agenda of the last two centuries rather than the evidence from earlier times.

7

Colonial Interpretations and Nationalist Reactions

By the start of the nineteenth century, readings of the event from the Turko–Persian sources were becoming familiar to colonial interpreters of Indian history and the narrative of Ferishta, for example, was taken as reliable history. As has been repeatedly noticed by historians, there is no mention of the event in what are regarded as 'Hindu' sources. Yet it came to be argued in the nineteenth century that the attack on Somanatha by Mahmud had brought about a trauma among the Hindus and an inveterate hatred for the Muslims. Initially, this statement was axiomatic to the colonial view of the event, but gradually it entered the mainstream reading of the history of these times.

In the colonial reading, the event assumes a place of prominence. Dow published his *History of Hindostan* in 1767–72 in which he retold the account as given by Ferishta.[1] Dow was widely read and the story was repeated by Gibbon, Mill, and many nineteenth-century historians.[2] Ferishta's version then

---

[1] Vol. I, pp. 68 ff.

[2] E. Gibbon, *The Decline and Fall of the Roman Empire*, VI, 57, p. 361; J. Mill, *The History of British India*, Vol. I, p. 177; quoted in R.P. Karkaria, 'Mahmud of Ghazni and the Legend of Somanatha', *Journal of the Bombay Branch of the Royal Asiatic Society*, 1895–96, 19, pp. 142–53.

becomes the hegemonic version. The colonial interest in the story may have grown from two factors: that by focusing on the Turko–Persian representation of the event, the antagonism between the Hindus and Muslims could be highlighted; and the statement that Mahmud found India a garden but converted it into a desert would require that the colonial power replant the desert, converting it into a garden and, in this process, emphasizing the destructiveness of Mahmud and of subsequent Muslim rule. This suited the continuing popular European myth from the time of the Crusades that Islam was a religion of barbarism as compared to the civilizing qualities of Christianity. There was little attempt to assess the evidence on 'Muslim rule' which would have revealed that, as is usual with rulers of any religious persuasion, the rule varied in quality and intention. Phrases such as 'Muslim rule' and 'Hindu rule' are historically speaking inappropriate, since much more was involved than the religion of the ruling class, although it was significant in some situations.

The court chronicles in Persian were taken as historically accurate by British historians since they had a familiar format of a clear chronology and sequential narrative. Historiography in the nineteenth century did not require enquiring into the intention of the author or the chronicle. Even the contradictions in the sources tended to be glossed over. The chronicles were purportedly reporting on political events related to Muslim rulers. In propagating the greatness of these rulers, they dramatized their power over their Hindu subjects. However, the exaggerations may well have arisen from an actually tenuous relationship between the ruler and the ruled. This was not unknown in Indian power centres even prior to the coming of Islam. And, as in earlier cases, loyalty to a single religion could not be assumed as a guarantee of support from the subjects. To avoid emphasizing the earlier pattern of multiple patronage to more than one religion, the superiority of the one was continually underlined. This can also be read as a lack of confidence in asserting authority as a ruling class. When such an authority came to be established, as for example, in the reign of Akbar, there was a more manifest return to multiple patronage.

Apart from the periodization of James Mill, there was also the added, unquestioned assumption—going back to the eighteenth century in the writings of William Jones and, almost a century later, in the work of Max Müller—that Muslim rule had been uniformly tyrannical and oppressive towards Hindu subjects. Since no evidence is quoted, it can only be assumed that these were again attitudes simmering from the time of the Crusades and the general rivalry between the European and Islamic world over trade and territory in subsequent times.

As we have seen, the aftermath of Mahmud's raid on Somanatha took the form of varying perceptions of the event and these differ from what has come down to us in the received version. None of the sources provide evidence of a starkly hostile reaction or a trauma among those that are viewed as the victimized. The theory of a Hindu trauma created by this event remains an enigma. There is little evidence of an overwhelming desire for revenge that had been smouldering for the last few centuries, and which is now the explanation for what is perceived as the current Hindu–Muslim antagonism. It is puzzling because there are other references to other occasions in texts in Sanskrit and the regional languages describing violent confrontations between local rulers and the new conquerors, the latter referred to as Tajiks, Turushkas, Yavanas or *mlechchhas*. Such conflicts are described in the traditional manner of battling enemies where blood, beheading and gory death were all part of the process of conquest. The process is invariably violent and hurts the defeated more than the victors, especially when it is followed by oppression, and victors have been prone to be oppressors throughout history. Not all these conquests of the Yavanas and Turushkas were of great significance. Yet the one occasion that is singled out in the Persian sources as a major victory is generally ignored in the non-Persian sources.

A noticeable feature in the texts of the pre-modern period is that the conquerors and the conquered are identified each as

specific and separate people and are not generally defined by
religion. Some religious differences would obviously be subsumed
in labels such as Yavana, Turushka, *mlechchhas*, but these were
not invariably the most important differences. The particular
participants therefore are not necessarily the same in different
confrontations. Members of the same religion had varied relationships with those of other religions, ranging from hostility to close
friendship. They were not identified solely by religion and
grouped together, and because of this expected to behave and
think only in a particular way. This may, in part, explain the
enigma: that since Mahmud's action was superceded by normal
interaction between diverse communities and groups subscribing
to varying religions, and Somanatha achieved a prosperity greater
than it had known before, the memory of the raid may have
receded. Significantly, it is not mentioned even when there are
claims to later Turkish raids on the temple. How then have we
arrived today at the simplistic theory that the raid of Mahmud
has been at the root of a hostility that has coloured the relations
between Hindus and Muslims since then, a theory which is not
suggested by the historical sources?

The emphatic insistence on a trauma and consequent hostility
in relation to this event comes from a source different from those
considered so far. By the early nineteenth century, the narrative of
the raid as described by Ferishta was well-known among colonial
administrators. It was at this point that Lord Ellenborough,
the Governor-General, issued what came to be called 'The
Proclamation of the Gates' in 1842. He had heard that the
sandalwood gates of the Somanatha temple had been taken back
to Ghazni by Mahmud and had been placed at the entrance to his
mausoleum. So he decided that the gates had to be brought back
to Somanatha.[3]

---

[3] Professor Sushil Srivastava drew my attention to the proceedings in the
House of Commons debate on the gates. Among the works that I have
cited on Somanatha, it is also referred to in R. Davis, op.cit., pp. 201 ff.

Where and how he obtained this information about the gates remains unexplained.[4] None of the Turko–Persian accounts refer to Mahmud taking away the gates of the Somanatha temple. John Wilson, who was asked to investigate this matter by Sir Bartle Frere, wrote in the late nineteenth century that there was no reference to gates in any of the histories, and that the idea probably originated with some travellers who may have mentioned it to the administrator Mountstuart Elphinstone.[5] If there were any gates at all, they might have been the gates of the fort at Somanatha. But it is unlikely that Mahmud would have transported the gates of the fort back to Ghazni. The style of the Proclamation is instructive of how the Governor-General viewed the colonial intervention in India. He ordered General Nott, in charge of the British army in Afghanistan, to return. If he took the route through Ghazni, he was to bring back the gates that had been installed at the mausoleum of Mahmud and which were supposed to have come from the temple at Somanatha.

The subject of how Ellenborough decided on the supposed gates remains puzzling and explanations are conjectural. The background to the act seems to involve events in Afghanistan and Punjab. The throne of the ruler of Afghanistan, Shah Shujah, had been usurped by Dost Mohammad and Shah Shujah was in exile, seeking the assistance of Ranjit Singh, who ruled the Punjab kingdom. Dost Mohammad wanted British support but the latter were anxious to keep Ranjit Singh quiescent. Not only had the Russian advance to be contained, but the lucrative trade with central Asia had also to be kept active.

Alexander Burnes, deputed as political officer to the court of Ranjit Singh at Lahore in 1831, referred to negotiations between

---

[4] Professor Malcolm Yapp has been very helpful in directing me to sources on this subject.

[5] George Smith, *The Life of John Wilson*, 'Appendix on Somanath Gates sent to Sir Bartle Frere', pp. 368 ff.

Shah Shujah and Ranjit Singh, in which the latter demanded the gates of Somanatha from Mahmud's tomb in Ghazni in return for armed help to the Afghan exile.[6] Normally, the demand was for money, so either the gates were highly prized, or else Ranjit Singh was using them as an excuse to postpone negotiation. If it was true that he confused the Somanatha temple with the Jagannath temple (at Puri in Orissa), as is alleged, it was not religious sentiment that drove him to make the demand.

R.H. Kennedy visited the tomb at Ghazni and reported in 1840 that the wooden doors (possibly sandalwood) had a design of six-pointed stars in a frame of arabesques,[7] and not many would have associated this with a typically Indian design. C. Masson reports that the shrine of Mahmud was in ruins and the gates in fragments. It was said that when Ghengiz Khan was threatening Ghazni, the tomb of Mahmud was saved from plunder by being covered with earth and thereby hidden. In later times, the grandson of Timur located it, removed the earth, and renovated the tomb. Was this when the gates were introduced and declared to be gates from Somanatha? Nadir Shah revoked the grants to the tomb and there was now a dependence financially on the offerings of pilgrims. The British succeeded in retaking Kabul and Ghazni and this came to be regarded as a major triumph and the gates became a symbol of the conquest of Afghanistan.[8] It would seem that in local eyes, the gates lent sanctity to the shrine, perhaps because they were thought to have come from a sacred place. Whatever the explanation, the myth came to stay. In an inverted replay, as it were, the mullahs and custodians of Mahmud's tomb pleaded with General Nott to leave the gates behind, but he refused.

---

[6] A. Burnes, *Travels into Bukhara*, Vol. I, pp. 175 ff.

[7] R.H. Kennedy, *Narrative of the Campaign of the Army of the Indus in Sind and Kaubool in 1838–39*, Vol. II, pp. 59 ff.

[8] J.W. Kaye, *History of the War in Afghanistan*, Vol. III, pp. 335 ff., pp. 374 ff.

Ellenborough's Proclamation addressed to the Chiefs and Princes of northern and western India speaks of the insult of 800 years finally being avenged; and the gates that were once the memorial of the humiliation (of the Hindus) have become the record of Indian superiority in arms over nations beyond the Indus. However, there was little reaction from the princes and still less from the Hindus.

Bringing back the gates may also have been seen as one-upmanship over Ranjit Singh. J.D. Cunningham wrote in 1853 that Ranjit Singh demanded a ban on the killing of cows to which Shah Shujah's reply was that the British killed cows and what was Ranjit Singh going to do about that.[9] He added that there was a prophecy that if the gates were brought back, the Sikh kingdom would decline. Possibly Ellenborough had heard of this! A request had been made in 1845 by some Afghan merchants that since the Hindus did not want the gates, these should be returned to Ghazni, as the income of Ghazni had declined, and the gates and the mausoleum were a major attraction for pilgrims.

Ellenborough's intentions were doubtless multiple: a signal to the Afghans to return what was looted from India, an act that would symbolize British control over Afghanistan despite the poor British showing in the Anglo–Afghan wars; the wish to reverse the memory of the Indian subjugation to the Afghans in pre-colonial times, particularly in view of the problems which the British were having with Afghanistan; where Ranjit Singh had merely made a demand for the gates, the British actually brought them back, and whereas the gates were valueless to the British, they were important to the politics of the Sikh kingdom;[10] and an appeal to Hindu sentiment that would further divide Hindus from Muslims and that might make Hindus more loyal and eager to

---

[9] J.D. Cunningham, *A History of the Sikhs*, pp. 200 ff.

[10] J.H. Stocqueler, *Memoirs and Correspondence of Major-General Sir William Nott*, Vol. I, pp. 109 ff., pp. 131–35.

join the British Indian army. The Hindus, he thought, would value the action as a guarantee of their future security and that of their religion against the Muslims. The Hindus were unimpressed and did not react. A telling comment is that Ellenborough wanted a triumph that would be cheap and without risk and would demonstrate British power.[11]

By the late nineteenth century, the gates had become an established fact. The *Tarikh-i-Sorath* of Ranchodji Amaraji, written in 1825, refers briefly to Mahmud's raid and gives some information on the fate of the temple from the eighteenth century.[12] It was translated from the original Persian into English and edited and published by J. Burgess in 1882. The publication included a note added by the editor to say that Mahmud carried off the gates of the Somanatha temple to Ghazni, and they were brought back by the British army 800 years later. Monier-Williams translated Kalidasa's play, *Abhijnana-shakuntala*, and when referring to the Soma *tirtha* as being a place of pilgrimage near the temple of Somanatha, explains that it has been made notorious by its gates, which were brought back from Ghazni at Lord Ellenborough's orders in 1842, and are now to be seen in the arsenal at Agra.[13]

The notoriety of the gates had made Somanatha into an item of popular interest in Britain. The idol at Somanatha becomes an undercurrent in one of the most widely read mystery novels of the nineteenth century, *The Moonstone*, by Wilkie Collins, published in 1868.[14] Wilkie Collins read the history of India by

---

[11] M. Yapp, *Strategies of British India*, pp. 443–44.

[12] J. Burgess (ed.), Ranchodji Amaraji, *Tarikh-i-Sorath*, pp. 63 ff. The author states that although the Hindus believe that the Shivalinga has been there since eternity, the Muslims maintain that it came from Mecca. The story of Manat, it would seem, was for some still hovering over the icon.

[13] M. Monier-Williams, *Sakoontala*, Act I, p. 9, Note 14.

[14] Professor Alan Hobson was coincidentally reading it at Bellagio when I was writing the first draft of this book and introduced me to it.

Talboys Wheeler and corresponded with a civil servant posted in Kathiawar for information on the story. The narrative revolves around the Yellow Diamond, which is removed from the idol and secreted when Mahmud plunders the temple. It is taken to Varanasi and from there passed from hand to hand through India and England, invariably followed by three brahman guardians. Eventually, it is brought back to Somanatha and placed in the forehead of the idol. The mystery is heightened by its being a jewel that carries a curse. The underlying argument of the restoration is that now that the British are ruling, the jewel cannot be stolen by the Muslims.

But to return to the Proclamation which came up for discussion in the House of Commons. Matters concerning India had been of considerable interest and Macaulay's 'Minute on Indian Education', seeking to replace Sanskrit and Arabic with English as the language of instruction, had been discussed a few years earlier. The Proclamation became highly controversial in the debate between the government and the opposition.[15] What motivated Ellenborough? asked the members of Parliament. Was he supporting religious prejudices by appeasing the Hindus and antagonizing the Muslims, or was he appealing to national sympathies? Was there discontent among the Hindus or the people of Gujarat? The style of the Proclamation was said to be more in keeping with an Oriental Potentate and lacked the sobriety of the English.

The act was defended by those who maintained that the gates were a national trophy and not a religious icon. That they were important to the people of India was an argument that was backed up by quoting the request of Ranjit Singh to Shah Shujah for the return of the gates. It was argued that Ranjit Singh had wanted them back as a national trophy and not for any religious

---

[15] The United Kingdom House of Commons Debate, 9 March 1843 on The Somnath [Prabhas Patan] Proclamation, *Hansard*, reprinted 1948, Junagadh.

reasons. But then it was found that in his letter to Shah Shujah, Ranjit Singh had confused the gates of Somanatha with the gates of Juggernaut/Jagannath. One wonders whether this letter was factual or hearsay as it does seem unlikely that the two temples, being so different, would have been confused. It was suggested that Jagannath might have been a mistake for Junagadh. The gates would be brought back by an Indian army as a trophy of war, although some saw it merely as a regional trophy pertaining to Somanatha and not a national one.

It was argued that no historian mentions the gates in the various accounts of Mahmud's raid, therefore the gates could only be an invention from hearsay or myth. Among the historians frequently quoted at the time was Ferishta but he does not mention any gates. Others such as Gibbon and Elphinstone had merely commented on Mahmud undertaking a war to promote Islam and attack the Hindus—a religious war—or as an attempt at projecting himself as the great champion of Islam and iconoclasm.

Questions were raised about the kind of religion that Ellenborough was defending and there were fierce attacks, particularly by Lord Macaulay, on this religion encouraging idolatry, superstition, human sacrifice, *suttee* and *thugee*. This was what some called the monstrous 'Linga-ism' and supporting it contravened the orders of the Court of Directors of the East India Company that the British administration must be neutral in matters pertaining to local religions.[16] This, they maintained, was polytheism in its worst form since it presented the most degrading, odious, polluted representation of the Supreme Being. It was described as the worship of a monster deified in the temple. The worship of a phallic symbol was seen by them, through the eyes of Victorian prudery, and was described in

---

[16] T.B. Macaulay, *Speeches by Lord Macaulay*, ed. by G.M. Young, 'The Gates of Somnath', 9 March 1843; *Hansard*, pp. 601 ff., 620 ff.

contemptuous terms. They said that Ellenborough was paying homage to a native religion. There were moral consequences to promoting Linga-ism and political consequences to antagonizing the Muslims, both of which were disapproved of by some members.

The Proclamation was seen to have political consequences, irrespective of whether Mahmud's raid was motivated by the promotion of religion or by the attraction of loot. There would be violent indignation among the Mohammedans who would see the British Government as supporting the Hindus against the Muslims. Macaulay maintained that,

> ... Our Governor-General has proclaimed his intention to retaliate on the Musulmans beyond the mountains, the insults which their ancestors, eight hundred years ago, offered to the idolatry of the Hindus.[17]

Ellenborough tried to muster Indian opinion in his defence and wrote to the Hindu lawyer of the raja of Satara for his view. The reply stated categorically that it would be unsuitable to bring the gates back, because according to Hindu practice whatever material has been placed over a dead body or has had contact with it, even in a tomb, is regarded as polluted and unfit for anything but destruction. This letter was quoted in Parliament.[18]

Those that defended Ellenborough did so with arguments that were to have extensive consequences and, incidentally, moulded what came to be the received version of the aftermath of Mahmud's raid. They argued that the memory of the gates was preserved by Hindus as a painful memorial of the most devastating invasion that had ever desolated Hindustan. Ellenborough, they said, was removing the feeling of degradation

---

[17] T.B. Macaulay, op.cit., p. 213.

[18] *Hansard*, p. 651.

from the minds of the Hindus and it would relieve that country which had been overrun by the Mohammedan conqueror from the painful feelings that had been rankling amongst the people for nearly a thousand years. The restoration of the gates of Somanatha was not merely the bringing back of a trophy of success from Afghanistan, it was a restoring to its original position of that which has been regarded for 800 years as a pledge of conquest by the now conquered enemy.[19]

The supporters of Ellenborough won the motion, but their arguments coloured the historical assessment of the consequences of Mahmud's raid. The gates were said to have been brought back, but were found not to be of Indian workmanship.[20] So they were placed in the storerooms of the fort at Agra. The attempt became the butt of jokes.

A postscript to the episode of the gates is rather curious. In 1951, a broadcast from Peshawar stated that local tribesmen from Quetta to Chitral, numbering 33 lakh, decided to prevent the Afghan government from returning the gates of the Somanatha temple to India, which they claim had been carried away by Mahmud as a mark of victory for Islam. The Government of India objected to this news item as being irresponsible, and Jawaharlal Nehru, in a letter to the Prime Minister of Pakistan, stated:

> ... The story of the gates of Somnath temple being brought back to India from Afghanistan is completely false and there is not an atom of truth in it. This has been publicly denied. In fact nobody knows if there are any such gates anywhere and nothing of the kind is being sent from Afghanistan to India.[21]

---

[19] Ibid., p. 656, p. 674.

[20] J. Fergusson, *A History of Indian and Eastern Architecture*, Vol. 2, p. 192.

[21] Sarvepalli Gopal, *Selected Works of Jawaharlal Nehru*, XVI, 1, p. 606.

This contradicts the earlier story of some gates, supposedly of Somanatha, having been brought back. The mystery of the gates, it would seem, remains in the shadows.[22]

The British assessment of the aftermath of the raid on Somanatha grew out of an idée fixe with seeing the relationship between Hindus and Muslims not just from the single dimension of religion but of religious antagonism. This was to become the generally accepted nineteenth-century comprehension of India. Yet even James Tod, writing just before the debate in the House of Commons, makes a special point of mentioning that neither he nor his friend who assisted him in his collection of the bardic and folkloric material of Gujarat and Rajasthan from non-Persian sources had come across traditional legends about Mahmud, even though Mahmud merited an eternity of infamy from the Hindu.[23] Nor did the British make much attempt to read what was being said by Indians in languages other than English. In 1843, Ramakrishna Vishvanatha, writing in Marathi, argued forcefully that Mahmud's real intention was not to convert Hindus to Islam, but to loot as much wealth as possible from Hindusthan in order to enrich himself and defeat his rivals at home. Such arguments were made by others as well.[24] K.N. Hali, writing in 1878, mentions the plundering by Mahmud resulting in the oppression of the poor but adds that this was no worse than the bloodshed and plundering of the western

---

[22] The claim to the identity of the gates will doubtless be revived from time to time. I was recently told that the gates are now part of a haveli in Rajasthan (!) but its location and the identity of the owners were not revealed.

[23] J. Tod, *Travels in Western India*, p. 344.

[24] Ramakrishna Vishvanatha, *Hindusthanchi Prachin va Sampratchi Sthithi va Pudhen kai Tyacha Parinama Honara ya Vishayim Vichara*, p. 12; D.K. Bedekar (ed.), *Chara June Marathi Arthashastriya Grantha, (1843–1855)*. I am grateful for this information to Professor J.V. Naik.

Christian nations in later times and especially through their policy
of free trade.[25]

As for any familiarity with popular religions and the articulations that they endorsed, this was too remote an idea even to be
considered by historians and was left to ethnographic compila-
tions which were segregated from historical sources. Had there
been a more sensitive and realistic understanding of Indian
society, such a distancing would have been less prevalent.
Interestingly, these firmly held theories of antagonism were being
projected in the decade prior to the Revolt of 1857, a movement
that can hardly be said to have subscribed to the notion of a
Hindu trauma in relation to Muslims brought on by the actions of
Mahmud.

The question remains as to whether Ellenborough's defence
of his actions stirred up Hindu sentiment about Somanatha on a
large scale, which earlier appears to have been marginal and
localized. Ellenborough saw the raid of Mahmud as a disaster
embedded in the Indian psyche.[26] Judging by the context,
Ellenborough, when he uses the term Indian, means, Hindu.

Interventions such as this wiped out the nuances of
community relationships and the particularities of each occasion
when a range of people with varying identities were involved.
The colonial intervention forms a striking contrast to the
discussions on 'Hindu–Muslim' relations in some of the texts in
the regional languages in the latter half of the second
millennium AD. An obvious example is Eknath's *Hindu–Turk
Samvada*, where matters of religion are frequently treated in a
disputatious manner but where the inevitable interdependence of
religious identities is assumed as an essential component of the

---

[25] K.N. Hali, *Urdu ka Klassiki Adab*. The text was sent to me by Rennier
Kimmij. The essay was read and discussed with me by Idrak Bhatty.

[26] R.H. Davis, op.cit., p. 202.

society.[27] But in the nineteenth-century interpretation, the inter-dependence was lost sight of and there remained just two segregated, monolithic communities and even these were formulated by the way history was interpreted. Whatever the reasons for the adoption of a religious dichotomy of Hindu and Muslim as the characteristic feature of Indian society, emerging from ideology, administrative needs and misrepresentations of history, the dichotomy came to stay. Not that these labels were absent earlier but they were not applied with such dualistic determinism as in colonial usage. It would be worth investigating the occasions in pre-colonial times when such labels were used, in what context and with what connotations. The problem with resorting to these was that it was impossible to invariably assign the majority of people into these two categories enforcing clearly demarcated boundaries. The identities of the Kabirpanthis, the Nathapanthis, some Sufi and Shakta sects and the followers of Isma'il Jogi, Satya Pir and Ghazi Miyan, for instance, as indeed of many others, were multilayered and changeable. Earlier references were more often to communities defined by language, region and occupation and to sects and castes.

A survey of the discussion or comments on Mahmud in histories by various European historians from the eighteenth and nineteenth centuries presents an interesting pattern.[28] The early interest seems to have been largely with viewing Mahmud in the central Asian context, and his raids on temple towns were not seen as a confrontation between Hindus and Muslims. At most, in some cases, a distinction was made between quiescent Hindus

---

[27] E. Zelliot, 'A Medieval Encounter between Hindus and Muslims: Eknath's Drama-Poem Hindu–Turk Samvad' in F.W. Clothey (ed.), *Images of Man: Religion and Historical Process in South Asia*. N. Wagle, 'Hindu–Muslim Interactions in Medieval Maharashtra' in G.D. Sontheimer and H. Kulke (eds), *Hinduism Reconsidered*, pp. 134–52.

[28] P. Hardy, 'Mahmud of Ghazna and the Historian', *Journal of the Punjab University Historical Society*, 1962, 14, pp. 1–36.

and aggressive Muslims. Edward Gibbon, for example, was more interested in the Islamic–Christian contest as articulated in the Crusades. There is therefore in some works a condemnation of the ferocity and barbarity of the Turks, although James Mill argues that the coming of Islam brought in a marginally improved condition as compared to that of Hindu rule. This argument was part of his periodization of Indian history into Hindu, Muslim and British, of which the Hindu was the most inferior, the Muslim somewhat less so, and it was the British who had the potential of introducing a superior civilization.

From the mid-nineteenth century, there were two theories about Mahmud's invasions: one advanced the idea of a clash between Turkish Islam and Hindu India and that Mahmud's iconoclasm harmed the image of Islam in India; the other was that Mahmud's invasions were mainly for plunder and the religious concerns were subordinate to the acquisition of wealth. Given the growing interest in theories of race at this time in Europe, some historians introduced the idea of a racial conflict as well. In the writing of the late nineteenth and early twentieth century, opinion veered from emphasizing the religious programme of Mahmud to that of plundering India to finance his central Asian empire.

The explanation of the history of the second millennium in India as being confined to religious antagonism gradually gained ground, nurtured by the communal politics of the 1920s and subsequent years. Mohammad Habib was an exception in as much as he saw plunder as a more central motif than religion and pointed out that Islam in India does not begin with Mahmud.[29] Some histories began to treat Mahmud's campaigns as the start of Hindu–Muslim antagonism. The Hindus are said to have been politically weak, lacking in national unity and unaware of the wider political spectrum prevailing at the time. Forcible

---

[29] M. Habib, *Sultan Mahmud of Ghaznin: A Study*.

conversion, it was held, had been used as a political mechanism to expand the Muslim kingdoms. Yet there is little reference to forcible conversion in the narratives about Somanatha from non-Persian sources. Conversion was doubtless made more complicated by the impressive number of Arab and Isma'ili Muslims in Gujarat between whom and the local Hindus there were cordial relations. In accounts of Mahmud's activities, there is the mention of the killing of 50,000 infidels, usually accompanied by references to the killing of 50,000 Muslim heretics—generally Isma'ilis and Shi'as. These are formulaic numbers, frequently mentioned, so it is difficult to tell precisely how many infidels and heretics, or for that matter Sunni Muslims, may have been killed in these campaigns.

The central Asian aspect that was of prime importance to Mahmud was by now receding from the perspective of Indian history, and he was seen largely in terms of his activities on the Indian subcontinent. These were regarded as seminal to confrontation between the Hindus and the Muslims, one that continued unabated to the present. British writers had repeatedly stated that the Somanatha temple was destroyed each time it faced a Muslim general, yet this was not the case judging by the non-Persian narratives and by the archaeological evidence. In the translation of the Turko–Persian narratives, as in the compilation by Elliot and Dowson, first published in 1867–77, Islamic terms were brought in where they were not used in the original and this gave a more pointed religious turn to the statement. So deep was the imprint of Mill's periodization that historians did not think of looking at sources other than those in Persian for the period, even where such other sources were equally important to its history. This compartmentalization that results in obscuring other sources remains a detrimental legacy of nineteenth-century historiography.

The colonial assessment of the raid on Somanatha and its aftermath, as being traumatic and germinating Hindu–Muslim antagonism, was useful to colonial political policy. Neither

Ellenborough nor any of the members of the House of
Commons who participated in the debate sought evidence from
sources reflecting opinions alternate to the Turko–Persian texts.
And even these were largely interpreted from a predictable
perspective: that a raid on a temple would ensure eternal hostility,
and the resulting antagonism would reinforce the colonial theory
of Hindus and Muslims having been permanently hostile. The
projection of this history, although it evolved from the politics
and policies of colonialism, began also to appeal to a section of
Indian nationalists.

Anti-colonial nationalism was the inclusive, mainstream nationalism which, as a movement, began in the late nineteenth century.
Its intention ultimately was to work towards the termination of
colonial rule and establish India as an independent nation-state.
Parallel to this movement in the early twentieth century was the
emergence of religious nationalisms—Muslim and Hindu
communalisms—that did not conform to the aims of mainstream
nationalism. The central concern of each of these two was less
tied to anti-colonialism and more to the creating, if need be, of
two nations, each dominated by a majority religious community—
Muslim in one case and Hindu in the other. Both Muslim and
Hindu communal ideologies were rooted in the familiar colonial
interpretations of the Indian past. Coming from the same source
they emerged as mirror images of each other. It was argued that
the Muslims were, and remained, alien from the non-Muslims of
India despite the overwhelming majority of Muslims being local
converts; the interface of Islam and Hinduism so crucial to many
societies in India was, and is, marginalised if not ignored;
medieval history records the triumph of Islam and, by the same
token, the subjugation of the Hindus; the Hindus and the
Muslims have constituted two separate nations ever since the
arrival of Islam.

    Although mainstream nationalism was largely not sympathetic
to religious nationalism because there was a fear that the

sectarianism of the latter would fragment the country, there was nevertheless some degree of ideological overlap with some sections of the former. There were attempts to homogenize identities and cultures in a manner that eroded the demarcation between mainstream and religious nationalism. A manifestation of this becomes visible in the rebuilding of the Somanatha temple and the controversy that resulted.

Among the nationalist politicians of the twentieth century, K.M. Munshi, who wrote extensively on the history of Gujarat, was an ardent advocate of this idea. His writing on Somanatha echoes statements made by Lord Ellenborough and those who supported him in the House of Commons. In terms of a wider context, Munshi was concerned to show the greatness of Aryan culture in India, which for him was Hindu culture and which he felt was being overturned by the presence of Islam. In the ideology of Hindu religious nationalism, the Aryans were equated, then as now, with present-day Hindus.

Munshi's literary career began in the early twentieth century with a series of historical romances, doubtless under the influence of reading Walter Scott and Alexander Dumas, probably the most popular historical novelists among middle-class Indians at the time.[30] The historical novel is of course not history but introduces a flavour of history into a literary genre. The historical fiction of Bankim Chandra Chatterjee was also being translated and widely discussed. And, as R.C. Majumdar puts it, Bankim Chandra's nationalism was Hindu rather than Indian. 'This is made crystal clear from his other writings which contain passionate outbursts against the subjugation of India by the Muslims.'[31] The influential writings of Dayanand Sarasvati, Vivekananda and Aurobindo gave shape to what Munshi understood as Indian culture and

---

[30] M.M. Jhaveri, *History of Gujarati Literature*, pp. 152–6.

[31] *History and Culture of the Indian People*, Vol. VIII, R.C. Majumdar, 'British Paramountcy and Indian Renaissance', Part II, p. 478.

nationalism, as they did in the case of many other political and literary personalities of the period.

Munshi's trilogy on the reign of Jayasimha Siddharaja, the Chaulukya king, published in 1917–23, projected the Jaina world as a parallel to the Islamic one and presented the Jainas as intending to make Gujarat into a Jaina state.[32] The depiction of the Jainas was unacceptable to many of his Jaina contemporaries. In another novel, the hostility between Gujarat and Malwa is the subject and the appeal is for unity against the Muslims. Munshi's argument is that it was the failure of the Hindu kings to unite that allowed the Muslims to conquer India. The third theme was a story familiar to many, that of Ranakadevi refusing to marry Jayasimha Siddharaja and becoming a *sati* at Vadhavan. Rajput society, imbued with heroic values, was idealized.

Munshi seems unaware of the contradictions in his discussion of Hindu–Muslim relations. For instance, he quotes at length from Ranchodji Amaraji's book on how the campaigns against the Turks were disastrous for the Turks with many being taken captive. We are then told that those women captives who were virgins were immediately taken as wives, but those who were not, were first cleansed and then married to men of appropriate rank. Of the men captives, those of respectable rank were accepted into the Shekhavat and Wadhel tribes of Rajputs, and the less respectable were inducted into the lower castes of Kolis, Mers and so on. The point being made is that the Turks and Afghans were assimilated into various castes and their women accepted in marriage. Yet Munshi's comment is that there was a wave of righteous hatred against the vandals which spread all over northern India.[33]

---

[32] A. Skaria, 'On the Curious Love of Indulal Yagnik', *Indian Economic and Social History Review*, 2001, 38, 3, pp. 271–97.

[33] *The Glory that was Gurjara-desh*, III, pp. 132–41; *Gujarat and its Literature*, p. 261. Ranchodji Amaraji, *Tarikh-i-Sorath*, p. 112.

Earlier historical novels set in Gujarat, such as *Karan Ghelo* by Nandashankar Mehta on Karanadeva, the last of the Vaghelas, and his relations with Ala al-Din Khalji, published in 1868, seem to have been less concerned with relations between religious groups. In this, the emphasis was on the decline of Rajput values, the moral corruption of society and the establishment of the new power.[34] The Vaghela king abducted the wife of his minister, Madhava, who in revenge, invited Ala al-Din to invade Gujarat. Munshi's novels had a different purpose and perspective.

Subsequently, in 1937, Munshi wrote his most widely read novel, *Jaya Somanatha*,[35] the focus of which was the raid of Mahmud and the destruction of the icon at Somanatha. The background is a story of intrigue, focusing on the rivalry between the two Shaiva sects, the Pashupata and the Kapalika. Romance is inevitable with the women being beautiful and accomplished *devadasis*, dedicated to the temple. Mahmud lays siege to the fortress around the temple. Bhimadeva, the Chaulukya king, is present but is wounded in the siege and evacuated to Khambat. A Pashupata priest goes berserk and reveals the secret tunnel into the temple to Mahmud's commander. Mahmud enters and destroys the icon. The depiction of Mahmud in this novel is not as negative as Munshi's later historical assessment of him, but that he was the anti-hero is evident. The segregation of Muslims was thought to be necessary to the purity of race and of culture. Hence the need to project a constant and visible distance between the Hindus and the Muslims throughout history. It has been said that this novel brought together Munshi's brahmanhood, family heritage,

---

[34] Yashaschandra, op.cit., pp. 597 ff. *Karanghelo*, trans. N.M. Tripathi. M.M. Jhaveri, *History of Gujarati Literature*, p. 83. C.A. Kincaid, *The Outlaws of Kathiawar and Other Stories*.

[35] Trans. by H.M. Patel.

worship of Shiva, literary activity, and understanding of nationalism.[36]

In his other works, Munshi veers between suggesting that Hindus and Muslims lived in harmony until the issue of separate electorates was introduced by the British, and stating that Hindu–Muslim antagonism had early historical roots.[37] The Aryans were regarded as the progenitors of the Hindus and there was no Aryan migration into India:

> ... the races that were settled from the banks of the Sarasvati to those of the Narmada were homogenous in blood, language and culture, long before the period of the Rigvedic *mantras* ...[38]

This conflation of race, language and culture would be unacceptable to social historians today, although it is common to ideologies of religious nationalism. Theories such as these were being discussed but in limited circles. Because they did not observe a historical method or procedures of analyses, they were not of much interest to most professional historians. Possibly Munshi's interest was encouraged by his closeness to members of the R.S.S.[39] In 1964, Munshi was the President of the Vishva Hindu Parishad, actively involved in its founding and its work.

The temple being derelict, Somanatha had ceased to be a major place of pilgrimage. Munshi's insistence on resuscitating it by building a new temple on the site was to revive it and make it

---

[36] G. Shah, 'Kanaiyalal Munshi on Gujarati and Indian Nationalism', Seminar paper 1988.

[37] K.M. Munshi, *The Changing Shape of Indian Politics*, pp. 20–21, 30, 43, 66.

[38] K.M. Munshi, *The Early Aryans in Gujarat*, p. 69.

[39] His junior in the legal profession, Shiv Shankar Apte, was a *pracharak* of the R.S.S. (Rashtriya Svayamsevak Sangh). Manjari Katju, 'The Early VHP: 1964–83', *Social Scientist*, 1998, 26, 5–6, pp. 34 ff. Apte together with Chinmayananda were key figures in organizing the VHP.

symbolic for another kind of pilgrimage. In this, he had the advantage of being politically important, and as a minister of the Central Government after 1947 could galvanize funds and labour of various kinds. Had he been just an ordinary citizen of that period, there may not have been a new temple at Somanatha. Part of Munshi's intention was to focus attention on Gujarat, its identity, and its historical role in the events that led to the creation of the nation-state of India. The assertion of a Gujarati identity was possibly fuelled in part by Gujarat being included in the Bombay Presidency, and therefore subordinate to the dominance of Maharashtra. The ultimate ambition was a separate state. It would seem that for Munshi Somanatha was the centre-piece of the glory that was Gurjara-desh. The process of revival consisted of setting out the history of Somanatha as he saw it; assuming that the excavation of the site prior to the reconstruction of the temple would endorse this history; and collecting funds for the building of a new temple at the site which he would supervise.

For him, the glory of Gujarat lay in the contribution of the Gurjaras who were indigenous, steeped in Aryan culture, and active in the Indian resistance to the alien Muslim.[40] Somanatha was a symbol of this. He visited the temple in 1922 and gradually became obsessed with the idea of rebuilding it.[41] He refers to Shiva as the guardian of national resurgence and writes,

> From this time [1026] Shiva the Destroyer was the god of Resistance and in his name millions laid down their lives in defence of their faith and land till AD 1665 and thereafter again in His name, the south under Shivaji and

---

[40] K.M. Munshi, *The Glory That was Gurjaradesha*, 550–1300, Part II, Foreword to First Edition, pp. 250 ff.

[41] K.M. Munshi, *Somanatha—The Shrine Eternal*, p. 42.

his successors with *har har mahadeva* on its lips rose in
resistance and destroyed the Mughal empire.[42]

One wonders what Virabhadra, Tripurantaka, members of
the *pancha-kula* of Somanatha and other dignitaries would have
made of all this, given their relations with Nur-ud-din Firuz and
the Muslims living in their midst. Munshi's book on Somanatha
includes the text of three inscriptions from Somanatha, but,
interestingly, he omits the inscription of Nur-ud-din Firuz.

In reconstructing the history of Somanatha, he dates the
earliest temple to the start of the Christian era and the second to
a rebuilding in the sixth century by the Maitrakas which he says
was destroyed by the Arabs. The archaeological evidence differs
from these statements.[43] Jaina sources refer to Somanatha as a
safe area for images prior to the eleventh century. This would
not suggest that the temple was subject to repeated raids by
Arabs. According to Munshi, the third temple was built in the
ninth century and vandalized by Mahmud. He maintains that
apart from destroying temples, the coming of Islam destroyed
the integrating factors of northern India, namely, *aryadharma*, the
four *varnas* and the reliance on the *dharmasmritis*. He adds that
Hemachandra encouraged scholarship in Prakrit rather than
Sanskrit, thereby weakening cultural unity, which required
Sanskrit. Historical scholarship today would argue that social
integration calls for more than just a veneer of similarity among
the upper castes.

The rebuilding of the Somanatha temple in 1951 required
clearing the ruins from the site and this encouraged the idea of
excavating the site before the rebuilding.[44] It might have been

---

[42] Ibid., p. 28. The primary deity worshipped by Shivaji was Bhavani at
Tuljapur.

[43] Dhaky and Shastri, op.cit., pp. 3 ff.

more imaginative architecturally to have incorporated and shored up the surviving plinth and the lower structural level of the medieval temple as part of the plan for the reconstruction. The medieval temple would then have been supported by the modern structure giving the site a greater historical presence. But this was evidently not the intention. The Somnath Trust had decided on clearing the ruins even before the excavation had started.[45] The excavation was intended to recover the sequence of building and record whatever evidence was available. The removal of the medieval temple can be viewed as an attempt to annul its history. If the iconoclasm of the Turks and of Aurangzeb symbolized Muslim tyranny and, more than that, the inability of Hindus to challenge it, then the symbol of this inability had to be removed. Replacing the old temple with a new one was an act of legitimizing the new politics and the power of Hindu nationalism.

Archaeologists and historians protested at the dismantling of the old temple, arguing that a historical site should be left as it was, irrespective of what the past politics may have been.[46] Munshi was even accused of vandalism by some.[47] The professional attempt to protect the site was overruled by identifying it as a Hindu national monument.[48] Munshi, expressing his view

---

[44] K.M. Munshi, *Somanatha—The Shrine Eternal*, pp. 12 ff.; B.K. Thapar, 'The Temple of Somanatha: History by Excavations', ibid., Part III, pp. 71–90; A.K. Majumdar, op.cit., pp. 370 ff.; Dhaky and Shastri, op.cit., pp. 25 ff.

[45] Dhaky and Shastri, op.cit., Foreword.

[46] R.H. Davis, op.cit., p. 213.

[47] P. Mukta, 'On the Political Culture of Authoritarianism', in G. Shah, M. Rutten and H. Strefkerk (eds), *Development and Deprivation*, pp. 63 ff. See also J.H. Dave et.al., *Munshi: His Life and Work*, II and IV.

and claiming the assent of Sardar Vallabhbhai Patel, converted Somanatha into an icon of the resurgence of Hindu religious nationalism, and of freedom from 'foreign' Muslim rule. This is evident from the objectives of the Somnath Trust that supervised the building and functioning of the temple, and which stipulated that non-Hindus could not perform acts of worship in the new temple.[49]

The results of the excavation, however, were not what Munshi expected—an endorsement of his theory of the continued destruction of the temple from the early centuries AD onwards. The archaeological evidence is reasonably clear as to the sequence and this is set out in the report.[50] Although there is an inscription that refers to Someshavara in the ninth century, early structures of this period were not found. Pilgrimage sites did not necessarily require the focus of a majestic temple. If structures had existed, they were probably of less importance and were likely to have been removed in the subsequent construction of the tenth century. Any earlier temple would have been small as were other temples of Gujarat in the initial period of temple construction, as for instance, the one at Gop.

The archaeological evidence of a temple dates the first structure to the tenth century or possibly at the earliest to the late ninth century. The pillar bases of local stone suggest a tenth century style. This may have been built by Mularaja Chaulukya. The other possibility would have been the raja Graharipu of Junagadh, but according to Hemachandra, he attacked and looted

---

[48] P. Van der Veer, 'Ayodhya and Somnath: Eternal Shrines, Contested Histories', *Social Research*, 1992, 59, 1, pp. 85–109, draws parallels between Ayodhya and Somanatha and comments on the use of archaeology. See also his *Religious Nationalism: Hindus and Muslims in India*.

[49] P. Mukta, op.cit.; J.H. Dave, op.cit., II, p. 98.

[50] B.K. Thapar, 'The Temple of Somanatha: History by Excavations'.

the pilgrims going to Somanatha.[51] This raises the question why the local rulers seemed hostile to the temple and prevented pilgrims from going there or were they merely concerned with acquiring wealth by looting pilgrims? The Chaulukyas, as we have seen, were constantly trying to protect it both from local raiders and from the rulers of Malwa. The stone of this temple was thin-grained reddish sandstone and there is evidence of breakage in the sculptures. The presence of lead has drawn attention to the description in some Persian sources of fifty-six wooden pillars sheathed in lead supporting the roof, but this remains a conjecture. The presence of stone pillar bases makes it unlikely that there were wooden pillars and fifty-six pillars of teak were too many to be accommodated.[52] This tenth-century temple would have been the one raided by Mahmud. There is evidence of some burning and the desecration of sculpture.

The second temple built soon after the raid in the eleventh century appears to have been a renovation of the earlier, probably carried out by Bhimadeva I, the Chaulukya king. This was most likely still on the small side although *mandapas* may have been added later. It follows the plan of the earlier temple and the stone is predominantly light-coloured sandstone. The style was the one commonly used in Gujarat at that time. This temple fell into decay, perhaps because it was more a renovation than a reconstruction and there was less attention to quality. There are no textual references to any attacks on the temple until the end of the thirteenth century, by which time the third temple had been constructed and had been established for well over a century.

The third temple in the time of Kumarapala registers changes in the temple plan. It was bigger than the second temple, possibly to accommodate more pilgrims, and to make a more effective impression since it was being built by a ruler of considerable

---

[51] Dhaky and Shastri, op.cit., p. 16.

[52] Ibid., p. 10.

standing. As has been pointed out, the three water channels placed in alignment indicate three periods of renovation or rebuilding. Desecration at the end of the thirteenth century when the Khalji army was said to have raided the temple is not registered in any striking way in the excavation of the site.[53] In the mid-fourteenth century, the *lingam* was replaced, according to textual evidence. The repeated destruction of the temple subsequently, as mentioned in the Persian sources is not apparent from the excavation.

In 1951, a new temple was constructed on the site. It was built by the traditional Somapuri builders of temples in Gujarat, and the style was what was thought to be appropriate to represent the finest architecture from Gujarat. Architectural historians, however, have differing opinions about the architectural style of the new temple and not all are enthusiastic about the result. Munshi spoke of the new structure as associated with the Government of India, and thought of it as a far more appropriate action for the collective subconscious of the nation than many other activities of the government.

The statement that it was the Government of India that was rebuilding the temple was strongly contradicted by the Prime Minister, Jawaharlal Nehru, for whom such activity was unacceptable as government activity and inimical to the policy of a secular government ruling a secular state.[54] This was a rather different position from that of Sardar Vallabhbhai Patel, the Home Minister and a Congressman from Gujarat, who had initially supported the reconstruction of the temple although he was not

---

[53] H. Cousens, *Somanatha and Other Medieval Temples in Kathiawar*, ASI, Vol. XLV, pp. 11–33.

[54] By comparison, Ahalyabai Holkar did not restore or rebuild the Somanatha temple. She built another temple since her intention was to make available a place of worship rather than furthering religious nationalism.

keen on involving the government. Nehru insisted that the Government of India should be left out of this enterprise and that the funding should come from a trust financed by public donations, as had been earlier suggested by Gandhiji. The Somnath Trust was thus established.

It has been stated recently that Nehru regarded the rebuilding of the temple at Somanatha as a matter of national sentiment and that the temple was financed by the Government of India.[55] This is an incorrect statement and the letters of Nehru on this matter to various persons involved leave no doubt about his position. His opposition to the Government of India supporting this project of rebuilding the temple at Somanatha was endorsed by Radhakrishnan and by Rajagopalachari. In his letter to the Chief Ministers, dated 2 May 1951, Nehru states categorically:

> You must have read about the coming ceremonies at Somnath temple. Many people have been attracted to this and some of my colleagues are even associated with it in their individual capacities. But it should be clearly understood that this function is not governmental and the Government of India as such has nothing to do with it. While it is easy to understand a certain measure of public support to this venture we have to remember that we must not do anything which comes in the way of our State being secular. That is the basis of our Constitution and Governments therefore, should refrain from associating themselves with anything which tends to affect the secular character of our State. There, are, unfortunately, many communal tendencies at work in India today and we have to be on our guard against them. It is important

---

[55] Sarvepalli Gopal in his biography of Nehru makes it evident that such a view is untenable. *Jawaharlal Nehru, A Biography*, Vol. II, p. 155. Much of what follows comes from my discussions with Professor Sarvepalli Gopal.

that Governments should keep the secular and non-communal ideal always before them.[56]

However, there were others that disagreed. The President, Rajendra Prasad, wrote to Nehru to say that he had been invited to preside over the opening of the new temple and wished to do so, to which Nehru replied on 2 March:

> ... I confess that I do not like the idea of your associating yourself with a spectacular opening of the Somnath temple. This is not merely visiting a temple, which can certainly be done by you or anyone else, but rather participating in a significant function which unfortunately has a number of implications. Personally, I thought that this was no time to lay stress on large-scale building operations at Somnath. This could have been done gradually and more effectively later. However, this has been done. I feel that it would be better if you did not preside over this function.[57]

However, Rajendra Prasad ignored Nehru's advice, as well as the criticism in the Gujarati press of the President of India participating in the ceremony, as reported by Mridula Sarabhai. Nehru does record in his *Autobiography* that there was only a small explicitly secular group in the Indian National Congress.

Nehru objected to two other actions on the part of the Somnath Trustees which he refers to in a letter to Rajendra Prasad.[58] One was the circular sent round to Indian ambassadors, asking them to collect and send to Somanatha containers of water from the major rivers of the countries to which they were

---

[56] Sarvepalli Gopal, *Selected Works of Jawaharlal Nehru*, XVI, 1, p. 559.

[57] Ibid., p. 270.

[58] Ibid., pp. 607–8.

accredited, as well as soil and twigs from the mountains of these countries. It was said that these were required for the rituals of the consecration of the temple. The Ambassador to China, K.M. Panikkar, was critical of embassies being asked to do such things, an opinion with which Nehru agreed. He instructed the Ministry of External Affairs to ignore these requests.[59]

He was equally angry about newspaper reports that the Saurashtra government was contributing Rs 5 lakh (in those days a substantial amount of money) towards the consecration of the temple. In the same letter to Rajendra Prasad, Nehru writes:

> ... According to newspaper reports, the Saurashtra Government has set aside five lakhs for these Somnath installation ceremonies. This seems to me completely improper for any Government to do and I have written to that Government accordingly. At any time this would have been undesirable, but at the present juncture, when starvation stalks the land and every kind of national economy and austerity are preached by us, this expenditure by a government appears to me to be almost shocking. We have stopped expenditure on education, on health and many beneficent services because we say that we cannot afford it. And yet, a State Government can spend a large sum of money on just the installation ceremony of a temple.
>
> I do not know what to do about this, but I must at least keep the Government of India clear of it. In answer to questions in Parliament, or perhaps in press conferences, I shall have to make this position clear.

This debate introduced a further dimension to the reading of the

---

[59] Ibid., pp. 604–6.

event, involving a discussion on what constitutes the secular credentials of society and state. Nehru's concern was not just with the Somanatha temple and its being rebuilt. He was underlining the larger view of the nature of the Indian state and society after independence and was demanding a commitment to democracy and secularism.

The secular credentials of Indian society were challenged by the most recent action focusing on the Somanatha temple. This was the *ratha-yatra* organized by the Vishva Hindu Parishad in association with leaders of the Bharatiya Janata Party (BJP) and aimed ostensibly at gathering momentum and support for the building of a temple at Ayodhya, on the presumed site of the Ramjanmabhumi. That the end purpose of the momentum was to support political mobilization for the BJP was not incidental. The *rath-yatra* began its journey from Somanatha in September 1990.

The second gathering in December 1992 led to the destruc-tion of the Babri Masjid at Ayodhya. The inevitable consequence was a series of riots in various places, culminating in the genocide in Gujarat in 2002. The driving force of this, as of much that the Hindutva ideology reads into Indian history, is the theory—current since the nineteenth century and derived from colonial historiography—of antagonism being the dominating relationship between Hindus and Muslims, a theory fanned by and giving support to the communal politics of the last century. It was the coming to fruition of the seed planted by the debate in the House of Commons and the nurturing by religious nationalisms of what grew from it.

8

Constructing Memory, Writing Histories

An opinion that generally receives popular support is, as we have seen, the idea that Mahmud's raid on the Somanatha temple created conditions that are sometimes represented as conquest and resistance.[1] Narratives emanating from 'Muslim' sources retelling the event have been read as epitomizing the archetypal encounter of Islam with Hindu idolatry.[2] In such sources, Mahmud is the archetypal Islamic warrior bringing new lands under Islam and is the Sunni Muslim who subverts the claim that Hindu images were indestructible. These views underline the thinking that went into the making of a historical dichotomy between Hindus and Muslims that was thought to be unshakable and kept them permanently opposed. Historians have questioned this reading in recent years. But popular perceptions often differ from historical assessments. The questioning has come from using a wider range of sources than just a single category, but, even more importantly, from subjecting the sources to what are now regarded as necessary forms of historical analyses.

---

[1] Aziz Ahmed, 'Epic and Counter-Epic in Medieval India', *Journal of the American Oriental Society*, 1963, 83, pp. 470–76.

[2] R.H. Davis, op.cit., p. 93.

The epic of conquest is evident in the glorification of Mahmud as the conqueror and the iconoclast Muslim at Somanatha and other places. This image is projected primarily in the Turko–Persian sources. These have been treated as consistent and homogenous narratives, which, as some scholars have shown, they are not. There are many contradictions: whose was the image and what was its form? Was it Manat or Shiva, female or male? Why does the manageable temple size of the earlier sources give way to fantasies about wealth and size in the later sources? The exaggeration of courtly literature is only too evident as also the manifest agenda of its authors. Why do the narratives of Mahmud plundering temples get transformed at a particular point in history to his being the founder of Muslim rule in India? Why were the Muslim Arabs not included in the story of the establish-ment of power by Muslim rulers, given that they preceded the Turks, settled in the area, and either did not indulge in the same iconoclasm as claimed by the Turks or else their iconoclasm was perceived as less fearful? Or was it that the Arabs did not have court poets to magnify every activity? Or were there differences in the perception and practice of Islam between the Arabs and the Turks? Arab culture gave birth to Islam, the Turks were recent converts, and enmeshed in the politics of eastern Islam. Inevitably, the difference would be marked. Mahmud was the champion of Sunni Islam but there was a range of dissident sects—as in all formal religions—and these broke down the supposed uniformity of Islam.

Differentiation in identity among groups viewed as Muslim was parallel in some ways to the segmentation of Hindu society. At the lower levels, and among the larger number of people, the differentiation between formal religions was less visible. The gloss of 'Muslim' and 'Hindu' has eroded the variant nature of relations within and between these societies. By the fourteenth century, the Turko–Persian narratives on Mahmud cease to focus only on his conquests, and start performing the role often required of pre-modern histories—they legitimize new political power as articulated through kingship and the emergence of a new state. There is now a more obvious political concern with the legitimacy of Islamic rule in India through the Sultans. This was complicated in the Indian situation where the majority of the population had not been converted to Islam, and further complicated by the politics of central Asian Islam and its relations with the Caliphate.

The epic of resistance is difficult to discern. Shaiva texts dismiss such raids as an inevitable occurrence in 'the age of the losing throw'—the Kaliyuga. Perhaps they were unconcerned because royal patronage ensured the continuation of the temple as a major institution. Where it was disrupted or the temple was raided, it was allowed to lapse unless there was patronage available to rebuild it. The Shaiva priests of the Somanatha temple and the Hindu elite were only too willing to accommodate a wealthy Persian trader building a mosque on land that was part of the temple estate at Somanatha. This might suggest that the profits of trade at this time and among the Somanatha elite had parity with religious sentiments and this would have been acceptable policy. The relations among the Hindus, Jainas and Arabs seemed to have been friendly, despite the raid of the Turk, Mahmud. The philosophy of unconcern, emanating from the condition of the Kaliyuga, was not highlighted in recent times because it did not suit religious nationalism. The politics of violence was what was chosen from the tradition and is now sometimes read as resistance.

Jaina authors, writing about the activities of the Chaulukya kings, give an account of the role of the Jaina minister in the renovating of the temple. This differs significantly from the account of the Shaiva chief priest in his inscription. The latter ignores the role of the Jaina minister, the self-manifestation of Shiva, and the conversion of the king to the Jaina faith. Rivalry over royal patronage may have superceded concern with Mahmud's iconoclasm. Jaina histories of the Chaulukyas and other events barely refer to the raid, although they frequently allude to activities involving the temple. Jaina merchants do not endorse resistance to the Yavanas: they are more concerned with navigating a return to peaceful conditions. An aversion to violence is central to Jaina ethics, and violence is generally avoided in the narratives relating to Jainas and Yavanas.

The Rajput narrative of Kanhadade describes a clash with the Khalji Sultan, but apart from a battle over the icon, much more is narrated about manoeuvres over negotiations with the Khalji and court intrigues among Rajputs. Curiously, there is no recall of the raid of Mahmud that is supposed to have initially inspired the resistance, even though the general of the Khalji Sultan raids the Somanatha temple to remove the icon. Is there an epic of resistance in this but so muted as to be almost inaudible? Other epic poems eulogizing Rajput rulers give more space to court intrigue, romance, and highlight the occurrence of disloyalty among Rajputs towards each other, rather than to a systematic resistance against the Turks. This is reflected in the oft-repeated statement by modern writers that Hindus could never unite to resist the Muslim conquest, but why this was so has not been analysed. Counterparts to resistance can take the form of millennarian movements but these again are absent among the Rajputs.

A hint of millenarianism comes from those placed lower down in society. But theirs are movements that interweave many religious sectarian groups of Hindu and Muslim persuasion rather than opposing them. In the process, they create literatures and systems of beliefs different from the formal religions. These widespread and popular stories subvert the depiction by the court chronicles of Mahmud being a great conqueror by insisting that he had to surrender to the power of piety, and that he was helpless without the aid of the pious and the holy. Even the fabricated story of his supposed nephew conquering territory and being martyred is ultimately converted into depicting him as a man of piety and moral authority, and as such widely worshipped by Hindus and Muslims alike, and particularly in the liminal area of religions beyond the conventional boundaries of either

Hinduism or Islam. In the tradition of the *Shabara Tantras* and the Natha Panthis, that included both Hindus and Muslims as worshippers, Mahmud is evoked among the pious. This was perhaps because it was believed that he subordinated himself to those worshipped for their piety, or he was acclaimed as an ascetic warrior where such figures were at a premium.

These stories, current in northern India, would have annulled at the popular level both the epics of conquest and whatever there might have been of the epics of resistance. These were the beliefs among a much larger number of people than those who accepted the veracity of the Turko–Persian chronicles or the Rajput epics. Oral traditions give their own gloss to events and this in itself draws from many voices, particularly as the notion of its coming from a homogenous society and attempting to create such a society is not the primary concern.[3] The relationships depicted in these various sources were not determined by the general category of what have been called Hindu and Muslim interests. They varied in accordance with more particular interests and these drew on many identities—ethnicity, economic concerns, religious sectarianism and social status. The narrowing of these identities to the single religion, Hindu or Muslim, silences the many voices.

Can these various categories of sources therefore be said to have created a dichotomy? We may well ask how and when does such a dichotomy crystallize? Does it take off from too literal a reading of one set of narratives by modern historians without juxtaposing them with the other narratives? The by now rather dog-eared version of the event, given in later chronicles, such as that of Ferishta, was repeated endlessly throughout the nineteenth and twentieth centuries. This is reflected in views such

---

[3] Cf. N. Wachtel, *The Vision of the Vanquished*, referring to similar questions in relation to the Catholicism of the Spaniards and the religion of the Incas. See also G. Viswanathan, *Outside the Fold: Conversion, Modernity and Belief.*

as those of the editors of *The History of India as Told By its Own Historians*, where Elliot and Dowson state that religious bigotry was characteristic of the Indian past. They do confess that in presenting the translations from Persian and Arabic sources, their intention is to highlight the oppressive rule of Muslim kings. They state that the intolerance of the Mohammedans led to idols being mutilated, temples destroyed, forced conversions, confiscations, murders and massacres, not to mention the sensuality and drunkenness of tyrants. Such descriptions were intended to convince the Hindu subjects that British rule was far superior and to their advantage.[4]

This was not an isolated attitude and is reflected in many British writings on Indian history. Religious bigotry was frequently read into the texts translated in the nineteenth century, which coloured the reading of the Turko–Persian texts. For example, where Utbi says, 'He (Mahmud) made it obligatory on himself to undertake every year an expedition to Hind', the translation of this passage in Elliot and Dowson's work reads, 'the Sultan vowed to undertake a holy war to Hind every year'.[5]

The British encounter with Islam in India has not received the same analytical attention as the encounter with Hinduism since Indian Islam was treated as an alien intervention untouched by Indian civilization. Those that saw India as only a Hindu, Sanskritic civilization, or an epitome of the Oriental Renaissance, ignored the Indian experience of Islam (or for that matter even some of the heterodoxies of earlier Indian traditions) until later times. There was little concession to the idea of a distinctly Indian form of Islam that needed to be studied in an Indian context. Nevertheless, there was a tendency to concede the credibility of the Persian historical accounts because these echoed notions of historical writing current in Europe. They were rarely

---

[4] Elliot and Dowson, op.cit., I, Original Preface, pp. xx–xxii.

[5] Quoted in Nazim, op.cit., pp. 86 ff.

questioned by counterposing other sources of the period. Perhaps this dependence was fuelled by the initial fascination with a possible common ancestry.

Dow's translation of Ferishta pointed to Indians being the descendants of Hind, the son of Ham, the son of Noah, and this linked the ancestry to Biblical genealogy, a subject of much interest to William Jones.[6] But in the post-Jonesian period, the negative characteristics prevailed. These further infiltrated into the writings of various Indians in the latter half of the nineteenth century. Histories in Bengal, for instance, transmitted the stereotypical figure of the Muslim as defined by the British, and the history of Muslim rule in India was treated more as the history of Islam than as the history of India.[7] There were some exceptions such as a few historians writing in Maharashtra, as mentioned earlier, and in other places. But the British imprint on Bengal was intense and continuous.

This raises some questions that are pertinent to the history of these times. Has the dichotomy between Hindu and Muslim become such a mindset that we do not comprehend the complexities and nuances of an event and its aftermath, however familiar we may be with its many representations? Why and when does the dichotomy become part of a social memory?

Al-Biruni is often quoted as having said that the raids of Mahmud caused such devastation that the Hindus came to dislike the Muslims permanently.[8] Al-Biruni was no admirer of Mahmud and would not have hesitated to blame him for the ills of India. Nevertheless, this passage needs to be examined more closely in the light of further questions. Who is he referring to when he speaks of Hindus? Does he mean the people of India, i.e. the

---

[6] T. Trautmann, *Aryans and British India*, pp. 52 ff.

[7] P. Chatterjee, *The Nation and its Fragments: Colonial and Post-Colonial Histories*, pp. 99–104. Shahid Amin, op.cit.

[8] E. Sachau, op.cit., I, p. 22.

people of al-Hind, as seems likely in the context of the passage, and those who suffered as a result of the raids, or only those who follow the brahmanical religion which, according to him, were not all the people of India? Those most affected would have been the people living in the north-west since Mahmud's raids seem to have had no impact on a major part of the subcontinent. More frequently, the connotation of Hindu in the early sources was primarily a reference to people inhabiting a specific geographical area. The opposition was between the Hindu in this sense and the Turk rather than the Hindu and the Muslim as religious categories. This distinction is significant.[9]

The raids would have been economically devastating in the areas where the temples were targeted. Yet, in the case of Somanatha, the revival seems to have been almost immediate, accompanied by a greater generation of wealth than before. Impressive temples were built in western India in the eleventh century at Kiradu, Sadri and such like, not to mention the later and more elaborate temples at Modhera and Mount Abu. Patronage came from both royalty and the mercantile community and the presence of the temples is indicative of a prosperous economy. It would be worth doing an assessment of the economy of other temple towns and their hinterland subsequent to raids by Mahmud.

If the descriptions are rooted in religious ideology, what constitutes this ideology? There are violent confrontations within Islam between Sunnis and Isma'ilis, and between the Bohras and the Turks. These are strong rivalries, initially, of matters relating to pristine belief and, later, determined by competition for access to resources and patronage. Shaivas and Jainas are even more important to the history of Gujarat in the earlier half of the second millennium AD. All these groups were aware of the

---

[9] C.W. Ernst, *Eternal Garden: Mysticism, History and Politics at a South Asian Sufi Centre*, p. 24.

historical event, but the function of the event or of the association with the temple is distinctively different. The context is that of various contested ideologies and the narratives they produced. These can therefore hardly be treated solely as a confrontation between Hindus and Muslims.

As a background to the major activities discussed here, there are the underlying stories of many people who came as migrants and settled in Saurashtra. Some were pastoral groups while others sought status as well as the kind of adventurous employment that would bring them into positions of authority and wealth. The area was peppered with petty rajas, usually chiefs of clans, some of whom stooped to brigandage in order to ensure an income and maintain their status. There are occasional references to more established rulers bringing them to heel. Doubtless, the migrant groups and even those now well-settled participated in the more renowned battles and hoped to obtain control over territory, status and loot from this participation. All over the pre-modern world, one of the purposes of war for kings was to acquire territory, but for the ordinary soldier it was inevitably booty. Raids filled in the interstices of campaigns. In some instances, they can even be seen as attempts at a more equitable distribution of wealth. The sources from early to late times continue to mention brigandage and raids in the area. Sea piracy, for example, was also an occupation of the Portuguese in the waters off Gujarat. Even the claim by the Turks to justify their raids—iconoclasm—was a known accompaniment to plunder. Those that raided could become the heroes of folk epics for a variety of reasons, and were often latched onto the larger historical events. Folk literature might therefore provide further variants on the perceptions of historical moments.

We have so far seen situations such as the raid on Somanatha as a binary projection of Hindu and Muslim, each viewed as a single, unified, monolithic community. But what the sources tell us is that there are multiple groups with varying agendas, either involved in the way the event and Somanatha are represented, or else in ignoring it. The Turko–Persian chronicles function with two sets of differentiations: the one that is highlighted as between the infidels/Hindus and the Muslims, and the other between the Turks as Sunnis and Muslims of a different Islamic persuasion from that of some of the Arab traders settled in India, and who were attacked by Mahmud as heretics. Was there a deliberate attempt to play down the role of the Arabs, who were on close and friendly terms with their counterpart Hindu and Jaina traders in Gujarat and elsewhere, because of tensions between the Arabs and the Turks? Some of this closeness had resulted in the evolution of communities ostensibly Muslim but with strong local practices, such as the Bohras and the Khojas. Were the politics of heresy and revolt which were affecting Islam in this period in west Asia linked to how such groups were viewed by the Turks? The hostility between the Bohras and the Turks, technically both of the same religion, may have been part of this confrontation since the Bohras had some Arab ancestry and probably saw themselves as among the settled communities of Gujarat and saw the Turks as invaders.

Texts and inscriptions in Sanskrit, focusing on matters pertaining to the royal court and to the religion of the elite, introduce from time to time elements of rivalry between Jainas and Shaivas. These were rivalries involving patronage: the appointment of ministers and the upper bureaucracy; financial and administrative support for the building of temples, monasteries and centres to propagate the religion; and grants of land and transfer of rights to support families or institutions. The concern of these authors would not relate centrally to whether or not Mahmud raided an important temple, but rather to how their patron legitimized his rule by his relationship to religious institutions as, for example, the Somanatha temple.

But the sources which focus on a different social group, that of the Jaina merchants, include narratives of the capturing of icons and raids on temples. These are destabilizing activities which act as obstructions to the smooth flow of commerce and to relations between distant traders. The views of these authors would seem to be conciliatory towards the creators of disturbance, perhaps because it was thought that this would be a quieter and more long-lasting way of coming to terms with the upheaval and preventing its reoccurrence.

From the Veraval-Somanatha inscription of 1264, co-operation in the building of a mosque came from a range of social groups—from orthodox Shaiva ritual specialists to those wielding administrative authority and from the highest property holders to those with lesser properties. Interestingly, the local members of the *jamatha*, if they were all Muslims—as is likely—were, in terms of occupation, from the lower end of the economic scale, and in caste terms were low, barring perhaps the teachers of religion. As such, their responsibility for the maintenance of the mosque would have required the goodwill of the Somanatha elite. And the elite, doubtless, recognized this as a further extension of their patronage.

These relationships were not determined by the general category of what have been called Hindu and Muslim interests. They varied in accordance with more particular interests and these drew on multiple identities and concerns. Colonial historiography conveniently reduced them to the two and subsequent historiography accepted this construction of Indian society. Some forms of nationalism recognized in this change the potential for political mobilization.[10] Neither of these historiographies viewed relationships in the past from the perspective of those low in the social order. Had they done so, these two convenient categories would have been found to be inappropriate. The evidence of popular perceptions challenges these categories. If these relationships are to be understood historically, the focus will inevitably have to include these groups and their interests, and not be

---

[10] S. Sarkar, 'Identity and Difference of Caste in the Formation of Ideologies of Nationalism and Hinduism', *Writing Social History*, pp. 358–90.

restricted to the supposedly monolithic communities as constructed by the politics of the last two centuries. Small local groups are generally involved in participating in a local event and the history that followed. But the memory which may come to envelop the event and its evolution is often the contribution of elite groups, later in time, motivated by wishing to use the past to legitimize their present concerns.

In the retelling of an event, there may be a claim, as is made about the raid on Somanatha in the last two centuries, that it encapsulates a memory; so too, the question of whether or why there may be amnesia. Where a historical event of a distant past is described as embedded in memory, there memory has to be understood from many perspectives: the historical point at which it was articulated, its context, and the process of its being handed down. Analysing a 'memory' can be a perplexing exercise.

In an early discussion on social memory, it was argued that such memories are constructed by social groups and, to that extent, collective memory is a social construct and should be analysed as such. This involves examining its function and its modes of transmission.[11] Memory need not be what is personally experienced, refined or retained. It also draws on notions that we inherit from preceding generations and pass on to the next.[12] The assumption here is that it is inherited, but it is equally likely that it is invented. The degree to which it is invented relates to the requirement of the memory as a perception and as that which is stored and retrieved. The opposite of retrieval is amnesia. It is a process of association where the object or the act generating the association need not be historical. Memory implies selection

---

[11] M. Halbwachs, *On Collective Memory*. P. Nora, 'Between Memory and History: Les Lieux de Memoire', *Representations*, 1989, 26, pp. 21 ff.

[12] T. Butler, 'Memory: a Mixed Blessing', in T. Butler (ed.), *Memory, History, Culture and the Mind*, p. 132.

between what is to be remembered and what is to be forgotten, hence the significance of time and context. It also involves an audience that is linked to determining the form and content.[13] The opposite of social memory is what has been called 'structural amnesia' which raises the question of why it is necessary to forget and who wants to do so.[14]

Recent work on history and memory and the reconstruction of the French past has demonstrated the circular process by which memory is created and is linked to the past and the present. It has been argued that attempts are made to create a collective memory by kneading the past into new forms and claiming these as legitimate memory. Such claims are created to endorse the attitudes of the present and are then used to restructure the past to justify the present. Collective memories are mutated with every major historical change and are constantly changing. Memory, therefore, can be formulated in any way, but this differs from the historical process which calls for analysis and critical discourse.[15]

The construction of a social memory can superscribe the history of the event as it appears to have done in the case of Somanatha. The event recedes or is absent in all but one set of sources. Only the Turko–Persian sources can attempt a claim to memory, drawing on narratives said to be contemporary with Mahmud, although such a claim is tenuous. Even where it is present, it is continually refigured, creating alternate and sometimes competing interpretations. Such reconstructions are part of the making of identities and identities in history are

---

[13] K.N. Petrov, 'History as Social Memory', in Butler, op.cit., pp. 77–96.

[14] J. Barnes, 'The Collection of Genealogies', *Rhodes Livingstone Journal*, 1947, 5, p. 52, quoted in J. Goody and I. Watt, 'The Consequences of Literacy', *Comparative Studies in Society and History*, 1962–63.

[15] P. Nora (ed.), *Realms of Memory*, Vol. I, pp. 1–23; 'Between History and Memory: Les Lieux de Memoire', *Representations*, 1989, 26, p. 21 ff.

neither permanent nor unchanging. The reshuffling of identities also leads to an event being reconstructed and incorporated into what is claimed as tradition.

Although the construction of the memory of the raid is a clear narrative by the nineteenth century, the accounts in the Turko–Persian sources are diverse and ambiguous. The event itself is not doubted. The diversity of representations or the absence of mention is not emphasized, perhaps because it is related to the histories of a range of communities and their interactions, attempting to define their own identities. They reflect the different political concerns of those writing the narratives. This does not allow of a monocausal explanation of the event.

The actual details of the event become less important and the identity of the idol is vague. The Turko–Persian accounts play out the fantasies of the authors and their audience in terms of power and wealth. Some early accounts of Mahmud drew on memory. Gradually, invention, imagination and fantasy are embroidered onto the description of the event. Magnification of the destruction, the loot, the intention, became the primary features. In the chronicles of the fourteenth century, the representation of political legitimacy is added. This was required to establish the legitimacy of the rule of Sultans in India, both as an inheritance from the earlier empires of west Asia such as those of Alexander and the Sassanids, and in the context of the threat to Islam in these areas from the Mongols.

Each narrative has its own politics, and trying to unravel this becomes one explanation in its historiography. A memory becomes a component of the identity of a group. The authors of the Turko–Persian texts attempt to distance themselves from local communities by focusing on destruction and power; the Sanskrit texts distance themselves from these acts perhaps by being silent about the destruction—if in fact they were deliberately silent or other events are recorded such as the coming of the trader from Hormuz. The Jaina texts seek legitimacy for their faith. The *pirs* and the Tantric *gurus* draw in the memory, recreate it in a manner that allows it to be common across a large range of communities, and make it different from the previous ones. The last is not a deliberate act of historical construction as is the first, but the forms emerge from popular perceptions and traditions. These stories reflect the sharing of a culture and a perceived history as being common to Hindus and Muslims.

The interesting counterpoint in the case of Somanatha is that the construction of the social memory of a Hindu trauma over Mahmud's raid and the destruction of other temples by Muslim rulers is a selection of a 'memory' that at the same time annuls the memory of Hindu kings raiding Hindu temples. That there might have been a memory of Mahmud's raid prior to the construction of the one put forward by Ellenborough, and in the debate in the House of Commons, is not reflected in Sanskrit sources. The amnesia regarding Hindu kings destroying Hindu temples is of a different order since such attacks are recorded and commented upon in 'Hindu' sources. Kalhana for one, does not suppress the fact or the memory of Hindu kings of Kashmir destroying Hindu temples. But this information has been the subject of amnesia among modern historians. The necessity for both the constructed memory in the one case, of Muslims alone destroying temples, and the amnesia in the other, was to give cohesion to a presumed Hindu community in modern times. And further, that the politics of modern times did not require that the amnesia be revoked, thus maintaining that only Muslims destroy temples. This precluded discussion of why, in the past, temples were destroyed for reasons other than religious bigotry.

Narratives such as the ones discussed here, claiming to be historical but incorporating various concerns and perceptions, drew from the past. But the past is part of the present, sometimes in tangible ways such as in our readings of the past. A narrative can create a structure for an action and this can then be used as the starting point for further action. The complexities of comparing the narratives are set aside with the introduction of a new perception—memory. In the reconstruction of events in the course of the debate in the House of Commons, memory is sought to be constructed. The event is seen from a single source—the Turko–Persian texts—it is interpreted from the perspective of a colonial understanding of the Indian past shored up by colonial historiography, and the memory of the event then finds its place as the primary cause of the action that follows. It is almost as if the constructed 'memory' takes over from an attempted history. The juxtaposing of the narratives raises its own problems, but now there is additionally a constructed memory that has to be accommodated. What adds to the complication is that there is also a forgetting of other instances of temple destruction.

Creating a memory involves claiming that what is being remembered actually happened in the past. The other side of the coin to remembering is forgetting and setting apart that which is not to be remembered. If remembering has its own politics, so does forgetting. Remembering or claiming to remember is a selective process and what is remembered and what is forgotten draws on history—actual or presumed. The historian can nudge the memory and point to what is forgotten. In the history of temple destruction by Muslims, there has been a forgetting of temple destruction by others, and it may be as well not to overlook this when considering the particular memory that is being discussed here.

The temple is a sacred space. But it has not been and is not the only kind of sacred space in India. It was both preceded by and was and is coexistent with many other forms: the animistic worship of nature and natural forms such as mountains and rivers; sanctuaries around burials in the vicinity of megalithic settlements; the sacred enclosures and tumuli that preceded Buddhism but were adapted as sacred monuments by Buddhists— *chaitya* halls that became the space for conducting worship and *stupas* that enclosed sacred relics; temples as structures in which images were enshrined in the sacred cella; and later monuments such as churches, synagogues, mosques, *gurdwaras*, intended for congregational worship.

A space that has been sanctified often continues to be regarded as sacred even when appropriated by another religion. A new religious sect takes over the space either by osmosis or by force, and the structure is converted to the new worship. Osmosis points to the underlining of the continuance of a sacred space; force generally implies the usurpation of such space. Burials associated with megalithic settlements are thought to be sacred spaces, suggested by the nature of the burial, the items of grave furnishings and the location and demarcation of the burial. Sometimes, a Buddhist *stupa* was built overlapping partially with a megalithic sanctuary, the obvious example being the one at Amaravati in Guntoor district. Buddhist monuments, in turn, were sometimes taken over by Hindu sects. The early Hindu temples at Chezarla and Ter are believed to be *chaitya* halls with their characteristic apsidal forms. Some images in small temples in the vicinity of Mathura have been identified as Buddhist and converted to Hindu icons with a different identity. The locality of Katra is thought to have been a Buddhist monastery prior to the Hindu temple.[16] Elsewhere, rivalries were more violent when Buddhist, Jaina, Shrivaishnava and Shaiva sects battled over structures, as in Karnataka and Tamil Nadu in the eleventh and twelfth centuries or later, and sometimes required the intervention of royalty.[17] Some temples in Gyaraspur (in Madhya Pradesh) were converted to Jaina worship. To understand the politics associated with sacred spaces, whether they be *stupas*, mosques or temples, we have to understand the multiple functions of such spaces.

The structure of the temple originated in the *garbha-griha*, a small shrine-room in which the image was placed, and the *mandapa*, a portal, was the entrance space. The icon was the

---

[16] F.S. Growse, *Mathura: A District Memoir*, p. 106.

[17] P.B. Desai, *A History of Karnataka*, pp. 342–43; R. Champakalakshmi, *Trade, Ideology and Urbanisation*, pp. 339–40, 390–92, 395–96.

focus of the temple. From about the seventh century, these structures began gradually to be enlarged to include an ante-chamber and a larger sanctum demarcated by a tower (*shikhara*), with the entire structure being placed on a plinth. The temples built from about the eleventh century assumed larger and grander proportions. Gradually, they incorporated courtyards surrounding the core and often an enclosing wall with a cloister-like structure, the area taking in subsidiary shrines as well. This converted them into conspicuous features of the landscape.

It hardly needs underlining that the importance of the temple relates to its being a place of worship and a religious centre. Increasing royal patronage and greater financial investment in building temples meant that they could be constructed of stone—the most expensive and durable building material—and, where stone was not available, of brick. The striking increase in such constructions in this period required manuals in Sanskrit to create typologies and to train architects, builders and masons. Even kings were proud to claim authorship of such manuals. The temple provided an institutional base for the priests, who, apart from performing the rituals had a stake in other concerns of the temple as an institution. This was not characteristic of the temple alone but was relevant to the places of worship of other religions as well.

Concerns that begin in religion can take on other functions and such changes were common to many religious institutions. The sacred centre becomes the focus of a community associated with a religious sect, the focus being established through worship, donations, offerings and loyalty to those administering the ritual and embodying the beliefs. Where the sect is powerful and widely patronized, the temples relate to the wider community: ideology spreads through regular narratives and recitals; performances of music and dance take on a form of offerings to the deity. The temple can become the focus of intellectual and artistic life.

Other functions less obvious on the surface are embedded in the institutional aspects of the temple. Those that were in charge of the temple's administration, or even senior priests, could advise on matters pertaining to social codes. The management had to supervise the finances of the temple, a major task where temples were richly endowed with grants or owned property in urban areas. Exemption from taxes increased the income of the temple. Possession of lands meant employing cultivators, labourers and functionaries, possession of herds required herdsmen, and shops needed traders and artisans for gainful functioning. Commercial exchange was important to the economy of pilgrimage centres and the proximity of the port of Veraval to Somanatha doubtless attracted the attention of Mularaja. His investment in a temple at the site, apart from its significance to him as an act of devotion and patronage, doubtless also brought some revenue to the Chaulukya administration, both from the growing maritime trade and also from the offerings and taxes from the pilgrims. All these activities, if they were to yield profits, required what today would be called a good business sense and managerial experience.

When impressively large and magnificent temples were built through the patronage of royal families and elite groups, the role of the temple in society was also magnified. It became a signature of power, legitimized royal authority and participated in local administration. Temple building takes on some of the elements of a potlatch with intense competition as to who expends the maximum wealth in building the best temples. In such situations, the temple is not restricted to being seen only as a sacred space.

Where a temple marked a place of pilgrimage—and this was so for many—the location attracted artisans and traders to cater to the thousands who visited the temple. Such locations often evolved into towns, as for instance, Kanchipuram, with an integrating of commerce and sacred centres where the temple participated in both. Lavish donations of land and properties and votive offerings assisted in the accumulation of wealth. As an institution with considerable wealth, the temple could intervene in economic matters. Temple administration made investments, acted as a bank in rural areas, employed functionaries and labour on its multiple properties, and collected a variety of dues; all of which are activities referred to in inscriptions and texts from various parts of the subcontinent. Being exempt from taxes placed it in a particularly advantageous position. Inevitably, the temple became a centre of local culture and, if sufficiently well-endowed, also supported facets of 'high' culture. Representations of myths, deities and epic narratives crystallized religious perceptions although there may have been a fault line between the interpretations of court culture and what the *kathakaras* and *pauranikas*, the tellers of tales, recited to visiting pilgrims. It could and did finance intellectual activity in the *mathas* and *ghatikas*, the centres of learning attached to it. In places where the temple was enclosed by fortifications, required by its larger treasuries, it could even act as a garrison centre.

One feature that distinguished the functioning of many temples from the places of worship of other religions, was that such temples also reinforced social demarcation. The rituals carried out in the sanctum were not open to everyone and anyone. Some lower castes were allowed entry into the precincts of the temple, but those still lower down in society and the Dalits were not permitted to enter the temple. As a counter to this, the early teaching of the Bhakti movement emphasized the point that worship lay in personal devotion to the deity and not in rituals. Groups that were excluded built their own places of worship.

The temple also embodied a political dimension in the relationship claimed between the king and the deity. This could be subtle, with some situations when the power of the one overlapped with the other in a not too ostentatious manner, or it could be more obvious where the king was proclaimed as incorporating divinity or being an incarnation of a deity. Sometimes the deity was said to reside in the temple and a routine of service was worked out which was based on the daily schedule of the king and the royal calendar. Where the association of kingship with deity was close, the temple became a more evident political symbol. Where the deity was specific to a territory such as Viththhala at Pandharpur in Maharashtra or Jagannath at Puri in Orissa,[18] the territorial range in the worship of the deity strengthened the political claim. This was perhaps more marked where the origin of the deity lay in a folk cult. It has been argued that this closeness was shared sovereignty that would convert the temple into a political symbol linked to the king.[19] By the same token, the looting of the image from the enemy's temple or the destruction of their sacred space established conquest over the enemy.[20] If the icon shared the king's sovereignty and the king incorporated the territory where the deity was worshipped, the capturing of the icon would indicate the delegitimation of the ruler.

The looting of images begins to be referred to in the seventh century. Chalukya armies brought back images from the temples in the areas where they campaigned, claiming them as trophies. The Pallava king took away the image of Ganesha from a temple in Vatapi. The travels of a Vishnu image, captured from the northern mountains by a Pratihara king and which found its way to Bundelkhand, is described in a Chandella inscription. A Chola king brought back images from the places conquered by him.[21] These and others are examples of the forcible taking of images that were then presumably installed in the victor's capital. The re-installation does not annul the fact that the image was seen as representing the political authority of the enemy and was to that

---

[18] A. Dandekar, 'Pastoralism and the Cult of Vitthala', Ph.D. thesis, Jawaharlal Nehru University, 1991. H. Kulke, 'Royal Temple Policy and the Structure of Medieval Hindu Kingdoms', in *Kings and Cults*, pp. 1–16.

[19] B.D. Chattopadhyaya, 'Historiography, History and Religious Centers: Early Medieval North India, circa AD 700–1200' in V.N. Desai and D. Mason (eds), *Gods, Guardians and Lovers: Temple Sculptures from North India, AD 700–1200*, p. 40.

[20] R. Eaton, *Essays on Islam and Indian History*, pp. 106 ff.

[21] Ibid.

extent an object to be seized. This is of course not the same as desecrating an image. The latter has two elements: capturing the political authority of the enemy, and denigrating his religion. Nevertheless, this was a step away from desecrating temples, an activity that also began prior to the coming of Islam.

Before the attacks on temples, there were acts of violence against those competing for royal patronage. The *Rajatarangini* of Kalhana, the much quoted twelfth-century history of Kashmir, refers to Mihirakula's hostility to Buddhism.[22] Hsüan Tsang, writing in the seventh century, describes the persecution of Buddhists and the destruction of Buddhist images and monasteries not only in Kashmir but also in eastern India by Shashanka.[23] In both cases, the rulers were Shaivas. The persecution of the Jainas by the Pallava king, Mahendravarman, otherwise known to be a man of cultural attainments, is well-known.[24] At the start of the eleventh century, an inscription records the arrival of a Chola king with his army in the Dharwar district of Karnataka. The countryside was ravaged, women were seized and some were murdered together with children and brahmans, and the order of caste was overthrown.[25] This invasion was avenged, presumably by similar acts. The *Basava Purana* of about the thirteenth century has no compunction in recommending the killing of Jainas and describing in gory detail their being impaled.[26]

---

[22] M.A. Stein, *Kalhana's Rajatarangini*, I, 289, n. 307; S. Beal, *Si-yu-ki*, I. 168, 171.

[23] Watters, I, 343; II, 43, 92, 115–16.

[24] R. Champakalakshmi, 'Religious Conflict in the Tamil Country: A Reappraisal of Epigraphic Evidence', *Journal of the Epigraphical Society of India*, 1978, No. 5.

[25] Inscriptions from Hottur, *Epigraphia Indica*, XVI, 1921, pp. 73–75. Ranabir Chakravarti drew my attention to this inscription.

[26] Narayan Rao V. and G.H. Roghair (trans.), *Siva's Warriors: The Basava Purana of Palkuriki Somanatha*.

Attacks on Hindu temples by Hindu rulers also date to this time. The more obvious examples may be mentioned here. In the early tenth century, Rashtrakuta Indra III takes pride in having destroyed the temple at Kalpa in his campaign against the Pratiharas.[27] The Jaina temples of Karnataka were desecrated and converted to Shaiva use.[28] The Paramara king of Malwa, Subhatavarman (1194–1209), destroyed the Jaina temple built by the Chaulukya king when he was campaigning against the Chaulukyas, as well as the mosque built by the Chaulukyas in Khambat for the Arab traders whose trade enhanced the wealth of the city.[29] A number of kings of Kashmir looted temples, starting with Shankaravarma in the ninth century. According to Kalhana, he plundered sixty-four temples, using the officers of his administration to do so and resumed the lands granted to the temples.[30] These, as we have seen, are activities that in some later inscriptions are associated with the Yavanas. The most notorious of these kings was Harshadeva, ruling in the eleventh century. He not only tided over the fiscal crises of the state by looting temple wealth, but also appointed a special category of officers to do so, the *devotpatananayaka*/officers for the uprooting of gods.[31] Their function was to forcibly obtain the wealth of temples and to defile the images wherever there was resistance. Kalhana writes disparagingly of these kings and applies the epithet of *turushka* to Harshadeva. The Chaulukya king, Ajayadeva, a patron of the Shaivas, destroyed the Jaina temples built by his father, and his son, in turn, destroyed the temples which Ajayadeva had built.[32]

---

[27] R. Eaton, op.cit., p. 107.

[28] P.B. Desai, *Jainism in South India and Some Jaina Epigraphs*, pp. 82–83, 101–2, 124.

[29] P. Bhatia, *The Paramaras*, pp. 140–42.

[30] *Rajatarangini*, V, 166–70.

[31] Ibid., VII, 1090–1108, 1091.

[32] *Prabandha-cintamani*, trans. Tawney, p. 245.

There were multiple reasons for attacking temples—
establishing political supremacy, legitimizing succession, obtaining
fiscal benefits, demonstrating religious differences—and it would
be worth examining the Turkish attacks on temples in the light
of these many reasons. What remains unexplained is that, in
the process of creating a memory of temple destruction in
modern times, only the temples desecrated by Muslim rulers are
remembered, those desecrated by Hindu rulers are forgotten.
Texts such as the *Rajatarangini* have been repeatedly read
and quoted, yet Kalhana's comments on Shankaravarma and
Harshadeva have been generally ignored. Memory is not value
free and the selection of what is chosen to be remembered from
the historical past reflects the imprint of historiography, among
other factors.

The vulnerability of the temple to attack begins prior to the
coming of Islam. But the resort to destroying temples increases
when temple destruction is central to a religious crusade as well
as a means of acquiring wealth and status. It has been argued that
in Muslim rulers selecting particular temples for desecration there
was, apart from loot, iconoclasm and contestation for kingly
authority, also a preference for those that were strategically
located in terms of geopolitics.[33] The location of the temples that
are attacked from the ninth century would form a worthwhile
aspect of the study of temple destruction. Temple ruins—and
many are in ruins as is the domestic architecture of earlier times—
are invariably explained as the result of Muslim iconoclasm and
other reasons are not generally considered. Some enthusiasts have
counted as many as over three thousand such examples.[34]

---

[33] R. Eaton, op.cit.

[34] S.R. Goel, *Hindu Temples: What Happened to Them. A Preliminary Survey*,
Vols I and II.

However, this is a complex subject and should be examined more closely.[35]

The intention is not to do a checklist of the numbers of icons and temples destroyed by Hindu kings as against Muslim kings. It is more appropriate to consider this data and try and understand why at a certain historic period temples became targets of attack by a variety of people. The destruction of temples requires a critical analysis. If the capturing of icons and attacks on temples is pre-Islamic and such activities have not been so common in still earlier periods, although known, these actions represent a change in the relations between a religious structure expressing religious sentiments and its public role. The Buddhist Sangha, for instance, was a wealthy institution but possibly it did not accumulate the same degree of wealth as the better-endowed Hindu temples and therefore *stupas* and *viharas* did not attract the greed of kings. The historical question remains—what led to the looting of temples?

A historian would not indiscriminately count all ruined temples as resulting from Islamic fanaticism, but would try to ascertain the cause of a temple falling into ruin. This relates to questions of why a temple was built at a particular place, what its function was other than the religious, what the source of its maintenance was and whether this source declined and, if it was desecrated, who was responsible and why. It also requires an assessment of actual iconoclasm as against presumed iconoclasm. Temples were seldom destroyed outright. Distinctions have to be made between a degree of destruction such that the structure could still be renovated and used as a temple or be converted into a mosque; or alternatively, where earlier ruins can

---

[35] As has been done by R. Eaton, 'Temple Destruction and Indo–Muslim States' in *Essays on Islam and Indian History*, pp. 94 ff. Eaton has been able to count only a fraction of this number of temples for the destruction of which there is authoritative historical evidence.

be used as building material for a mosque.[36] Religious fanaticism notwithstanding, there was also the natural process of decline when the temple was not being adequately maintained. If the function of the temple is complex, the interpretation of its history, even where it is attacked, is all the more so. Is it wilful destruction in every case or was there a natural cause beyond human control?

The building of temples and the patronage required for their upkeep was not restricted to kings. Other groups such as lesser intermediaries or mercantile groups are known to have contributed to the maintenance of temples. When such groups ran into political troubles or their wealth got diminished or they were party to intense rivalries—all of which happened—the decline of the temple they helped maintain would be inevitable. In such cases, the historian has to recount not only the history of the temple but also the history of its patrons. By the same token, a necessary aspect of building a temple was to ensure the authority of its patron.

There is also the technical aspect of how well the building itself could withstand age and weathering. According to Cousens, temples in Kathiawar were likely to have fallen into ruin naturally, because of their poor foundations, lack of proper jointing of stones, and inadequate beams for bearing the weight of the stones.[37] Both the Sanskrit inscriptions and the text of Merutunga refer to poor maintenance in the case of the Somanatha and some other temples. Burgess mentions places such as Devakota where fragments of old temples were pulled down to build new ones, as stated in the inscription at the site.[38]

---

[36] M. Meister, 'Indian Islam's Lotus Throne: Kaman and Khatu Kalan' in A.D. Dalapiccola and S. Zingle-Ave Lallemant (eds), *Islam and Indian Regions*, Vol. I, pp. 445–52.

[37] H. Cousens, op.cit.

[38] J. Burgess, op.cit., p. 43.

Such rebuilding of new temples from the ruins of old ones did not invariably mean that the older temple was in ruins as the result of a raid.

The relationship between religion and politics had complex dimensions in the past and cannot be explained away by a simple monocausal explanation that reduces everything to a minimalist religious motivation. Religion is a private matter so long as it remains within the thoughts of a person. When these thoughts are expressed publicly and inspire public actions such as building monuments for worship and organizing fellow believers into carrying out political and social functions, then religion ceases to be an exclusively personal matter. It is no longer only a matter of faith since its formulation as an organization of believers has a bearing on the functioning of the society. Its religious identity incorporates these functions that are expressed through its institutions such as monasteries, *mathas*, temples, mosques, *khanqahs*, churches, synagogues, *gurdwaras*. Their role has to be assessed not merely in terms of the religion with which they are associated, but also in the context of their functions as institutions of society. This has ramifications far beyond a monocausal historical explanation.

Multiple sources have been discussed above, providing differentiated perspectives on the history of Somanatha subsequent to the raid of Mahmud. The historiographical context of each has been attempted since the argument is that historiographies differ, and this is significant to the understanding of history. The one discussion that was to become hegemonic in the last two centuries and in some ways to create a disjuncture was the colonial intervention that was later appropriated by various nationalist histories and is today being reiterated in the version of the past propagated by religious nationalism. The rather limited colonial reading of the sources inaugurated a new historiography seeking to create a memory of trauma despite the absence of such a trauma in the earlier sources. The memory becomes more important than the event and is used to build identities, and to legitimize some and exclude others in the politics of the present.

A trauma arises from an action of such severity outside the normal mode of understanding that those so traumatized either exorcise it by referring to the experience again and again to expurgate their fear; or, alternately, they suppress it by withdrawing and refusing to have anything to do with those who have perpetrated the trauma. There is little evidence of either of these reactions to Mahmud's raid in the sources. There have been traumas related to hostilities between communities in the last hundred years and we are familiar with the aftermath of these. They do not reflect what happened a thousand years ago but emerge out of contemporary origins. We should be wary of projecting onto the past that which emerges out of the experience of the present.

Sometimes such projections are said to result from 'national memory'. But, as has been pointed out, one cannot speak of national memory since nations do not think as a collectivity.[39] What is sometimes called a national memory is not a spontaneous or an evolved experience of a collectivity but is the creation of a particular political process; what is presented as national and long-standing is historically specific. It is created by a group in society that resonates to the narrative,[40] and in this case, to colonial readings of selected narratives. Certain segments of nations, generally the more articulate middle-class intelligentsia that constitutes the political elite, create what is claimed to be a memory and this is then projected as the memory of the nation. It is a creation of a hegemonic group in society, can be manipulated and is often used against those that are politically inconvenient and are dubbed as 'aliens'. If it is reiterated sufficiently often, it comes to be accepted as factual by many.

---

[39] J. Fentress and C. Wickham, *Social Memory*, pp. 127 ff.

[40] Ibid., pp. 21 ff.

Since memory of this kind is deliberately created, it can be changed, according to time and context. Claim to a social memory needs to be monitored since it suppresses whatever it does not find satisfying. Articulating what is to be remembered and suppressing that which is better forgotten can go into the making of a narrative that is claimed to be national. To know when a memory is being articulated, and when there is amnesia and why this is so, is significant to comprehending history, and more so the history of an event.

It is as well to recognize that a single, homogenous view emerges by displacing multiple perceptions. Yet, different groups remember the past in differing ways; one of the ways of observing these differences is by juxtaposing varying narratives of the same segment of history. Multiple voices often take the form of alternate histories, either alternate to the dominant culture or to competing cultures. The recognition of multiple voices means multiple perceptions from an evaluation of which a more comprehensive history can be read. This means recognizing a wider range of causal connections and a more precise appraisal of the priorities in these connections. It would assist not only in fresh analyses and assessments of Islam in India but would also point to the nature of ensuing relationships, some confrontational, some conciliatory, and some that were a continuation of the usual. Sifting the different kinds of relationships and analysing the reasons for the difference can illumine the complexity of social relationships. A juxtaposition of sources requires an appraisal of their interface from which ultimately a more sagacious history can emerge. Every voice does not have equal authority, for each has to be assessed in its historical context; and some will be given priority in the necessary process of evaluating causes. But a justification for the priority has also to be provided and this involves appraising the evidence.

Where memory is said to be based on an event—even an event that happened about a millennium ago—there is inevitably a relationship of memory to the history supposedly drawn upon in the construction of that memory. This involves a complex process, made more complicated by the constant change of space and time in memory and historical perceptions. It begins with what is believed to be the historical event. There are subsequent encodings of the event, which are placed on it layer upon layer, through the centuries. When the decoding of the event and the memory begins, the presence of the historian becomes imperative. The pointing up of the historiographical context of each layer becomes a prime requirement, as also the analysis of the construction of the memory.

The experience of the raid of Mahmud is followed by attempts to encode the event as in the Turko–Persian sources, or by ignoring the event in other sources, or by giving it a different gloss in yet others. At a certain point, in this case the nineteenth century, a homogenized memory of a trauma is created. This book has been an endeavour in demonstrating a historian's attempt at decoding the meaning of the event for various people and of the creating of a memory asserting a communal reading of the past.

I have tried to show how each set of narratives turn the focus of what Somanatha symbolizes: the occasion for the projection of the iconoclast and champion of Islam; the assertion of the superiority of Jainism over Shaivism; the centrality of the profits of trade subordinating other considerations; confrontations in the politics of Rajput and Turkish courts; perceptions of the event in the larger society of northern India; colonial interpretations of Indian society as having always been an antagonistic duality of Hindus and Muslims; religious nationalisms—both Hindu and Muslim—appropriating the colonial interpretation in formulating their versions of the event; Hindu nationalism contesting the contemporary secularization of Indian society. But these are not discrete foci. They do require that the understanding of the event should be historically contextual, multifaceted and aware of the ideological structures implicit in the narratives.

I have tried to suggest that the event of Mahmud's raid on the temple of Somanatha did not create a dichotomy. There were varying representations, both overt and hidden. A deeper investigation of these representations could point to concerns quite other than the ones to which we have given priority so far, both in this and similar events in Indian history. An assessment of these may provide us with more accurate and more sensitive insights into the Indian past.

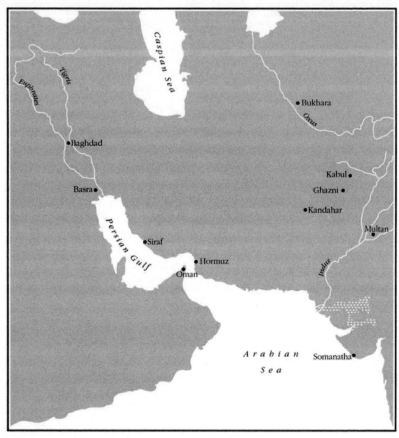

Map 1 Some locations in western India and west Asia

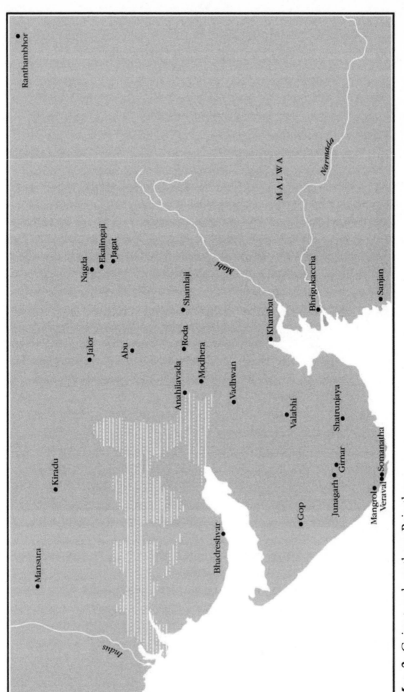

Map 2 Gujarat and southern Rajasthan

Approximate Dates

The Chaulukya Dynasty

Mularaja	940–995
Chamundaraja	
Durlabharaja	1008–1022
Bhimadeva	1022–1064
Karna	1064–1092
Jayasimha Siddharaja	1092–1142
Kumarapala	1142–1171
Ajayapala	1171–1174
Mularaja II	1174–1177
Bhima II	1177–1240
Tribhuvanapala	1240–1244

The Vaghela Dynasty

Dhavala	
Arnoraja	
Lavanaprashada	
Viradhavala	
Vishaladeva	1244–1262
Arjunadeva	1262–1273
Sarangadeva	1273–1297
Karna	1297–1302

Other Rulers

Mahmud of Ghazni	998–1030
Prithviraja Chauhan	1177–1192
Muhammad Ghuri	1178–1206
Ala-al-Din Khalji	1296–1316

Bibliography

Abdullah Wassaf in H.M. Elliot and J. Dowson, 1996 (reprint), *The History of India as Told by its Own Historians*, Vol. III, Delhi.

Abu'l Fazl, 1978 (reprint), *Ain-i-Akbari*, Vol. III, Delhi.

Abu-Lughod J., 1989, *Before European Hegemony. The World System AD 1250–1350*, New York.

Acharya G.V., 1933–42, *Historical Inscriptions of Gujarat*, Bombay.

Adame L.W., 1985, *Historical and Political Gazetteer of Afghanistan*, Graz.

Alam M., 2002, 'Shari'a and Governance in the Indo–Islamic Context', in D. Gilmartin and B.B. Lawrence (eds), *Beyond Turk and Hindu*.

Alam M., 2003, 'The Culture and Politics of Persian in Pre-Colonial Hindusthan', in S. Pollock (ed.), *Literary Cultures in History*.

Alam M. and S. Subrahmanyam (eds), 1998, *The Mughal State 1526–1750*, Delhi.

Al-Ansary A.R., 1981, *Qaryat al-Fau*, New York.

Al-Biruni, 1964, *Tahqiq ma li'l Hind*, tr. E. Sachau, *Alberuni's India*, Delhi.

Ali Muhammad Khan, 1965, *Mirat-i-Ahmedi*, tr. M.F. Lokhandwalla, Baroda.

Amin S., 2002, 'On Retelling the Muslim Conquest', in P. Chatterjee (ed.), *History and the Present*, pp. 24–43.

Attar, Farid al Din, 1984 (tr.), *Mantiq al-Tayr*, tr. A. Darbandi and D. Davis, *The Conference of Birds*, London.

Aziz Ahmed, 1963, 'Epic and Counter-Epic in Medieval India', *Journal of the American Oriental Society*, 83, pp. 470–76.

Babb L. et al., 2002, *Multiple Histories*, Jaipur.

Badayuni, 1973 (reprint), *Muntakhab al-Tawarikh*, tr. G. Ranking, Delhi.

Banerjea J.N., 1956, *Development of Hindu Iconography*, Calcutta.

Barnes J., 1947, 'The Collection of Genealogies', *Rhodes Livingstone Journal*, 5, pp. 52 ff.

Bayley E.C., 1886, *The Local Muhammadan Dynasties. Gujarat*, London.

Beal, S. 1969 (reprint), *Si-yu-ki, Buddhist Records of the Western World*, Delhi.

Bedekar D.K. (ed.), 1961 (reprint), *Chara June Marathi Arthashastriya Grantha, 1843–55*, Pune.

Behl A., 2003, 'The Magic Doe: Desire and Narrative in a Hindavi Sufi Romance circa 1503', in R. Eaton (ed.), *India's Islamic Traditions*.

Bharati A., 1965, *The Tantric Tradition*, New York.

R. Bharucha, 2003, *Rajasthan: An Oral History, Conversations with Komal Kothari*, Delhi.

Bhatia P., 1970, *The Paramaras*, Delhi.

Bhattacharya A.K., 1964, 'Bilingual Coins of Mahmud of Ghazni', *Journal of the Numismatic Society of India*, XXVI, pp. 53–56.

Bhattacharya N.N., 1996, *History of the Sakta Religion*, Delhi.

Bhattacharya N.N., 1992, *History of the Tantric Religion*, Delhi.

Bhavnagar Archaeological Department, *A Collection of Prakrit and Sanskrit Inscriptions*, 1931.

Bilhana, 1965, *Vikramankadevacarita*, tr. S.C. Banerji and A.K. Gupta, Calcutta.

Blank J., 2001, *Mullahs on the Mainframe*, Chicago.

Bosworth C.E., 1966, 'Mahmud of Ghazna in Contemporary Eyes and in Later Persian Literature', *Iran*, 4, pp. 85–92.

Bosworth C.E., 1968, 'The Development of Persian Culture Under the Early Ghaznavids', *Iran*, 6, pp. 33–44.

Bosworth C.E., 1973 (2nd edition), *The Ghaznavids, Their Empire in Afghanistan and Eastern Iran, 994–1040*, Beirut.

Bosworth C.E., 1991, 'Farrukhi's Elegy on Mahmud of Ghazna', *Iran*, 29, pp. 43–51.

Briggs G.W., 1958, *Gorakhnath and the Kanphata Yogis*, Calcutta.

Briggs J., 1966 (reprint), *History of the Rise of Mohammadan Power in India*, Calcutta.

Buhler G., 1877, 'Eleven Land Grants of the Chaulukyas of Anhilvad: A contribution to the history of Gujerat', *Indian Antiquary*, VI, pp. 180–214.

Buhler G., 1892, *The Jagaducarita of Sarvananda: a Historical Romance from Gujarat*, Vienna.

Buhler G. 1902, 'The Sukritasankirtan of Arisimha', tr. E. Burgess, *Indian Antiquary*, XXXI, pp. 477–95.

Buhler G., 1936, *The Life of Hemacandra*, Santiniketan.

Burgess J., 1869, *Notes of a Visit to Somanatha, Girnar and other places in Kathiawar in May 1869*, Bombay.

Burnes A., 1834, *Travels into Bukhara*, Vols I–III, London.

Butler T. (ed.), 1989, *Memory: History, Culture and the Mind*, Oxford.

Canfield R.L., 1991, *Turko–Persia in Historical Perspective*, Cambridge.

Chakravarti R., 2000, 'Nakhudas and Nauvittakas: Ship-Owning Merchants in Coastal Western India', *Journal of the Economic and Social History of the Orient*, XLIII, 1, pp. 34–64.

Chakravarti R., 2002, 'Nakhuda Nuruddin Firuz at Somanath: AD 1264' in *Trade and Traders in Early Indian Society*, Delhi.

Champakalakshmi R., 1978, 'Religious Conflict in the Tamil Country; A Reappraisal of Epigraphical Evidence', *Journal of the Epigraphical Society of India*, Mysore.

Champakalakshmi R., 1996, *Trade, Ideology and Urbanisation*, Delhi.

Chand Bardai, 1993 (reprint), *Prithviraja-raso*, Vols I and II, eds M.V. Pandya and S. Das, Banaras, tr. A.F.R. Hoemle, Calcutta, 1886.

Chandra Prabha, 1976, *Historical Mahakavyas in Sanskrit (Eleventh to Fifteenth Century AD)*, Delhi.

Chatterjee P., 1993, *The Nation and its Fragments: Colonial and Post-Colonial Histories*, Delhi.

Chatterjee P. (ed.), 2002, *History and the Present*, Delhi.

Chattopadhyaya, B.D. 1998, *Representing the Other? Sanskrit Sources and the Muslims*, Delhi.

Chattopadhyaya B.D., 2003, *Studying Early India*, Delhi.

Collins W., 1868, *The Moonstone*, London.

Corpus Inscriptionum Indicarum, 1970 (reprint), Vol. III, *Inscriptions of the Early Gupta Kings and their Successors*, ed. J.F. Fleet, Delhi.

Cousens H., 1931, *Somanatha and Other Medieval Temples in Kathiawar*, ASI, Vol. XLV, Calcutta.

Crooke W., 1896, *The Tribes and Castes of the North-West Province and Oudh*, Calcutta.

Crooke W., 1968 (reprint), *The Popular Religion and Folklore of North India*, Delhi.

Cunningham J.D., 1853, *A History of the Sikhs*, London.

Dandekar A., 1991, 'Landscapes in Conflict: Flocks, Herostones and Cult in Early Medieval Maharashtra', *Studies in History*, ns. 7, 2, pp. 301–24.

Das Gupta S.B., 1946, *Obscure Religious Cults*, Calcutta.

Dave J.H. et.al., 1956, *Munshi: His Life and Work*, Vols I–IV, Bombay.

Davis R.H., 1997, *The Lives of Indian Images*, Princeton.

Desai P.B., 1957, *Jainism in South India and some Jaina Epigraphs*, Sholapur.

Desai P.B., 1970, *A History of Karnataka*, Dharwar.

Desai S.H., 1980, *Arabic and Persian Inscriptions of Saurashtra*, Junagadh.

Desai V.N. and D. Mason (eds), 1993, *Gods, Guardians and Lovers: Temple Sculptures from North India, AD 700–1200*, New York.

Desai Z.A., 1961, *Arabic and Persian Supplement, Epigraphia Indica*, pp. 11–15.

Dhaky M.A. and H.P. Shastri, 1974, *The Riddle of the Temple at Somanatha*, Varanasi.

Dhavlikar M.K. and G. Possehi, 1992, 'The Pre-Harappan Period at Prabhas Pattan', *Man and Environment*, 17, 1, pp. 71–78.

Digby S., 1982, 'The Maritime Trade of India', in *The Cambridge Economic History* I, ed. T. Raychaudhuri and I. Habib, Cambridge.

Diskalkar D.B., 1939, 'Inscriptions of Kathiawad', *New Indian Antiquary*, I, pp. 576–90.

Doniger W., 1976, *The Origins of Evil in Hindu Mythology*, Berkeley.

Dow A., 1973 (reprint) *The History of Hindustan*, New Delhi.

Dundas P., 1992, *The Jains*, London.

Dundas P., 1999, 'Jain Perceptions of Islam in the Early Modern Period', *Indo–Iranian Journal*, 42, 1, pp. 35–46.

Eaton R., 1997, *The Rise of Islam and the Bengal Frontier 1204–1760*, Oxford.

Eaton R., 2000, *Essays on Islam and Indian History*, Delhi.

Eaton R., 2002, 'Indo–Muslim Traditions, 1200–1750: Towards a Framework of Study', *South Asia Research*, 22, 1.

Eaton R. (ed.), 2003, *India's Islamic Traditions, 711–1750*, Delhi.

Elliot H.M. and J. Dowson, 1996 (reprint), *The History of India as Told By its Own Historians*, Vols I to VIII, Delhi.

Epigraphia Indica.

Ernst C.W., 1992, *Eternal Garden: Mysticism, History and Politics at a South Asian Sufi Centre*, Albany.

Fentress J. and C. Wickham, 1992, *Social Memory*, Oxford.

J. Fergusson, 1910 (revised ed.), *A History of Indian and Eastern Architecture*, 2 Vols, Bombay.

Ferishta S.A., 1973 (reprint), *Tarikh-i-Ferishta*, tr. in A. Dow, *The History of Hindustan*, New Delhi; J. Briggs, *History of the Rise of Mohammadan Power in India*, 4 Vols, Calcutta 1966 (reprint).

Forbes A.K., 1864–66, 'Putton Somnath', *Journal of the Bombay Branch of the Royal Asiatic Society*, 8, pp. 49–64.

Forbes A.K., 1973 (reprint), *The Ras Mala*, New Delhi.

Frye R.N., 1984, *The History of Ancient Iran*, Munich.

Gazetteer of the Bombay Presidency

Gibbon E., 1960, *The Decline and Fall of the Roman Empire*, Harmondsworth.

Gilmartin D. and B.B. Lawrence, 2002, *Beyond Turk and Hindu: Rethinking Religious Identities in Islamicate South Asia*, Delhi.

Gode P.K., 1946, 'Some References to Persian Horses in Indian Literature from AD 500 to AD 1800', *The Poona Orientalist*, XI, 1–2, pp. 1–13.

Goel S.R., 1990, *Hindu Temples: What Happened to Them, A Preliminary Survey, Parts 1 and 2*, Delhi.

Gopal Sarvepalli, 1979, *Jawaharlal Nehru, A Biography*, London.

Gopal Sarvepalli (ed.), 1994, *Selected Works of Jawaharlal Nehru*, Vol. 16, Parts I and II, Delhi.

Goudrian T., 1981, *Hindu Tantric and Sakta Literature*, Wiesbaden.

Granoff P., 1991, 'Tales of Broken Limbs and Bleeding Wounds: Responses to Muslim Iconoclasm in Medieval India', *East and West*, 41, 1–4, pp. 189–203.

Granoff P., 1992, 'The Householder as Shaman: Jaina Biographies of Temple Builders', *East and West*, 42, 2–4, pp. 301–17.

Growse F.S., 1978 (reprint), *Mathura: A District Memoir*, Ahmedabad.

Gujarat State Gazetteer, Junagadh District, 1975, Ahmedabad.

Gupta P.L., 1969, *Coins*, New Delhi.

Halbwachs M., 1992, *On Collective Memory*, Chicago.

Habib M., 1967 (reprint), *Sultan Mahmud of Ghaznin: A Study*, Delhi.

Hali K.N., 1970 (reprint), *Urdu ka Klassici Adab*, Lahore.

Hall F., 1861, 'Decipherment of an Inscription from Cedi', *Journal of the Asiatic Society of Bengal*, 30, 1–4, pp. 317 ff.

Hansard, The United Kingdom House of Commons debate 1843 on the Somnath [Prabhas Patan] Proclamation, reprinted 1948, Junagadh.

Hardy P., 1997 (reprint), *Historians of Medieval India, Studies in Indo–Muslim Historical Writing*, Delhi.

Hardy P., 1962, 'Mahmud of Ghazna and the Historian', *Journal of the Punjab University Historical Society*, 14, pp. 1–36.

Harishankar Sastri, 1898, *Brihat Savara Tantra*, Haridwar.

Hemachandra, 1915–1921, *Dvyashraya-mahakavya*, ed. A.V. Kathvate, Bombay.

Hemachandra, 1885–1915, *Kumarapala-carita*, ed. A.V. Kathavate, Bombay.

Hiltebeitel A., 1999, *Draupadi Among Rajputs, Muslims and Dalits*, Chicago.

History and Culture of the Indian People, Vol. VI, 1960, The Delhi Sultanate, Bombay.

History and Culture of the Indian People, Vol. VIII, 1965, British Paramountcy and Indian Renaissance, Bombay.

Hoernle A.F.R., 'The Pattavali or List of Pontiffs of the Upakesa-gaccha', *Indian Antiquary*, 1875, 4, pp. 72 ff., 110 ff., 232 ff., 265 ff.

Hottinger A., 1963, *The Arabs*, London.

Ibn al-Athir, 1853–69, *Al Kamil fi al Tarikh*, ed. C.J. Tornberg, Leiden.

Ibn al-Kalbi, 1952, *Kitab al-Asnam*, tr. Nabih Amin Faris, *The Book of Idols*, New Jersey.

Isami, 1967 and 1976 (tr.), *Futuh-al-Salatin*, tr. Agha Mahdi Husain, 2 Vols, Calcutta.

Jackson P., 1999, *The Delhi Sultanate: A Political and Military History*, Cambridge.

Jain V.K., 1990, *Trade and Traders in Western India*, Delhi.

Janaki V.A., 1969, *Gujarat as the Arabs Knew It*, Baroda.

Jayanaka, 1914, *Prithviraja-vijaya*, ed. S.K. Belvalkar, Calcutta.

Jhaveri M.M., 1978, *History of Gujarati Literature*, New Delhi.

Jinaprabha Suri, 1923, *Vividha-tirtha-kalpa*, ed. D.R. Bhandarkar and K. Sahityabhushan, Calcutta.

Joshi M.C., 1983, 'Islam in the Hindu Tantras', *Journal of the Asiatic Society of Bombay*, 58, pp. 51–56.

Kalhana, 1960 (reprint), *Rajatarangini*, ed. and tr. M.A. Stein, Delhi.

Kangle R.P., 1965, *The Kautiliya Arthasastra*, Bombay.

Karkaria R.P., 1895–96, 'Mahmud of Ghazni and the Legend of Somanatha', *Journal of the Bombay Branch of the Royal Asiatic Society*, 19, pp. 142–53.

Katju M., 1998, 'The Early VHP: 1964–83', *Social Scientist*, 26, 5–6, pp. 34 ff.

Kaye J.W., 1874 (2nd edition), *History of the War in Afghanistan*, London.

Kennedy R.H., 1840, *Narrative of the Campaign of the Army of the Indus in Sind and Kaubool in 1838–39*, London.

Kensdale W.E.N., 1953, *The Religious Beliefs and Practices of Ancient South Arabians*, Ibadan.

Kincaid C.A., 1905, *The Outlaws of Kathiawar and Other Stories*, Bombay.

Klatt J., 1882, 'Extracts from the Historical Records of the Jains', *Indian Antiquary*, XI, pp. 245–56.

Kolff D.H.A., 1990, *Naukar, Rajput and Sepoy*, Cambridge.

Kumarapalacaritasangraha, 1956, ed. Jina Vijaya Muni, Bombay.

Kulke H., 1993, *King and Cults*, New Delhi.

Kumar K., 1990, 'Hindu Revivalism and Education in North Central India', *Social Scientist*, 18, pp. 4–26.

Lal K.S., 1980 (3rd edition), *History of the Khaljis*, Delhi.

Lambton A.K.S., 1988, *Continuity and Change in Medieval Persia, Aspects of Administrative, Economic and Social History, 11th to 14th Century*, London.

Lokhandawalla S.T., 1967, 'Islam, Law and Isma'ili Commentaries', *Indian Economic and Social History Review*, 4, 2, pp. 154–79.

Lorenzen D., 1978, 'Warrior Ascetics in Indian History', *Journal of the American Oriental Society*, Vol. 98.

Macaulay T.B., 1935, *Speeches by Lord Macaulay*, ed. G.M. Young, London.

Mahmood T., 1989, 'The Dargah of Sayyid Salar Mas'ud Ghazi in

Bibliography

236 *Bibliography*

Bahraich Legend, Tradition and Reality', in C.W. Troll (ed.), *Muslim Shrines in India*, Delhi.

Majumdar A.K., 1956, *Chaulukyas of Gujarat*, Bombay.

Majumdar R.C., 1965, *British Paramountcy and Indian Renaissance*, Vol. VIII, part II, History and Culture of the Indian People, Bombay.

Marco Polo, 1929, *The Travels of Marco Polo: the Venetian*, ed. and tr. W. Marsden, revised M. Komroff, New York.

Masson C., 1842, *Narratives of Various Journeys in Balochistan, Afghanistan and the Panjab*, Vols I–III, London.

Meher-Homji V.M., 1970, 'Notes on Some Peculiar Cases of Phytogeographic Distributions', *Journal of the Bombay Natural History Society*, 67 (1), pp. 81–86.

Mehta N., 1968, *Karanaghelo*, trans. N.M. Tripathi, Bombay.

Mehta R.N. and S.N. Chowdhury, 1961, *Excavations at Devanimori*, Baroda.

Meister M.M., 1993, 'Indian Islam's Lotus Throne: Kaman and Khatu Kalan', in A.D. Dalapiccola and S. Zingle-Ave Lallemant (eds), *Islam and Indian Regions*, 2 Vols, Stuttgart, I, pp. 445–52.

Merutunga, 1933, *Prabandha-cintamani*, ed. Muni Jinavijaya, Santiniketan, tr. C.H. Tawney, Calcutta, 1901.

Metcalfe B.D., 1995, 'Too Little and Too Much: Reflections on Muslims in the History of India', *Journal of Asian Studies*, 54, 4, pp. 951–67.

Mill J., 1817–23, *The History of British India*, 3 Vols, London.

Minhaj Siraj, 1863–4, *Tabaqat-i-Nasiri*, Bibliotheca Indica, Calcutta, tr. H.G. Raverty, *A General History of the Muhammadan Dynasties of Asia including Hindustan*, 2 Vols, 1970 (reprint), Delhi.

Minorsky V., 'Gardizi on India', *BSOAS*, 1948, 12, pp. 625–40.

Mirkhond, 1891, *Rauzat-al Safa*, tr. E. Rehatsek, London; *Indian Antiquary*, VIII, p. 153.

Misra S.C., 1964, *The Muslim Communities in Gujarat*, Bombay.

Mohan Singh, 1937, *Gorakhnath and Medieval Hindu Mysticism*, Lahore.

Monier-Williams M., 1894, *Sakoontala*, London.

Moore V.N., 1948, *Somanatha*, Calcutta.

Moraes G., 1931, *The Kadamba Kula: A History of Ancient and Medieval Karnataka*, Bombay.

Morgan P., 1991, 'New Thoughts on Old Hormuz', *Iran*, 29.

Mukta P., 2002, 'On the Political Culture of Authoritarianism', in G. Shah et.al., *Development and Deprivation*, Delhi.

Munshi K.M., 1941, *The Early Aryans in Gujarat*, Bombay.

Munshi K.M., 1945, *The Changing Shape of Indian Politics*, Poona.

Munshi K.M., 1951, *Somanatha—The Shrine Eternal*, Bombay.

Munshi K.M., 1951, *Glory That was Gurjaradesha*, Bombay.

Munshi K.M., 1967, *Gujarat and its Literature*, Bombay.

Nahar P.C. (ed.), 1918 and 1927, *Jaina Lekha Sangraha*, 2 Vols, Calcutta.

Nanavati J., R.N. Mehta and S.N. Chowdhury, 1956, *Somanatha*, MS University Monograph 1, Baroda.

Narang S.P., 1972, *Hemachandra's Dvayshrayakavya: A Literary and Cultural Study*, Delhi.

Narayana Rao V. and G.H. Roghair, 1990, *Siva's Warriors: The Basava Purana of Palkuriki Somanatha*, Princeton.

Nayanchandra, 1968 (reprint), *Hammira-mahakavya*, Jodhpur.

Nazim M., 1971 (2nd edition), *The Life and Times of Sultan Mahmud of Ghazna*, Delhi.

Nazim M., 1928, 'Somanath and its Conquest by Sultan Mahmud', *Journal of the Royal Asiatic Society*, Part 1, pp. 233–38.

Nizam-al-din Ahmed, 1990 (reprint), *Tabaqat-i-Akbari*, tr. B. De, Delhi.

Nizami K.A., 1983, *On History and Historians of Medieval India*, Delhi.

Nora P., 1989, 'Between Memory and History: Les Lieux de Memoire', *Representations*, 26, pp. 21 ff.

Nora P. (ed.), 1996, *Realms of Memory*, New York.

Padmanabha, 1959, *Kanhadade Prabandha*, ed. K.D. Vyas, Bombay, tr. V.S. Bhatnagar, 1991, New Delhi.

Pandey S.N., 1987, *Shaivite Temples and Sculptures at Somanatha*, Delhi.

Pearson M.N., 1976, *Merchants and Rulers in Gujarat*, Berkeley.

Petrov K.N., 1989, 'History as Social Memory', in T. Butler (ed.), *Memory: History, Culture and the Mind*, Oxford.

Pollock S. (ed.), 2003, *Literary Cultures in History*, Berkeley.

Poona Orientalist

Postan W., 1838, 'Notes of a Journey to Girnar', *Journal of the Asiatic Society of Bengal*, 7, 2, 865–82.

Prinsep J., 1838, 'Note on Somnath', *Journal of the Asiatic Society of Bengal*, 7, pp. 883–87.

Raeside I.M.P., 1992, 'A Gujarati Bardic Poem: The Kanhadade-Prabandha', in C. Shackle and R. Snell (eds), *The Indian Narrative: Perspectives and Patterns*, Wiesbaden.

Ranchodji Amaraji, 1882, *Tarikh-i-Sorath*, ed. J. Burgess, Bombay.

Ray H.C., 1936, *Dynastic History of Northern India*, Calcutta.

Raychaudhuri T. and I. Habib (eds), 1982, *The Cambridge Economic History of India*, Cambridge.

Russell R.V., 1896, *Tribes and Castes of the Central Provinces of India*, London.

Ryckmans G., 1951, *Les Religions Arabes Pre-Islamique*, Louvain.

Sa'di, 1911, *Bustan*, tr. A.A. Edwards, *The Bustan of Sa'di*, London.

Sadid-al-Din Muhammad Awfi, 1966 (reprint), *Jawami al-Hikayat wa Lawami al-Riwayat*, ed. M. Nizam-al-Din, Hyderabad, AP.

Sandesara B.J., 1953, *Literary Circle of Mahamatya Vastupala and its Contributions to Sanskrit Literature*, Bombay.

Sankalia H.D., 1941, *The Archaeology of Gujarat*, Baroda.

Sankalia H.D., 1949, *Studies in the Historical and Cultural Geography and Ethnography of Gujarat*, Poona.

Sarkar S., 1997, *Writing Social History*, Delhi.

Scerrato U., 1959, 'Summary Report on the Italian Archaeological Mission in Afghanistan', *East and West*, 10, 1–2, pp. 39–40.

Schimmel, A-M., 1973, 'Turk and Hindu: a poetical image and its application to historical fact', in S. Vryonis (ed.), *Islam and Cultural Change in the Middle Ages*, Weisbaden, pp. 107–26.

Schwerin K.G., 1985, 'Saint Worship in Indian Islam: the Legend of the Martyr Salar Masud Ghazi', in Imtiaz Ahmed (ed.), *Ritual and Religion among Muslims of the Sub-Continent*, Lahore, pp. 143–61.

Scot-Meisami, J., 1990, 'Ghaznavid Panegyrics: Some Political Implications', *Iran*, 1990, 28, pp. 31–44.

Scot-Meisami, J., 1999, *Persian Historiography*, Edinburgh.

Shah G., 1988, 'Kanaiyalal Munshi on Gujarati and Indian Nationalism', Unpublished paper.

Sharma D., 1969, 'Some New Light on the Route of Mahmud of

Ghazna's raid on Somanatha ...' in B.P. Sinha (ed.), *Dr Satkari Mookerji Felicitation Volume*, Varanasi, 165–68.

Sharma D., 1975 (2nd edition), *Early Chauhan Dynasties*, Delhi.

Shastri H.G., 1989, *The Inscriptions of Gujarat*, Ahmedabad.

Sheth C.B., 1953, *Jainism in Gujarat 1100–1600*, Bombay.

Shokoohy M., 1988, *Bhadreshvar*, Leiden.

Siddiqui I.H., 1989, 'A Note on the Dargah of Salar Mas'ud in Bahraich in the light of the Standard Historical Sources', in C.W. Troll, *Muslim Shrines in India*, Delhi.

Sikand Y., 2002, 'The Changing Nature of Shared Hindu and Muslim Shrines in Contemporary Karnataka', *South Asia*, XXV, 1, pp. 49–67.

Skaria A., 2001, 'On the Curious Love of Indulal Yagnik', *Indian Economic and Social History Review*, 38, 3, pp. 271–97.

Smith G., 1879, *The Life of John Wilson*, London.

Smith J.D., 1991, *The Epic of Pabuji*, Cambridge.

Sreenivasan R., 2002, 'Alauddin Khalji Remembered: Conquest, Gender and Community in Medieval Rajput Narratives', *Studies in History*, ns. 18, 2, pp. 275–96.

Stocqueler J.H., 1854, *Memoirs and Correspondence of Major-General Sir William Nott*, London.

Talbot C., 1995, 'Inscribing the Other: Inscribing the Self; Hindu Muslim Identities in Pre-Colonial India', *Comparative Studies in Society and History*, 37, 4, pp. 692–722.

Tambs-Lyche H., 1997, *Power, Profit and Poetry*, Delhi.

Thapar R., 1996, *Time as a Metaphor of History*, Delhi.

Thapar R., 1997, (2nd edition), *Asoka and the Decline of the Mauryas*, Delhi.

Thapar R., 2000, *Narratives and the Making of History*, Delhi.

Thapar R., 2000, *Cultural Pasts*, Delhi.

Tod J., 1839, *Travels in Western India*, London.

Trautmann T., 1997, *Aryans and British India*, Delhi.

Troll C.W. (ed.), 1989, *Muslim Shrines in India*, Delhi.

Turner V., 1984, *Dramas, Fields and Metaphors*, Ithaca.

Varahamihira, 1981, *Brihatsamhita*, ed. and tr. M. Ramakrishna Bhat, Delhi.

Varma S., 1997, *Settlement Patterns in Kathiawar from the Chalcolithic to the Early Historical Period*, JNU Ph.D. thesis, New Delhi.

Van der Veer P., 1992, 'Ayodhya and Somnath: Eternal Shrines, Contested Histories', *Social Research*, 59, 1, pp. 85–109.

Van der Veer P., 1993, *Religious Nationalism: Hindus and Muslims in India*, Berkeley.

Vigne G.T., 1842, *Travels in Kashmir, Ladakh, Iskardo, Vols I and II*, London.

Visuvalingam S., *The Marriage of Lat Bhairava and Ghazi Miyan-Sexuality, Death and Transgression in Hinduism and Islam*, (forthcoming).

Viswanathan G., 1998, *Outside the Fold*, Princeton.

Yashaschandra S., 2003, 'Gujarati Literary Culture', in S. Pollock (ed.), *Literary Cultures in History*.

Yapp M., 1980, *Strategies of British India*, Oxford.

Wachtel N., 1977, *The Vision of the Vanquished*, Hassocks.

Wachtel N., 1986, 'Memory and History', *History and Anthropology*, II, 2, pp. 207–24.

Wagle, N., 1997 (2nd edition), 'Hindu–Muslim Interactions in Medieval Maharashtra,' in G.D. Sontheimer and H. Kulke (eds), *Hinduism Reconsidered*, Delhi.

Watson J.W., 1879, 'The Fall of Patan Somanath: Ballad of the Fall of Pattan', *Indian Antiquary*, VIII, pp. 153–61.

Watters T., 1973 (reprint), *On Yuan Chwang's Travels in India*, Delhi.

Wilberforce-Bell H., 1980 (reprint), *The History of Kathiawar*, New Delhi.

Wink A., 1991 and 1997, *Al-Hind*, Vols I and II, Leiden.

Winnett F.V., 1940, 'The Daughters of Allah', *The Moslem World*, 30, pp. 113–30.

Zelliot, E., 1982, 'A Medieval Encounter between Hindus and Muslims: Eknath's Drama-Poem, Hindu–Turk Samvad', in F.W. Clothey (ed.), *Images of Man: Religion and Historical Process in South Asia*, Madras.

Zia al-Din Barani, 1960, *Fatawa-i-Jahandari*, tr. M. Habib and A.U.S. Khan, Allahabad.

Zia-al-din Barani, 1862, *Tarikh-i Firuz Shahi*, ed. Saiyid Ahmad Khan, Calcutta, Bibliotheca Indica.

Index